CREATED AND LED BY THE SPIRIT

MISSIONAL CHURCH SERIES

The missional church conversation continues to grow in importance in providing for many fresh ways to rethink what it means to be church in our rapidly changing context. The Missional Church Series, published by the Wm. B. Eerdmans Publishing Co., is designed to contribute original research to this critical conversation. This series will make available monographs as well as edited volumes produced from specially designed consultations.

Created and Led by the Spirit

Planting Missional Congregations

Edited by

Mary Sue Dehmlow Dreier

WILLIAM B. EERDMANS PUBLISHING COMPANY
GRAND RAPIDS, MICHIGAN / CAMBRIDGE, U.K.

Wm. B. Eerdmans Publishing Co.
2140 Oak Industrial Drive N.E., Grand Rapids, Michigan 49505 /
P.O. Box 163, Cambridge CB3 9PU U.K.

Printed in the United States of America

19 18 17 16 15 14 13   7 6 5 4 3 2 1

Library of Congress Cataloging-in-Publication Data

Created and led by the Spirit: planting missional congregations /
    edited by Mary Sue Dehmlow Dreier.
        p.   cm.   — (Missional church series)
    Includes bibliographical references.
    ISBN 978-0-8028-6894-7 (pbk.: alk. paper)
    1. Church development, New.
    2. Missional church movement.
    I. Dreier, Mary Sue Dehmlow, 1951-

    BV652.24.C74   2012
    254'.1 — dc23

                                        2012038535

www.eerdmans.com

Contents

Foreword, *by Craig Van Gelder*   vii

Contributors   ix

Abbreviations   xii

Introduction: Engaging the Missional Church
Conversation for Church Planting, *by Mary Sue Dehmlow Dreier*   xiv

**Section I: Theological Frameworks
for Planting Missional Congregations**   1

1. Planting Missional Congregations: Imagining Together   3
Mary Sue Dehmlow Dreier

2. Human Flourishing   27
Miroslav Volf

3. Raised for Our Justification: Christ's Spirit for Us and for All   45
Lois Malcolm

Section II: Glimpses of the Holy Spirit in Action   69

4. New Churches for a New Millennium:
The Holy Spirit Does It Again   71
Leith Anderson

Contents

5. Hints from the Past for the Present and Future:
   Five Congregations and Their Church-Planting Stories   95
   Susan Tjornehoj

Section III: New Appearances on the Scene   123

6. Church Emerging: A Missional View   125
   Daniel Anderson

7. Multicultural Church Planting: African Pneumatology
   in Western Context   151
   Harvey Kwiyani

8. Postbureaucratic Churches: Emerging Forms of
   Organization and Leadership   178
   Todd Hobart

Epilogue: A Sermon   203

9. Missional Church: Planted in the Gospel for All   205
   Paul Chung

Foreword

The missional church conversation is continuing to expand within the church today. Scores of books have been published in the past decade that refer to the word "missional" as a key concept for discussing the identity, purpose, and ministry of the church. At Luther Seminary, we are especially committed to contributing to this conversation via the graduate programs we offer — MA, MDiv, DMin, MTh, PhD — as well as through special events. Our focus is primarily on trying to frame the ongoing missional discussion in light of biblical and theological perspectives, believing that central to this conversation is reclaiming the identity of the church, which is basic to informing its purpose and ministry.

The church's identity has to do with its very nature, what the church *is* in light of its being created by the Spirit. So much of the writing about missional church today tends to assume that this territory is self-evident, and thus it moves all too quickly to focusing on what the church is to *do* on behalf of God in the world. This approach can be hazardous to the missional discussion in terms of shifting the focus too quickly away from the agency of the Spirit in the midst of the church and redirecting it toward the primacy of human agency and responsibility.

Being clear about the agency of the triune God through the Spirit with respect to God's mission in the world and the church's participation in that mission was central when the concept of "missional church" was first introduced in the 1998 publication of the book of the same name, edited by Darrell Guder. Since that time, maintaining this perspective has grown in importance as the Trinitarian conversation has become more nuanced through incorporating more fully the perspectives of the social Trinity in relation to the sending Trinity. This is the biblical and theological approach that Luther Seminary has sought to contribute to the missional conversation over the past decade: framing the role of human agency within divine agency with regard to the ministry of the Spirit.

One key event sponsored by Luther Seminary each year that contributes to this focus is our annual Missional Church Consultation. This consultation began in 2005 by addressing the dynamics of the missional church in context. Each succeeding year has dealt with another theme regarding the missional church, including the missional church and denominations (2006); the missional church and leadership formation (2007); the missional church and global civil society (2008); planting missional congregations (2009); missional spiritual formation (2010); the missional church and the first third of life (2011); and the missional church and global media cultures (2012). Each consultation consists of the presentation of prepared essays by several established scholars as well as by a number of emerging scholars, many of whom have been students in our PhD program in Congregational Mission and Leadership at Luther Seminary.

One of the primary goals of Luther Seminary has been to contribute published works that provide biblical and theological frameworks with respect to the growing missional church literature. To help us accomplish this, the Wm. B. Eerdmans Publishing Company has graciously agreed to publish in a series a number of the volumes of essays that have come out of these annual consultations. The 2009 consultation was our fifth annual and was entitled "Created and Led by the Spirit: Planting Missional Congregations." This volume of essays is the fruit of that consultation, the fifth volume in the Missional Church series.

We believe that the focus on planting new congregations that have a clear missional identity is a crucial theme in the church today. The work of this consultation sought to bring historical clarity, biblical and theological substance, and practical guidance to this important dimension of church life. It is our hope that readers will find this volume helpful in understanding more fully the complex character of how new congregations come into existence within concrete communities through the creative work of the Spirit.

CRAIG VAN GELDER
Editor, Missional Church Series

Contributors

Daniel Anderson holds a PhD degree from Luther Seminary in the field of congregational mission and leadership. He is an ordained minister in the Evangelical Lutheran Church in America (ELCA) and has served in calls both as a pastor and as a worship leader. He is program developer for the Center for Missional Leadership at Luther Seminary.

Leith Anderson holds a DMin degree from Fuller Theological Seminary and is a graduate of Denver Seminary. He served as senior pastor at Wooddale Church, Eden Prairie, Minnesota, for thirty-five years, during which time Wooddale planted fourteen new churches. His recent publications include *How to Act Like a Christian* (2006), *Jesus: An Intimate Portrait of the Man, His Land, and His People* (2006), and *The Jesus Revolution: Learning from Christ's First Followers* (2009).

Paul Chung holds a PhD degree from the University of Basel, Switzerland, in the field of systematic theology. He is an ordained minister in the ELCA and has planted a multicultural congregation in California. He is currently serving as associate professor of mission and world Christianity at Luther Seminary, where he has taught since 2009. His recent publications include *The Spirit of God Transforming Life: The Reformation and Theology of the Holy Spirit* (2009), *Public Theology in an Age of World Christianity: God's Mission as Word-Event* (2010), and *The Cave and the Butterfly: An Intercultural Theory of Interpretation and Religion in the Public Square* (2011).

Mary Sue Dehmlow Dreier holds a PhD degree from Luther Seminary in the field of congregational mission and leadership. She is an ordained minister in the ELCA and has served as a pastor in rural, suburban, and church-planting calls. She is presently serving as associate professor of congregational mission and leadership at Luther Seminary, where she has taught since 2008. She is the editor of this volume.

Todd Hobart holds a PhD degree from Luther Seminary in the field of congregational mission and leadership. He has worked in a variety of areas with youth and children, including after-school programs, a faith-based drug and alcohol treatment center, and several church ministries. He is presently serving as Life Stage Youth Coordinator at St. Matthew Lutheran Church (ELCA), Renton, Washington, where he has worked since 2007.

Harvey Kwiyani holds a PhD degree from Luther Seminary in the field of congregational mission and leadership. He grew up in a charismatic Christian home in an African village in rural Malawi, and he has served for nine years on the mission fields of Europe and the United States. He is currently the pastor-developer of a new multicultural Vineyard Church in St. Paul, Minnesota, which he has led since 2009.

Lois Malcolm holds a PhD in theology from the University of Chicago. Her background also includes an MA in theology from Luther Seminary and an MA in applied linguistics from the University of Minnesota. She is presently serving as associate professor of systematic theology at Luther Seminary, where she has taught since 1994. Her publications include *Holy Spirit: Creative Power in Our Lives* (2009) and *God: The Westminster Collection of Sources of Christian Theology* (2012). Forthcoming are a book entitled *One Died for All: A Trinitarian Theology of the Cross* and a theological commentary on 2 Corinthians.

Susan Tjornehoj holds an MTh degree from Luther Seminary. She is an ordained minister in the ELCA and has served congregations in Alaska and Minnesota. She has worked on the bishop's staff in three synods of the ELCA, including the Minneapolis Area Synod, where she oversaw the planting of missional congregations as director for evangelical mission. She is currently the senior pastor at Christ Lutheran Church, Baltimore, Maryland.

Miroslav Volf holds a PhD from the University of Tübingen, Germany. He is the Henry B. Wright Professor of Systematic Theology at Yale Divinity School and the founding director of the Yale Center for Faith and Culture in New Haven, Connecticut. His book *Exclusion and Embrace* (1996) was selected by *Christianity Today* as one of the 100 best religious books of the twentieth century. His most recent publications include *Captive to the Word of God: Engaging the Scriptures for Contemporary Theological Reflection* (2010), *Public Faith: How Followers of Christ Should Serve the Common Good* (2011), and *Allah: A Christian Response* (2012).

Abbreviations

AELC   American Evangelical Lutheran Church
ALC   American Lutheran Church
ATS   Association of Theological Schools
CIL   Christ is Lord (congregation pseudonym)
DL   Distributed Learning
DMin   Doctor of Ministry degree
ELCA   Evangelical Lutheran Church in America
ELW   Evangelical Lutheran Worship
GCSCC Greater City Simple Church Cooperative (congregation pseudonym)
GOC   Gospel and Our Culture
GOCN   Gospel and Our Culture Network
HPWS   High Performance Work Systems
ICE   Immigration and Customs Enforcement
IMC   International Missionary Council
KC   Kingdom Community (congregation pseudonym)
LBW   Lutheran Book of Worship
LCA   Lutheran Church in America
MA   Master of Arts degree
MAS   Minneapolis Area Synod
MDiv   Master of Divinity degree
MTh   Master of Theology degree
NCS   National Congregations Study
NIV   New International Version Bible

NRSV   New Revised Standard Version Bible
PhD   Doctor of Philosophy degree
POG   Place of Grace (congregation pseudonym)
RIC   Reconciling in Christ
SBH   Service Book and Hymnal
STC   Saint Timothy's of the City (congregation pseudonym)
TEEM   Theological Education for Emerging Ministry
WEA   World Evangelical Alliance

Engaging the Missional Church Conversation for Church Planting

Church planting is full of "go figure" moments — those moments when you sit back, awestruck, and realize you can't explain what just happened. Those exhilarating experiences of something like the rush of a mighty wind blowing through the room. Those provocative coincidences that whisper of *something* stirring out in the world beyond our imaginations.

I wonder about the decline of mainline denominations in the United States — while the church is growing explosively in Africa. I see Pentecost-like sparks flashing in unconventional places. I can't systematize all the moments that are reminiscent of Peter being led, as though in a trance, by the angel in Acts 12. The Spirit of God is stirring out in the world beyond our imaginations!

Churches in North America are in a mission field, as we become increasingly aware that people in our neighborhoods are not acquainted with the gospel. One of the ways the Spirit of God is creating a new future for Christianity in North America is through the planting of missional congregations: these are new faith communities, created and led by the Spirit, that are intentional about participating in God's Trinitarian mission for the sake of God's world. This is an exciting frontier for the church, and it invites new theological reflection, new imagination, and new partnerships as God's people engage this creative new apostolic era.

A Changing Context and Changing Church

In the late 1970s and early 1980s, a new conversation about mission began in the United Kingdom and the United States under the influence of missiologist Lesslie Newbigin. When he returned to his native England after almost thirty years as a pastor and bishop in India, he encountered modern Western culture and challenged the church to bring the gospel into a fresh encounter with this culture. His mission theology was Trinitarian, and it was shaped by international mission conferences and conversations that wrestled with the nature and mission of the church in light of the nature and mission of God as Trinity. Mission belonged to God, not the church. The church was not the sender, but the one sent — into the world to participate in God's mission *(missio Dei)* for the sake of bringing God's care and redemption to all creation.

As a result of Newbigin's concerns, the Gospel and Our Culture (GOC) discussion emerged in England in the 1980s to address these missionary issues. After Newbigin lectured at Princeton in 1984, a similar network took shape in the United States: the Gospel and Our Culture Network (GOCN). A new conversation about the mission of God and a missionary church had begun. With the publication of volumes in the Gospel and Our Culture series by Wm. B. Eerdmans Publishing Company, a distinctive U.S. voice and conversation began to emerge. The title of one of these books, *Missional Church,* popularized the concept that has become synonymous with the movement that bears its name. The books in the Eerdmans series focused on the triune mission of God, the missional nature of the church, and North America as a missional context. They include:

George Hunsberger and Craig Van Gelder, eds., *The Church Between Gospel and Culture: The Emerging Mission in North America* (1996).

Darrell L. Guder, ed., *Missional Church: A Vision for the Sending of the Church in North America* (1998).

George R. Hunsberger, *Bearing the Witness of the Spirit: Lesslie Newbigin's Theology of Cultural Plurality* (1998).

Craig Van Gelder, ed., *Confident Witness — Changing World: Rediscovering the Gospel in North America* (1999).

Darrell L. Guder, *The Continuing Conversion of the Church* (2000).

James V. Brownson, ed., *StormFront: The Good News of God* (2003).

Lois Y. Barrett, ed., *Treasure in Clay Jars: Patterns in Missional Faithfulness* (2004).

The missional church conversation has now gained wide attention and momentum within North America. There is a steadily growing body of literature by numerous authors and editors that has contributed significantly to the burgeoning conversation. Luther Seminary seeks to contribute to this literature with its Missional Church Consultation, held annually at Luther Seminary in St. Paul, Minnesota, since 2005.

The Missional Church Series

The purpose of this series is to extend and deepen the missional church conversation through original scholarship that addresses areas of emerging interest. All of the already published volumes listed below have come out of the Missional Church Consultation:

Craig Van Gelder, ed., *The Missional Church in Context: Helping Congregations Develop Contextual Ministry* (2007).
Craig Van Gelder, ed., *The Missional Church and Denominations: Helping Congregations Develop a Missional Identity* (2008).
Craig Van Gelder, ed., *The Missional Church and Leadership Formation: Helping Congregations Develop Leadership Capacity* (2009).
Dwight Zscheile, ed., *Cultivating Sent Communities: Missional Spiritual Formation* (2011).

The present volume, an outcome of the November 2009 Missional Church Consultation, entitled "Created and Led by the Spirit: Planting Missional Congregations," is another in this series. It builds on the work of the previous consultation publications and brings the missional church into conversation with the expanding enterprise of church planting. More than 160 church planters, mission directors, denominational leaders, scholars, and educators gathered for missional presentations, conversation, Bible study, worship, and prayer. In addition to thanking those who contributed essays at the consultation (now the chapters of this book), I wish to offer special thanks to Rev. Dr. Stephen Bouman, Bible study leader, and Rev. David Housholder, responder and facilitator of the consultation conversations.

How to Read and Use This Book

The primary purpose of this book is to extend the missional church conversation as it relates to the generative work of planting new missional congregations. The reader will find that the authors draw significantly on the developing body of missional church literature, as well as a diverse range of other applicable sources, case studies, and contextual anecdotes. The book provides original scholarship with a missional church-planting focus, and thus it contributes fresh insights to the missional church conversation as well as to the expanding field of church-planting resources.

The first section of three essays provides the theological framework for planting missional congregations. In the first essay, Mary Sue Dehmlow Dreier sets up the conversation across diverse perceptions of the Spirit's work by focusing on God's primary agency as church planter and our secondary role as midwives; it offers fresh reflections based on the third article of the Apostles' Creed. In the second essay, Miroslav Volf offers the act of loving God and our neighbor rightly as the core theological challenge for establishing human community that flourishes. He implicitly redefines and contextualizes church planting amid a culture dominated by the pursuit of experiential satisfaction. In the third essay, Lois Malcolm retrieves the missionary thrust of Paul's apostolic theology to explore the promising breadth and depth of the Spirit's work "for us and for all." Thus she creates a Pauline theological framework for church planting.

The two essays in the second section provide congregational stories that give witness to the Holy Spirit's activity in the world through church planting. In the first essay, senior pastor Leith Anderson traces how the Spirit led his congregation in numerous church-planting efforts and summarizes his rich experience into a mini-primer for planting missional congregations. In the second essay, Susan Tjornehoj sifts through the unique beginnings of five very different congregations in the metropolitan area of Minneapolis and St. Paul, Minnesota. She identifies how common biblical themes in the deeply contextual soil of a congregation form a furrow from its past, through its present, and into its future.

The third section of three essays narrates new missional appearances on the church-planting scene, pointing the reader's attention to emerging churches, multiculturalism, and new organizational possibilities for church planters to consider. In the first essay, Daniel Anderson tackles the phenomenon of emerging churches; he provides descriptions, distinguishes areas of emphases, and suggests a process for seeing beyond innovation to missional identity. In the second essay, African-born Harvey Kwiyani brings his native experiences and understandings of the Spirit to bear on the North American context, creating a pneumatological missiology that discerns and celebrates the multicultural activity of the Holy Spirit in the United States. In the third essay, Todd Hobart explores the theological and structural possibilities of postmodern organizational forms. This essay grew out of his research within four postbureaucratic congregations that offer innovative alternatives to traditional structures for planting missional congregations.

The fourth section, an epilogue, concludes this collection with the proclamation of the gospel. Paul Chung, professor of mission and world Christianity at Luther Seminary, delivered this sermon during worship at the 2009 Missional Church Consultation. With the wisdom of a scholar and heart of a church planter, Chung orients our church-planting efforts in witness that flows from the heart of God.

Each of the contributions to this volume uniquely addresses the theme "Created and Led by the Spirit: Planting Missional Congregations." When considered together, these essays are complementary to each other and present a diverse but cohesive celebration of the Spirit's missional church planting in our time — and into a creative new future. This book provides a critical focus and helpful trajectory within the growing missional church conversation for church planters, judicatories, students, educators, and scholars. May it facilitate rigorous theological reflection on the imaginative, challenging, and rewarding adventure of planting missional congregations that are created and led by the Spirit.

Mary Sue Dehmlow Dreier
Luther Seminary

THEOLOGICAL FRAMEWORKS FOR PLANTING MISSIONAL CONGREGATIONS

This opening section addresses missional church planting as a theological practice, with particular attention to the activity of the Holy Spirit within the context of God's Trinitarian life. This pneumatological focus for church planting highlights the constitutive work of the Spirit in the eschatological frame of the new creation and creates a theological conversation that is highly suggestive for church planting and related practices. It emphasizes the necessity to move beyond how-to books and, alternatively, to start with the Trinity and to orient church planting around the nature and mission of God.

Church planting is fertile ground for new hospitable initiatives within God's larger purposes for humankind. This section offers opportunity for a theological imagination for church planting to learn from and expand on creedal, contextual, and biblical roots. The three essays in this section challenge the reader to explore connections to church planting that are both explicit and implicit, to think deeply about the theological ground for church planting, and to envision missional congregations yet to be born that are distinctively rooted in the life and mission of God the Holy Spirit.

"Planting Missional Congregations: Imagining Together," by Mary Sue Dehmlow Dreier, invites people with diverse perceptions of the Holy Spirit into a shared imagination for the recognizable reality of the Holy Spirit. She engages the Acts of the Apostles, the third article of the Apostles' Creed, and her own experiences as a church planter, teacher, and researcher to identify the Holy Spirit as the primary church planter and then

1

to see human church planters as missional midwives to that divine creativity. The four sections of the third article provide a biblical and theological framework within which to discern the fourfold reality of the Spirit as a public, reconciling, life-promoting, and joyful force who creates new churches to bear those same traits in the world. Church planters as midwives participate with God by discerning, assisting, and promoting the possibilities and potential of new missional congregations so created and led by the Spirit.

In "Human Flourishing," theologian Miroslav Volf envisions the life of congregations within the theological context of God's larger purposes for human flourishing amid a culture dominated by the pursuit of experiential satisfaction. His historical analysis and Augustinian critique of Western culture, along with his call for coherence between our understanding of reality and our definition of a fulfilling life, place before us a rigorous theological challenge applicable to planting missional congregations. There is a need for Christian communities that, rather than appeasing the drive for experiential satisfaction, offer a culture of grace in which God is the hope for human flourishing. According to Volf, our core theological challenge is to love God and our neighbor rightly. This requires us to make that love concrete, plausible, and central to our hope for flourishing in human community. It is a theological framework that is profoundly challenging and stunningly functional for church planting in our culture.

How might we experience and discern the Spirit's work today? In "Raised for Our Justification: Christ's Spirit for Us and for All," Lois Malcolm retrieves the missionary thrust of Paul's theology for apostolic proclamation in this post-Christendom and postsecular pluralistic era. In her well-researched and carefully argued essay, Malcolm aligns with Luther's critique of the theological trajectories extending from the books of Acts and John in favor of Pauline missionary theology, which attends to the Spirit's work amid a plethora of competing plausibility structures and options. With the precision of a systematic theologian deeply rooted in Scripture, the Lutheran tradition, and a missionary upbringing, Malcolm's own confidence in the Spirit's faithful presence and activity provides a necessary theological framework for church planting. The breadth and depth of the Spirit's work shape the breadth and depth of our own promising labors in this "Spirit-filled messianic age" for us and for all.

CHAPTER 1

Planting Missional Congregations: Imagining Together

Mary Sue Dehmlow Dreier

Introduction

It was Sunday, January 23, 1994. Gary, my co-pastor husband, and I were driving home from the first worship service of a church plant, People of Hope Church in Rochester, Minnesota.[1] That day God had given birth to a new worshiping community. As with most birthing days, the experience had been both exhilarating and exhausting. "It feels like *we* just gave birth," one of us said. Perhaps midwives often feel like that. It had been almost nine months since we had been commissioned as the pastors who were to develop this new congregation. This gestation period had called forth all our pastoral training, gifts, and experience to monitor and guide the process along, just as midwives do with the birth of a child. That day, the months of groundwork and preparation had culminated in its initial public worship service — the appearance of a new creation among the churches in Rochester.

The title of this book is *Created and Led by the Spirit: Planting Missional Congregations*. It addresses different facets of human agency in

---

1. In this essay I use a variety of terms interchangeably to identify the initiatives to start new congregations, e.g., "church (or congregation) planting," "mission development," "birthing," and "midwifing." Some of these are preferred in certain church bodies, but all refer essentially to the efforts of beginning new congregations.

3

the energy-intensive task of planting new congregations. But we begin with the perspective of Psalm 127:1: "Unless the Lord builds the house, those who build it labor in vain."[2] A different focus emerges from this psalm, one that points to the agency of the *Spirit.* God's generative building activity makes our own building activities possible, from putting up actual structures to shaping human community. So it is with planting missional congregations: the energy-intensive task of building new households of faith is initiated and undergirded by the primary agency of the Spirit.

The chapters in this book are thus primarily about the Holy Spirit, who creates and leads us in the development of new congregations. These chapters celebrate the power, presence, and primary role of the Holy Spirit as we labor with God to plant congregations in the rich soil of the North American mission field. With the wisdom of Psalm 127:1 echoing in our ears, we might say: "Unless the Lord plants the church, those who plant it labor in vain." It is important to note that our focus is on planting *missional* congregations. Church planting today, in this new era of apostolic mission, calls for congregations that have an intentional, mission-focused identity, and that, in turn, informs their participation in God's mission in the world for the sake of the world.[3] God's mission, therefore, clearly influences the identity, activity, and organization of these new congregations.[4] Developing new missional congregations focuses on having God's mission as essential to their congregational DNA.[5]

I divide this chapter into three main sections. In the first section I discuss questions raised by diverse human experiences of God the Spirit in today's world, which provides the experiential backdrop for pursuing a pneumatology for missional church planting. In the second section I explore how the Holy Spirit, as the primary church planter in the Acts of the Apostles, sends out apostles to participate in God's mission. This places the

2. Bible quotations in this volume are from the New Revised Standard Version (NRSV), unless otherwise noted.

3. See Patrick R. Keifert, *We Are Here Now: A New Missional Era* (Eagle, ID: Allelon Publishing, 2006), pp. 36-37.

4. Craig Van Gelder, *The Essence of the Church: A Community Created by the Spirit* (Grand Rapids: Baker, 2000), pp. 155-56.

5. For a discussion of missional DNA, see Craig Van Gelder, "An Ecclesiastical Geno-Project: Unpacking the DNA of Denominations," in Van Gelder, ed., *The Missional Church and Denominations: Helping Congregations Develop a Missional Identity,* Missional Church series (Grand Rapids: Eerdmans, 2008), pp. 12-45.

primacy of the Spirit's work in North American church planting today in biblical and theological perspective. In the third section I engage the third article of the Apostles' Creed to discern the fourfold public reality of the Spirit. This section further develops the biblical and theological framework for recognizing, celebrating, and participating in the reality of the Spirit's planting missional churches today.

In all three sections of the essay I draw on my own experiences as a mission developer-midwife of the People of Hope congregation from 1993 to 2006, a researcher of newly planted ELCA congregations, and a professor of future missional leaders at Luther Seminary. I engage Michael Welker's realistic theology (introduced in section 1) as a working framework throughout this chapter, to offer a pneumatology in which the experienced and expected reality of the Spirit may come forward in new and renewing ways through the planting of missional congregations.

Unless the Lord plants the church, those who plant it labor in vain.

God the Spirit in Today's World

Differing Experiences, One Spirit

I remember a high school athletic cheer we bantered across football fields and basketball courts: "We've got spirit, yes we do. We've got spirit, how 'bout you?" Our opponents would shout it back a little louder, and the contest for competitively higher decibels was on — until we were all screaming back and forth at the top of our lungs. Sometimes it seems church bodies do the same thing regarding the Holy Spirit, each claiming, "We've got the Spirit, yes we do. We've got the Spirit, how 'bout you?" The competitive banter can get quite serious and heated, as if we could measure, contain, or possess the Spirit, as if we could vie for the greatest measure of the outpouring of the Spirit, as if we could claim to harness the wind of the Spirit. We cannot, of course, because the reality of the Spirit is far beyond human understanding, power, or control.

In the forming of diverse churches, the Spirit blows and leads creatively. The missional pneumatology for church planting that I propose in this chapter is, first and foremost, about a power encounter between God and evil. As Craig Van Gelder has said, the Spirit prevails in this power encounter, and new types of community take shape in this world through the formation of these congregations, communities that live by the power of the presence of God the Spirit.[6] In order to plant, cultivate, and nurture such communities in the power of the Holy Spirit, it is important that we find ways to acknowledge the reality and vitality of the Spirit, to provide clarity to diverse human experiences of the Spirit and the forces over which God's Spirit has power, and to live in that Spirit within the structures of human community.

Toward a Realistic Theology of the Spirit in Church Planting

With all its uncertainty, potential, and creativity, the task of church planting is deeply immersed in the generative activity of the Spirit. There is a *reality* of the Spirit mediating God's power and presence in the world through the growth of a new community of faith. There is also the necessity to discern that reality through both experience and theological reflection as wide-ranging spiritual encounters are cast like seeds across the fertile soil of a new church plant. German theologian Michael Welker has comprehensively engaged this task of a biblical and systematic theology of the Holy Spirit in his book *God the Spirit,* where he provides a framework within which to identify the many different perceptions of the Spirit in today's world, while seeking unity through interconnections rather than by eliminating competing interpretations.[7]

To begin the conversation, Welker identifies two extremes: on one end is the secular Western understanding that characterizes God's Spirit as a distant, intellectual construct; on the other extreme is the worldwide charismatic movement that experiences the Spirit through intense and personal interaction. Welker says, "The Holy Spirit is neither an intellectual construct nor a numinous entity" (p. ix). In confronting the tensions and conflicts between these attestations of God's distance and God's proximity, as well as the other predominant experiences of God the Spirit in contemporary society, Welker invites us into a new openness to appearances of God's reality and power based on the varied experiences and complex interconnections of biblical testimonies to God the Spirit.

6. Van Gelder, *The Essence of the Church,* p. 83.
7. Michael Welker, *God the Spirit,* trans. John F. Hoffmeyer (Minneapolis: Fortress, 1994), pp. 1-49. Hereafter, page references to this work appear in parentheses in the text.

I teach a course entitled "Starting New Missional Ministries," which begins with a demonstration of Welker's starting point. I place Welker's extremes at opposite ends of the classroom blackboard, draw a line between them, and ask the students to place an X on the chalkboard continuum to indicate where they would place themselves and their understanding of the Spirit. Each semester there are class members who resist the notion of a straight-line continuum between two extremes; instead, they draw the interplay between them as vacillating, circular, and somehow mutually inclusive. At least one student invariably protests that his/her understanding is at *both* ends, and thus places an X on each extreme — somehow indicating a connection between the two. Others seek more precise definitions or more diverse possibilities. Yet, even with creative qualifiers and inevitable outliers, most students eventually land somewhere along Welker's continuum. It is interesting that, while the majority of the students in this Midwestern Lutheran seminary are predominantly (though not exclusively) Western Protestants, the X's are almost always grouped more toward the charismatic side. (One semester a student perceptively pointed out that this was a class of would-be church planters who, quite possibly, would be more inclined toward the experiential side than most leaders in their denominations.)

The ensuing classroom conversation is lively. Even those Western Protestants eschew the perception of bounded rigidity, prescriptiveness, and lack of creative possibilities associated with the Western intellectual construct as Welker describes it. The Spirit cannot be placed on a neat continuum between two poles. Blowing wind is not so easily tamed and contained. However, as students wrestle with Welker's polarity, they essentially bring to the surface the questions behind the *realistic theology* presented in Welker's study (pp. 46-49). Is there a recognizable reality of the Spirit that makes itself knowable and clearly mediates God's presence to us? How might we gain theological access to that reality? And what difference might that make for our life in the church and the world — particularly as church planters? (p. 46).

Three underlying questions emerge when we seek to frame a pneumatology for planting missional congregations using Welker's realistic theology. First, is there a *recognizable reality* of the Spirit that clearly mediates God's power and presence to us, as the Spirit labors to bring forth new congregational life? New churches attract people with many different spiritual experiences and expectations. How might we identify with clarity and confidence the reality of the Spirit of God among us? Second, how might we gain *theological access to this reality of the Spirit?* People engage a variety of plausibility structures in making sense of life. How might a theology of the Holy Spirit help us discern, critique, and confirm or reject the experiences, formulas, or systems with which people identify? Third, can such theological access provide discernment of God's power and presence for our *callings* as mission developers, our *life* in new missional congregations, and our *missional focus* "for the sake of the world"? How might careful theological reflection awaken new alertness and attention to the power and presence of the Spirit? How might that openness to God the Spirit help structure the life of a new community?

These questions encourage people to interact with the biblical texts and their experiences of God's Spirit. Welker's theological framework seeks clarity concerning those things that are "characteristic and unavoidable" regarding appearances of God's reality and power in the structural patterns of life (p. xi). This is crucial for planting missional congregations. Such a realistic pneumatology for church planting in the twenty-first century invites us to search for interconnections in the midst of different experiences of the Spirit as a new community begins to gather, structure itself, and participate in God's mission for the sake of the world.

Missional Church Planting in Biblical Perspective

The Holy Spirit as Church Planter

> *Unless the Lord plants the church, those who plant it labor in vain.*

The Holy Spirit bears the very life of the crucified and risen Christ into our individual lives and into our shared life in congregations. The book of Acts gives powerful testimony to this: the Holy Spirit functions as the main character (as it does in church planting today) and faithfully labors to bring about God's new creation in the concrete reality of congregations.[8] In the stories of Peter, Paul, and a host of other supporting characters, it is the Spirit who faithfully and persistently pours out, unleashes, and extends the reality of God's power and presence in Jesus Christ to the world. As the church in the North America has increasingly recognized itself on a mis-

8. Justo L. González, *Acts: The Gospel of the Spirit* (Maryknoll, NY: Orbis, 2001), p. 8.

sion field similar to that of New Testament apostolic times, Acts provides a valuable biblical perspective for our own missionary understandings and activities. Indeed, the Holy Spirit is the church planter for the Christian church.

This missionary Spirit has three overall activities in the book of Acts: the church shares the gospel, the church grows and develops, and the gospel and church have influence in a variety of cultural settings.[9] Each of these is an important facet of the Spirit's presence and reality in Acts. To some extent, the chapters in this book address all three of them: the first apostles share the gospel; Christian communities spring up, take shape, and grow from the rich soil of the good news; and eventually we see the church planted in various cultures that exist from Jerusalem to Rome. This book focuses primarily on the second of those three movements: the growth and development of the church as the early apostles share the gospel, and then the church quickly spreading beyond the culture of the Jews.

The book of Acts is structured around the promise, prophecy, and proclamation made to the perplexed disciples in Acts 1: "You will receive power when the Holy Spirit has come upon you; and you will be my witnesses in Jerusalem, in all Judea and Samaria, and to the ends of the earth" (1:8). The book of Acts is like an unrolling map of the church-planting activities through which the Holy Spirit fulfills these departing words of Jesus to the disciples. A brief look at the beginning, middle, and end of Acts illustrates this. In the early chapters after Pentecost we hear how "day by day the Lord added to their number those who were being saved" (2:47). In the middle of Acts, with the map halfway unrolled, Jerusalem hears surprising reports from both Peter (Acts 11) and then Paul (Acts 15) that the Holy Spirit was coming to the Gentiles as well as to the Jews. And at the end of Acts, we leave Paul in Rome "teaching about the Lord Jesus Christ with all boldness and without hindrance" (28:31). The Holy Spirit has brought the gospel to Samaria, Damascus, Antioch, Cyprus, Athens, Corinth, and all the way to Rome.

The Jerusalem church kept trying to oversee this process and somehow resolve conflicts that surfaced out on the mission field. And so it convened the first mission development summit — the Council at Jerusalem in Acts 15 — to settle the question of circumcising Gentiles. The leading mission planters were assembled, and the groundswell of joy over the con-

9. Craig Van Gelder, *The Ministry of the Missional Church: A Community Led by the Spirit* (Grand Rapids: Baker, 2007), p. 40.

9

version of the Gentiles out in the mission fields (15:3) stood in sharp contrast to the requirement for their circumcision mandated in Jerusalem (15:5). After listening to the stories of both Peter and Paul, the summit lifted the circumcision requirement because "it seemed good to the Holy Spirit and to us" (15:28). After careful deliberation, the Council acknowledged that the Holy Spirit was up to something new and heretofore unimagined. The testimony of Scripture does not neatly systematize the Spirit's activity, and yet it clearly reveals the reality of God's power and presence in the world (Welker, pp. ix-xii). This new Christian church is the Holy Spirit's creation.

Things did not always go well for those who carried that message to the ends of the earth. They were stoned, fettered, publicly condemned, unjustly jailed, and even killed — thus constantly on the move to the next town. Yet a new reality had overtaken them: the life of Christ crucified and risen. As Saint Paul writes, "If anyone is in Christ, there is a new creation" (2 Cor. 5:17). Even in the face of worldly opposition and personal peril, the New Testament church lived a new-creation life. It flourished "in the fear of the Lord and in the comfort of the Holy Spirit" (Acts 9:26), and it just kept growing.

"Boldness and without hindrance" are the last words in the book of Acts (28:31), ending that biblical book on a forward trajectory. Those words refer to Paul's bold and unhindered proclamation in Rome, but they also hang in the air like an unresolved musical note at the end of Acts, anticipating what follows. The Word continues to be proclaimed with boldness and continues unhindered by the dramatic, diabolical, and even deadly attempts to stop it. Church planters after Paul have preached with "boldness and without hindrance" over time, terrain, and oceans until, by the power of the Spirit, we come to this place and this time.

> *Unless the Lord plants the church, those who plant it labor in vain.*

Church Planters as Midwives

As I mentioned in my opening reflection on the first worship service at People of Hope, church planting is a vocation of midwifery. Although waning and declining in many places, the church is pregnant with the promise of new life. The midwife image reinforces the fact that ours is a vital but secondary role. We lend a hand as necessary, we use our training and experience for the successful delivery of new life into the church, and we seek to assist and not hinder the outpouring of the Spirit as it creates new communities. As midwives attending to births, missional developer-midwives labor expectantly as each unique and particular new congregation emerges.

Midwifery takes us anywhere where life is stirring and ready to be brought forth in diverse contexts. New-creation church life is being planted in all kinds of places and germinating in all kinds of forms. For example, it appears as new or emerging congregations begun by existing churches. It appears as unconventional offshoots of tradition in renovated mansions, coffee shops, and converted warehouses. It appears among tattooed artists, surfing buddies, imaginative college students, and visionary retirees. It appears as Swahili-speaking congregations in new suburbs, immigrant communities, and rural cooperatives. Church planters today are thus going into all kinds of places, some expected and some surprising, as the outpouring of the Holy Spirit continues today as it did in Acts. Midwives attest to and assist in God's generative activity.

Even though it is the Holy Spirit giving birth to the church, our task as church-planting midwives is nonetheless crucial and challenging — and ongoing. Midwifing the Spirit's work not only takes place at a point in time, like a first worship service. Tending the growth of the new church plant comes next. And just as for the apostles in the book of Acts, things do not always fare well for church planter-midwives in our day. Outcomes do not always match strategies, expectations, and hopes. Some missional developers do not bear witness to the start of viable new congregations. Some congregations may sprout up, grow quickly, but then fail to thrive, falter, and die. Others grow very slowly until, finally, the efforts to keep them growing are no longer sustainable. However, many congregations do succeed in taking root, becoming viable, and flourishing. Throughout that journey, however, church planter-midwives must still guide a fledgling congregation through stages of vulnerability, unpredictable growth or decline, and instability.

Church-planting midwifery is thus a precarious walk among spiritual and institutional realities, and a biblically framed perspective provides a map for the way. The book of Acts opens up both hopeful and harsh realities of church planting. We, too, push forward "in the fear of the Lord and in the comfort of the Holy Spirit" (Acts 9:31). As Paul says to the Corinthians, our job is to abound in the work of the Lord — in this case, God's church-planting work — knowing that "in the Lord your labor is not in vain" (1 Cor. 15:58). Important as human efforts certainly are to church planting, it is God who continually creates congregations by the power of the Spirit. In the end, while churches and church planters struggle along, it is by the power of the Holy Spirit that the Word continues to go out with all boldness and without hindrance.

Missional Midwifery

As I have observed above, this chapter is not just about planting congregations but planting *missional* congregations. In line with the developing understanding of our North American context as a mission field, missional congregations are intentional about how God's Trinitarian nature and mission shape their own nature, mission, and organization.[10] They reflect deeply on what God is doing in the world, and they define their own mission from that perspective, living with two orienting questions: "What is God doing?" and "What is God calling us to be and to do?" This leads to sustained, creative, and intentional openness to what God is up to among them and in their communities, as they journey in discernment toward their own missional vocation.[11] A missional hermeneutic shapes their understanding and implementation of biblical and confessional beliefs.[12] Missional congregations are communities of faith who do not just draw people in but send people out, who have an external as well as internal focus, who seek people as God has sought them, and who welcome people as God has welcomed them.[13]

Planting missional congregations means that such a focus is not an afterthought or something that is done only after a viable congregation has been established; rather, it is part of the formation of the community's

10. Van Gelder, *Essence of the Church*, pp. 155-56.

11. A process of missional discernment that is shaped by these questions in specific congregational contexts is described in Keifert, *We Are Here Now.*

12. For a Lutheran approach to missional hermeneutics, see Gary M. Simpson, "The Reformation is a Terrible Thing to Waste: A Promising Theology for an Emerging Missionary Church," in Craig Van Gelder, ed., *The Missional Church in Context: Helping Congregations Develop Contextual Ministry,* Missional Church series (Grand Rapids: Eerdmans, 2007), pp. 65-93.

13. Congregational mission is the expression of God's self-giving, self-sacrificing, liberating presence. For a discussion of biblical exegesis and public theology in the shaping of missional hospitality, see Patrick R. Keifert, *Welcoming the Stranger: A Public Theology of Worship and Evangelism* (Minneapolis: Fortress, 1992).

identity and is sunk deep in its developing bones.[14] These congregations orient themselves and their activities around mission: they view their specific context as a mission field; they understand their purpose as participation with God on that mission field; and they mobilize their members as missionaries of the gospel in that mission field, bringing the gospel in both word and deed.

That requires *missional* midwifery. The nature and mission of the Trinitarian God shapes the mission development task in two significant ways. First, the mission of the church is rooted in the *sending nature* of the triune God active in the world: as the Father sends the Son, and the Son sends the Spirit, so the Spirit sends the church for the sake of the world. We do not simply go; we are sent on God's mission, known as the *missio Dei*.[15] Congregations are not just keepers of religious tradition or attractive vendors of religious goods and services for consumer-driven church shoppers. They are justified by grace through faith alone and freed to live for the sake of others, sent for the care and redemption of the neighbor and God's world. Therefore, missional church planting is a task of being *sent* into the mission field to cultivate congregations for this mission.

Second, the Holy Spirit draws church planters and new missional congregations into the *relational life* of the Trinity (often denoted by the Greek word *perichoresis*). *Perichoresis* is the circulation of divine life within the Trinity in mutuality and fellowship, openness, and neighborly sharing, maintaining individuality and yet fulfilling one another.[16] Concentrated in

14. My own PhD dissertation explored five newly planted congregations that were identified for their involvement in the wider communities in which God planted them, and within which the churchly vocation of public companionship with God in the civil arena was part of their developing missional identity. See Mary Sue Dehmlow Dreier, "Missional God Outside the Box: New Congregations as Public Companions with God in Civil Society" (PhD diss., Luther Seminary, 2008).

15. The widespread use of the term *missio Dei* to refer to the mission of the triune God in the world for the sake of the world set the stage for the missional church movement, according to David J. Bosch, *Transforming Mission: Paradigm Shifts in Theology of Mission*, American Society of Missiology series (Maryknoll, NY: Orbis, 1991), pp. 389-93. Denoting the church that understands itself in the light of the Trinitarian *missio Dei*, the term "missional church" derives from the book by that name: Darrell L. Guder, ed., *Missional Church: A Vision for the Sending of the Church in North America*, The Gospel and Our Culture series (Grand Rapids: Eerdmans, 1998).

16. Jürgen Moltmann, "Perichoresis: An Old Magic Word for a New Trinitarian Theology," in M. Douglas Meeks, ed., *Trinity, Community, and Power: Mapping Trajectories in Wesleyan Theology* (Nashville: Kingswood, 2000), pp. 113-14.

the crucified and risen Christ, the perichoretic Trinity imprints us with a congregational life that is marked by openness, participation, and mutuality in the face of oppression, domination, and inequality. The very Trinitarian life is imprinted on us. Church planting is a task of creating and leading concrete communities that are shaped by Trinitarian relationality. In light of both the sending and relationality of the Trinity, then, church planting is the activity of being sent into the world (Matt. 28:19) to establish human communities of faith that live in and bear witness to God's relational life in the world (Eph. 4:1-16).

As the imagination of People of Hope was being shaped, they decided to use the word "mission" whenever and wherever possible, even within their organizational structure. Instead of a church council, they established a mission leadership team. The annual meeting is an annual "mission event," the operating budget is a "mission budget," and adherents officially become member-missionaries. Monthly encouragement to the missionary task appeared in the newsletter under the title "On a Mission!" Efforts such as these helped shape the self-perception of the new congregation as a missional congregation into whom the very life of the missionary triune God was being poured by the power of the Spirit.[17] It helped establish a missional DNA within the young faith community.

I have identified the Holy Spirit as the primary church planter today, just as in the Acts of the Apostles in the New Testament. We participate in this generative activity of God as missional midwives who assist while God brings the creation of new congregations into this world. Planting missional congregations is situated within the larger context of the missional church in North America, which is shaped by Trinitarian understandings of the nature and mission of God. In this next section I will focus on recognizing, celebrating, and participating in the reality of the Holy Spirit's planting of missional congregations today in the tradition of the Apostles' Creed and on a deeper examination of several chapters from Acts.

---

17. The self-perception of a congregation profoundly affects its behavior and, ultimately, its destiny. See Patrick Keifert, "The Trinity and Congregational Planning: Between Historical Minimum and Eschatological Maximum," *Word and World* 18, no. 3 (Summer 1998): 283.

The Holy Spirit Today in the Tradition of the Apostles' Creed

Michael Welker's realistic theology of God the Spirit offers a critique of the dominant Western views of the Spirit characterized by heightened self-consciousness, power, and control, owing predominantly to the philosophers Aristotle and Hegel.[18] He proposes a contrasting view in the selflessness of the Spirit of God discernible through the four perspectives in the Apostles' Creed: the communion of saints, the forgiveness of sins, the resurrection of the body, and the life everlasting. Each one of those four illustrates, respectively, the public, reconciling, life-promoting, and joyful Spirit of God.[19] In this final section I draw on Welker's vision of God the Spirit in the Apostles' Creed, bring it into conversation with specific chapters from the book of Acts and my own experiences as a mission developer-midwife, and present a pneumatology for planting missional congregations today in the tradition of the Apostles' Creed.

The Communion of Saints: The Public Spirit of God

In the Apostles' Creed we confess, "I believe in the communion of saints." God's own self becomes publicly inscribed in this world through human beings and, in leading us beyond ourselves, takes concrete, realized expression in the local expression of the communion of saints called *congregations* (Welker, pp. 297-315). Similarly, Van Gelder reminds us that "the church does not exist only for itself. It belongs to God and is to involve itself fully in the redemptive work of God in the world."[20] As we plant new missional congregations, we participate with the public Spirit of God in newly constituting such a community of faith, one that bears the public power and presence of Christ in new ways in local community. Church planting invites, inspires, and expresses new openness to the public potential of the communion of saints gathered and sent for the sake of the world.

This understanding of the *public* nature of the Spirit can be seen in the experience of Pentecost in Acts 2. The book of Acts begins in suspense

---

18. See Welker's contrast of the dominant Western notions of the Spirit with a biblical understanding in Welker, *God the Spirit*, pp. 279-302.

19. See Welker, *God the Spirit*, chapter 6, "The Public Person of the Spirit," pp. 279-341.

20. Van Gelder, *Essence of the Church*, p. 139.

as we wait for the appearance of the main character, this Holy Spirit of God. The Spirit arrives at Pentecost with unmistakable power: the forces of nature herald its entry, and the polylingual disciples burst out of their waiting room with the gospel. Acts 2 tells us, "[A]t this sound the crowd gathered" (2:6). The Jews from foreign countries in Jerusalem were bewildered, amazed, astonished, curious, perplexed, and in some cases sneering because, after navigating the streets and shops of Jerusalem in their second languages, they heard their *native* languages being spoken (2:6).

Ralph drove a city bus in Rochester, Minnesota. With that big man sitting in the driver's seat, people who stepped onto his bus entered a community on wheels. *Whoever* you were — and *whatever* state you were in — Ralph welcomed you into his small bus community. Ralph believed Jesus was there with the folks on that bus, and he didn't mind telling them. He had a word for the garrulous and an assuring smile for the silent. He wore a WWJD bracelet, and he usually gave it away sometime during his day. Often his bus riders came to People of Hope worship on Sundays. It seems that when Ralph invited them — often picking them up as well — they knew they were really welcome.

Ralph helped write the People of Hope mission statement. While the rest of us were suggesting provocative and sometimes clever church jargon, Ralph challenged us: "Give it to me in bus language. I've gotta be able to use it on my bus, so I can tell people about Jesus and our church!" Ralph understood that speaking the language of the culture is basic to mission work.

Ralph understood the Holy Spirit of Pentecost. He knew that God's power was wafting through his bus. At Pentecost in Acts 2, that Spirit blew through closed doors and broke through language barriers with a power that inscribes Godself in this world and compelled the lowly disciples to address the world with the news of Jesus Christ crucified and risen (Welker, p. 310). In Rochester, the Spirit inscribed itself in Ralph's heart and compelled him, as he opened that bus door to stranger after stranger, to present Jesus through his smile, the sight of his WWJD bracelet on his outstretched arm, a word of encouragement, and sometimes an actual conversation. When people asked him, as did the ancient people at the first Pentecost, "What does this mean? (Acts 2:12) What's this God stuff all about, Ralph?" Ralph was an apostle for Jesus Christ.

According to Barbara Brown Taylor, the outpouring of the Spirit creates a poured-out church: "Leaving the church, I believe, is what church is for — leaving on a regular basis, leaving to see what God is up to in the world and joining God there, delivering all the riches of the institution to those who need them most. . . ."[21] The public Spirit breaks down doors and sends people into the public sphere as a communion of folks inscribed with the selflessness of Christ. Ralph practiced that selflessness in the ways he took care of the people on his bus. As the Minnesota winter got colder, he became concerned about one woman who never wore a coat. So he got her one by calling People of Hope, the community where he knew someone would find a coat for a nameless shivering woman. People of Hope was becoming a concrete public expression of the public Spirit of God, hospitable as the open door of a city bus. The word on the street was that People of Hope was the church "where anyone can go."

The public Spirit gives birth to a new public community within the world, one that is imprinted with the selfless crucified and risen Christ. Church planting is about entering openly and expectantly into this formation process, into the whirlwind of wind and fire and buses and rental units and homeless shelters where that selfless Spirit takes concrete public shape in the world. *Going public* is quite challenging to a church accustomed to its assumed position of quiet authority in the private realms of life in Christendom; but with the waning of Christendom, the church is commissioned again into its Pentecost-given public vocation in the world.

One new congregation, Signs of Transformation, reopened the doors of a church that had died of "white flight" and left behind an empty red-brick sanctuary shell on an urban street corner. Signs of Transformation flung open those doors, and the fresh breath of the Spirit brought new life to the neighborhood through a newly planted African-American congregation. The Holy Spirit stirred the new church to do a variety of things needed in the community: sending people out into the neighborhood with bottled water on a dangerously hot urban day, creating reliable daycare for children, and advocating for housing issues to the municipal board. These efforts were like bus language: they addressed the needs of that particular community in ways that spoke powerfully within the neighborhood.

The public Spirit creates and leads new missional congregations into the life and mission of the triune God, in whom these congregations bear Christ crucified and risen to the neighbor and to the world as a concrete public reality. These new missional congregations understand their mis-

21. Barbara Brown Taylor, "The Poured-Out Church," *Christian Century,* May 29, 2007, p. 35.

sion as more than the internal viability of their project.[22] Their viability is also related to perichoretically bearing the public Spirit of the Trinity within their surrounding communities in both proclamation and acts of mercy and justice. While fulfilling individual hungers, the public Spirit can be expected to gather and send people with the language, new visions, and wide-open possibilities for structuring a public life for the sake of the surrounding community.

The Forgiveness of Sins: The Reconciling Spirit of God

The Apostles' Creed continues: "I believe in the forgiveness of sins." Such a concrete reality comes upon us in forgiveness, Michael Welker says, that it is nothing less than a *rebirth,* which "establishes a new beginning to life, gives a new identity, creates new surroundings" (Welker, p. 320). Planting new missional congregations vividly exemplifies the newness in life that is possible because of the reconciling power of the Spirit of God. This is a relational understanding of forgiveness that creates community amid our creaturely diversity. Through planting missional congregations, the reconciling Spirit of God unites people into new communities of forgiveness that overcome our disunifying creatureliness and the local structures that create, reinforce, and maintain it.

On the first Sunday in Advent, while many people scurried around to set up for People of Hope worship at a local elementary school, two men in particular caught my eye and gave me a picture of the reconciling Spirit at work. One was a world-renowned Mayo Clinic physician; the other was on the housekeeping staff of a local motel. They knelt together stringing white lights on an inverted plant trellis, slowly and quite surprisingly transforming it into a makeshift Christmas tree to decorate the worship area.

"That's it," I thought, and took a lasting mental picture. "That's a picture of the church." Church is people kneeling together despite the world's stations and barriers, gathered and welcomed by the relational triune God into fellowship with one another, invited into praise of God and sent into service within God's world, diverse and gifted, reaching as the transforma-

---

22. Lesslie Newbigin, who had a vision for a church in mission in the Western world, encouraged the church to "be concerned with the doing of God's justice in the world and not primarily with increasing the membership of the church." Lesslie Newbigin, *The Open Secret: An Introduction to the Theology of Mission* (Grand Rapids: Eerdmans, 1995), p. 7.

tive hands of God turning things upside down and creating light and beauty out of the flat and ordinary.

We often think of forgiveness as the grace that wipes our individual slates clean of personal sins. Indeed, forgiveness does that and penetrates us deeply. But it is more than that. It is the unifying presence of the Spirit amid our disunifying creatureliness. The church-planting Holy Spirit was not only at work within the hearts of that Mayo doctor and that motel housekeeper, which would itself be powerful enough, but was also at work bringing two such forgiven ones together — as brothers, as a *church*.

The unlikeliness of such gathering is demonstrated in Acts 10 and 11. In the power of the reconciling Spirit, Peter (the lowly Jewish fisherman) is sent to the house of Cornelius (a mighty centurion of the Italian Cohort) with the inviting, uniting, and transforming gospel of Jesus Christ. In Peter's vision a large sheet full of animals that are unclean to the Jews descends from heaven, and a voice tells Peter, "What God has made clean, you must not call profane" (10:15). With that message ringing in his ears, Peter is sent to the unclean house of a Gentile, goes without objection, and announces: "God has shown me that I should not call *anyone* profane or unclean" (10:28; italics added). The Spirit of God was poured out on the Gentiles while the circumcised Jews looked on in amazement. Peter counsels the believers back in Jerusalem: "If then God gave them the same gift that he gave us when we believed in the Lord Jesus Christ, who was I that I could hinder God?" (11:17) The Jerusalem believers agreed (11:18).

The reconciling Spirit plants the church through the forgiveness that unifies. As Paul writes, "All have sinned and fall short of the glory of God" (Rom. 3:23). As Martin Luther declares in the Large Catechism, "Although we have sin, the Holy Spirit sees to it that it does not harm us because we are a part of this Christian community."[23] The church is thus the gift of forgiven and forgiving community. Through Peter and Cornelius, the doctor and the cleaning man, we see how the Spirit's world-overcoming power breaks through the barriers that humans erect between themselves. The reality of the Spirit "makes its appearance in tension-filled interconnections of different realms of experience that are not necessarily compatible with each other" (Welker, p. xi). The unifying presence of the reconciling Spirit

23. Martin Luther, "The Large Catechism," in Robert Kolb and Timothy J. Wengert, eds., *The Book of Concord: The Confessions of the Evangelical Lutheran Church* (Minneapolis: Fortress, 2000), p. 438.

draws together in mutual forgiveness the diverse members of the communion of saints.

In some places, this reconciling Spirit gathers people into newly planted congregations that are not usually part of established congregations. As in Acts, churchly institutions sometimes become nervous about developments on the mission field that create unexpected communities of faith. For example, Christ Gig is a diverse assembly of struggling urban twenty- to thirty-somethings brought together by a common interest in music. Many young people come to Christ Gig for free concerts, where they discover a community of folks who share in similar struggles. As one young woman said, "You're not uncomfortable here because of the way you're dressed, the money you don't have, or what sins you're carrying because everybody in here commits the majority of the same ones and we are working as a team to get over it." A former Wiccan started coming to this new missional congregation because of the "positive energy" she experienced through the music, but she became a Christian when this community of faith witnessed to her that there was something even more to life than good music and positive energy — that is, being a follower of Jesus.

Martin Luther brilliantly proclaimed in his explanation to the third article of the Apostles' Creed: "Daily in this Christian church the Holy Spirit abundantly forgives all sins — mine and those of all believers."[24] To confess "I believe in the forgiveness of sins" is to accept that the distasteful creaturely sins of my neighbors are just as forgiven as my own, and that I am united with them in a community that doesn't qualify God's unqualified grace. When someone is tempted to balk at someone else who stinks or is found disgusting in some other way, the pastor of Christ Gig reminds him or her: "At the great feast, she may be sitting next to you. You better get used to having her around now." Only the reconciling power of the Holy Spirit forgiving sins makes it possible for this kind of community to happen.

The ultimate expression of God's hospitality to us is the utter forgiveness of our sins. Our true hospitality to one another resides in the fact that we have all been redeemed, justified by grace through faith alone, and woven together by the common thread of forgiveness that has become the lifeline for us all. The power and presence of the reconciling Spirit brings us into this community life with each other and sanctifies us into a *new*

24. Martin Luther, "Luther's Small Catechism," in Kolb and Wengert, *The Book of Concord*, p. 356.

creaturely reality with one another, a reality characterized by liberation and freedom (Welker, p. 324).

New missional congregations, created and led by the reconciling Spirit, often open new doors to God's people who have been marginalized, disappointed, or disenfranchised from church communities. New communities emerge that sometimes don't fit into expected or usual forms for the church. They may even be awkwardly disjunctive when evaluated from the human viewpoint. Within their wondrous messiness, however, is the forgiving, unifying, freeing reality of the reconciling Spirit of God, who ushers in a "more comprehensive creaturely reality" than exists anywhere else: liberation from the power of sin (Welker, p. 325). It is in this liberation that new missional communities explore, discover, and celebrate new structures for life together.

The Resurrection of the Body: The Life-Promoting Spirit of God

In the Apostles' Creed we make the bold assertion, "I believe in the resurrection of the body." The life-promoting Spirit of God secures our life with God beyond the reach of death. According to Welker, resurrection delivers us through the discontinuity signified by death into real life, life that is vital and fleshly, not just numinous and beyond this world (Welker, p. 326). Resurrection is thus a present reality as well as an eschatological promise. As such, it is constitutive of earthly life lived in continuity with future hope, delivered from the marks of transitoriness, and enabled to fulfill its calling of perceiving and reflecting God's power and presence in the world (Welker, pp. 327-29).

Resurrection is thus more than one's private, individualized promise; it validates and shapes the human community of faith that testifies to the life-promoting Spirit present and powerful here and now. It creates missional communities that are fleshly and alive, communities that partner with the life-promoting Spirit in ushering people beyond the destructive reaches of death.

The conversion of Saul on the road to Damascus in Acts 9 vividly demonstrates this. Saul had become the reach of death personified. Terror and destruction lay in his wake, as he pounded the road to Damascus in pursuit of Christians. He had promised to march them back to Jerusalem in chains. But Saul was stopped in his own tracks and turned into a vessel of resurrection life. The encounter blinded him, and suddenly this intent

21

man with an intent agenda of death was himself enveloped in darkness. He could not take one certain step without being led by another. The life-promoting Spirit overcame Saul's death reach and transformed him, his purposes, and his influence. Saul became Paul, who proclaimed the resurrection power that had given him life, and consequently given life to those previously threatened by his own reach of death.

The homeless community of Rochester asked People of Hope to conduct the funeral for a woman who lived and died under a bridge near an all-night coffee shop. The word was out on the streets (and under the bridges) that People of Hope cared about the community, and particularly those at its margins and in its Women's Shelter, Dorothy Day House, and Habitat for Humanity–built homes. As a result, People of Hope was also called to stand with the homeless community as they grieved this death and to proclaim the reality of the resurrection for life under Rochester's bridges. We all live amid death-dealing realities. But these homeless people face them on a daily basis, and one among them had fallen to their shared vulnerabilities. The picture is emblazoned in my mind: all of us, standing together, needing and receiving in common the life-promoting Spirit that breathes resurrection power into fleshly life. Life beyond the defeated reach of death, life lived here and now — together. The mission development task is to preach Jesus Christ in such a way that people may be transformed by the proclamation of Christ's resurrection life and then ushered into a community shaped and patterned for living beyond the reach of death.

The reach of death has many tentacles. Mission developer-midwives are commissioned to be attentive to the death grips within their particular communities. The life-promoting Spirit gathered folks into the People of Hope community from many of those death reaches, some that seem quite ordinary, but are powerful for those in their clutches. Some had come because they had become weary of the failings of the church itself, hoping to "get it right" with this new start. Others came because they heard it was "a church for people who don't like church," hoping to have their spiritual hungers fed. Ralph came because he had a mission on his bus that needed a church. Still others came out of deeply buried grief, or the need to belong, or the desire to find a church that welcomed children, and so on.

The DNA of newly planted congregations is shaped by those who come. Life in new communities of faith is thus often tentative and courageous, composed of people who themselves are tentative and courageous as they journey in their own body of death. In the power of the life-promoting Spirit, we celebrate and proclaim good news to them: "Here you are beyond the reach of death. Nothing can separate you from the love of God in Christ Jesus our Lord" (Rom. 8:38-39, paraphrased).

In planting new churches, the life-promoting Spirit creates and leads another community that pushes defiantly against death's encroachments with the power and presence of Christ's death and resurrection. "For if we have been united with him in a death like his, we will certainly be united with him in a resurrection like his" (Rom. 6:5). We are not only life-receivers but become life-promoters ourselves as the Spirit of God is imprinted on our minds and hearts. That is, of course, what happened to Saul when God met him on the road to Damascus. And that is what happens to us when God meets us on our own death-bound roads.

The life-promoting Spirit places some new congregations at the margins of society, where death dramatically breathes its threats. Banquet of Praise is a newly planted congregation that has courageously staked out a life-promoting presence right in the middle of one of the poorest and most dangerous cities in the United States. Children fall to bullets on the streets, and drug dealers have overtaken the town square, but the life-promoting Spirit of God raised Banquet of Praise like a beacon of light that shone hope on this dark neighborhood. Everyone there is so poor and vulnerable that the gospel cannot be proclaimed without also helping with the overwhelming struggles that attend poverty: the daily need for such things as food, medicine, crisis intervention, or a place to sleep. Prayer and help walk hand in hand throughout the neighborhood as the life-promoting Spirit of God brings both redemption and care via Banquet of Praise to the neighborhood.

The life-promoting Spirit creates and leads new missional congregations into the life and mission of the triune God, in whom these congregations bear witness to Christ crucified and risen to the neighbor and in the world as a life force that frees them to live beyond the threat of death. Participating with the life-promoting Spirit in planting missional congregations takes great courage, energy, and vision for living life together beyond the multiple threats of death experienced individually and collectively by the gathered community. Living courageously at the edge of death, the life-promoting Spirit weaves together a life-promoting community imprinted with the power and presence of the crucified and risen Christ.

The Life Everlasting: The Joyful Spirit of God

We conclude our confession in the Apostles' Creed with, "I believe in the life everlasting." Life eternal is the joy of having an indissoluble connection with Christ crucified and risen that is unhindered by death. This infuses earthly life with the enjoyment of God's eternal power and presence while anticipating the glory of its future unveiling. The joyful Spirit of God creates and leads new missional congregations with awakening enjoyment for God, each other, and their mission for the sake of the world.

The story of Peter's release from prison in Acts 12 illustrates the wonder of this release from those things that hold us captive as God ushers us in joy to freedom. James had been killed, and Peter had been thrown into prison. Security was pretty tight. Even while sleeping, Peter was in two chains, between two guards, with more guards in front of the door. But no prison is too strong for the power of God, and an angel led Peter, who was as though in a trance, out of the chains, past the guards, through the door, and back onto the street.

The disciples, even while praying for his release, didn't really expect him to appear at the door. Joy awaited them, and the power of God to release from bondage seemed too good to be true. That is often true of us as well. As a part of this present life, our indissoluble connection to Christ is mediated by the Spirit "in acts of deliverance, preservation, transformation, renewal, and instruction in the discernment of powers and spirits" (Welker, p. 338). The Spirit's work continues unhindered, and it hinders powers that seek to constrain us. The glory of the Spirit awakens enjoyment of life unhindered by death.

Lucille heard that there was a new church being planted in Rochester, and she warily began to come. She was searching for something. She invited me to her home and slowly, over many lunches together, the story of her stillborn first child unfolded. Now, more than fifty years later, her only other child was grown·and living far away, her husband was deceased, and this memory was weighing more and more heavily on her. One day she said, "You know, what really bothers me is that my Martha never had a funeral." So we planned a funeral. One bright October day we headed to the cemetery — just the two of us, as Lucille had requested. She brought flowers, and I brought a baptism candle.

Scripture says that the Spirit of God blows around us like the wind, and the Spirit was really blowing that day. We huddled together against the wind and thanked God for creating little Martha. We read special passages of thanksgiving and comfort from the Bible. We lit the candle to remember that, although Martha was unable to receive the gift of baptism in this life, she was still God's creation and loved by God. We had to cup our hands around the candle to keep the wind from blowing out the flame.

When we got to the commendation, I had to shout loudly into the wind and into Lucille's good ear, "Into your hands, O Merciful Savior, we commend little Martha." At that precise moment, with no change in the wind and our hands still protecting the flame, it suddenly went out — as if someone had blown it out. For a long time we looked at each other in silence. It was a holy moment. The Spirit of God was stirring with the wind, assuring Lucille that Martha had been taken into God's waiting arms. This daughter, locked securely in her heart, was also indissolubly connected to God's life eternal through the power of the Spirit.

Lucille was rather like Peter when he was led by an angel out of his jail cell. She was led out of worrisome doubt and unexpressed grief that had held her captive for over fifty years. Freed from this deeply buried grief, I watched her life be transformed over the weeks and months that followed. Her heart was lighter, her faith stronger, and she felt less lonely and more joyful. Her personal transformation of joy spilled out to the People of Hope community, multiplying as she infused others with joy.

One by one, the Spirit gathered others imprinted with this indissoluble connection to Christ's eternal life. Bill was told his heart condition was untreatable, and that he was a living time bomb. It could go off in hours, days, perhaps weeks, but soon he would die. That night he came to practice with Spirit of Joy, the Sunday music leadership team for People of Hope, which always met on Tuesdays to practice for the upcoming Sunday worship. It was a courageous, faith-filled act of confidence in God's eternal life living in him despite his heart condition. He practiced hard, he sang on Sunday, and he died on Monday morning of a massive coronary. He lived the concrete liberation from powerlessness and hopelessness given by the Spirit, and he reveled in the foretaste of God's feast to come, however veiled, suppressed, and impaired by the reality of earthly frailty. God had led him — and would continue to lead him — from life into life. His rejoicing was like what carried the apostles throughout the book of Acts, through trials and even death, because of their unbreakable connection to eternal life in Christ.

The joyful Spirit creates and leads new missional congregations into the life and mission of the triune God, in whom these congregations joyfully bear Christ crucified and risen to the neighbor and in the world as new-creation life. Newly planted congregations carry a fresh openness to the joyful Spirit of God that can create new visions for individuals, structures, and communities. Our indissoluble connection to Christ's eternal life is present and promising, transformative and triumphant, generative and joyful.

Conclusion

The glimpses in this essay from Scripture and experience attest to the recognizable reality of God the Spirit in the world today. As the Spirit freely moves among us, it gives birth to new missional congregations and leads the church in its midwife's task of attending to these new communities. While there are diverse perceptions of the Holy Spirit, they may be woven into a shared imagination that is shaped from the perspective of the book of Acts and the Apostles' Creed. This provides a fourfold framework within which to discern the present reality of the Spirit of God as public, reconciling, life-promoting, and joyful. This Spirit imprints that same reality on the church. As we experience differences in the free activity of the Spirit, these four perspectives attune us to identify, celebrate, and advance the possibilities and potential of new missional congregations created and led by that Spirit for the sake of God's world.

CHAPTER 2

Human Flourishing

Miroslav Volf

Hope, in a Christian sense, is love stretching itself into the future. When I hope, I expect something from the future. But I don't hope for everything I expect. Some anticipated things — like a visit to the dentist — I face with dread rather than welcome in hope. "I speak of 'hope,'" wrote Josef Pieper in his *Hope and History*, "only when what I am expecting is, in my view, *good*."[1] And yet, not even all good things that come my way are a matter of hope. I don't hope for a new day to dawn after a dark and restful night; I *know*, more or less, that the sun will rise. But I may hope for cool breezes to freshen up a hot summer day. In our everyday usage, "hope" is, roughly, the *expectation* of good things that don't come to us as matter of course.

Christian faith adds another layer to this everyday usage of "hope." In *Theology of Hope*, Jürgen Moltmann famously distinguishes between optimism and hope. Both have to do with positive expectation, and yet the two are very different. Optimism has to do with good things in the future that are latent in the past and the present; the future associated with optimism — Moltmann calls it *futurum* — is an unfolding of what is already there. We survey the past and the present, extrapolate about what is likely to happen in the future, and, if the prospects are good, become optimistic. Hope, on the other hand, has to do with good things in the future that

---

1. Josef Pieper, *Hope and History: Five Salzburg Lectures*, trans. David Kipp (San Francisco: Ignatius, 1994), p. 20.

First published in Miroslav Volf, *A Public Faith: How Followers of Christ Should Serve the Common Good* (Grand Rapids: Brazos, 2011). Used by permission.

come to us from "outside," from God; the future associated with hope — Moltmann calls it *adventus* — is a gift of something new.[2] We hear the word of divine promise, and because God is love, we trust in God's faithfulness, and God brings about "a new thing": aged Sarah, barren of womb, gives birth to a son (Gen. 21:1-2; Rom. 4:18-21); the crucified Jesus Christ is raised from the dead (Acts 2:22-36); a mighty Babylon falls and a new Jerusalem comes down from heaven (Rev. 18:1-24; 21:1-5); and, more generally, the good that seemed impossible becomes not just possible but real.

The expectation of good things that come as a gift from God — that is hope. And that is love, too, projecting itself into our future and our world's future. For love always gives gifts and is itself a gift; inversely, every genuine gift is an expression of love. At the heart of the hoped-for future, which comes from the God of love, is the flourishing of individuals, communities, and our whole globe. But how is the God of love, "who gives life to the dead and calls into existence things that do not exist" (Rom. 4:17), related to human flourishing? And how should we understand human flourishing if it is a gift of the God of love? Consider with me a prevalent contemporary Western understanding of human flourishing, how it differs from some previous understandings — and what its consequences are.

Satisfaction

Many people in the West today have come to believe — "to feel in their gut" might be a colloquial but more accurate way of putting it — that a flourishing human life is an experientially satisfying human life. By this they don't mean only that the experience of satisfaction is a desirable aspect of human flourishing, so that, all other things being equal, people who experience satisfaction flourish in a more complete way than people who do not. We flourish more, for instance, when we are energetic and free of pain than when we are enveloped in sadness and wracked with pain (even if it may be true that pain can be a servant of the good, and exhilaration can be deceptive). Though some ancient Stoics believed that one can flourish equally well on the torture rack as in the comfort of one's home, most people in all periods of human history have thought that experiencing satisfaction enhances flourishing.

2. Jürgen Moltmann, *Theology of Hope: On the Ground and the Implications of a Christian Eschatology,* trans. Margaret Kohl (San Francisco: HarperSanFrancisco, 1991). For a brief summary, see also Jürgen Moltmann, *The Coming of God: On Christian Eschatology,* trans. Margaret Kohl (Minneapolis: Fortress, 1996), p. 25.

In contrast, for many in the West, experiential satisfaction is what their lives are all about. It does not merely enhance flourishing — it defines it. Such people cannot imagine themselves as flourishing if they do not experience satisfaction, if they don't *feel happy,* as the preferred way of expressing it goes. For them, flourishing *consists* in having an experientially satisfying life. No satisfaction, no flourishing. Sources of satisfaction may vary, ranging from appreciation of classical music to the use of drugs, from the delights of haute cuisine to the pleasures of sadomasochistic sex, from sports to religion. What matters is not the source of satisfaction but the fact of it. What justifies a given lifestyle or activity is the satisfaction it generates — the pleasure. And when they experience satisfaction, people feel that they flourish.

As Philip Rieff observed in *The Triumph of the Therapeutic* some decades ago (1966), ours is a culture of managed pursuit of pleasure, not a culture of sustained endeavor to lead the good life, as defined by foundational symbols and convictions.[3] This is a broad generalization, with many important exceptions. Yet it describes well a major and growing trend.

Love of God and Universal Solidarity

We can contrast contemporary Western culture and its implicit default account of human flourishing with the two dominant models in the history of the Western tradition. Fifth-century church father Augustine, one of the most influential figures in Western religion and culture, well represents the first of these two accounts. In his reflections on the happy life in his major work *The Trinity,* he says: "God is the only source to be found of any good things, but especially of those which make a man good and those which will make him happy; only from him do they come into a man and attach themselves to a man."[4] Consequently, human beings flourish and are truly happy when they center their lives on God, the source of everything that is true, good, and beautiful. As to all created things, they should be loved as well. But the only way to properly love them and fully and truly enjoy them is to love and enjoy them "in God."

Now Augustine readily agrees with what most people think, namely,

3. See Philip Rieff, *The Triumph of the Therapeutic: Uses of Faith after Freud* (New York: Harper and Row, 1966), pp. 232-61.

4. Augustine, *Trinity* 13.10.

that those people who have everything they want are happy. But he adds immediately that this is true only if they want "nothing wrongly," which is to say, if they want everything in accordance with the character and will of their Creator, whose very being is love.[5] The supreme good that makes human beings truly happy — in my terminology, the proper content of a flourishing life — consists in love of God and neighbor and enjoyment of both. In the *City of God,* Augustine defines it as a "completely harmonious fellowship in the enjoyment of God, and each other in God."[6]

In about the eighteenth century, a different account of human flourishing emerged in the West. It was connected with what scholars sometimes describe as an "anthropocentric shift": the gradual redirection of interest from the transcendent God to humans and their mundane affairs. The new humanism that was born was different "from most ancient ethics of human nature," writes Charles Taylor in *A Secular Age,* in that its notion of human flourishing "makes no reference to something higher which humans should reverence or love or acknowledge."[7] For Augustine and the tradition that followed him, this "something higher" was God. Modern humanism became exclusive by shedding the idea of human lives centered on God.

And yet, even as the new humanism rejected God and the command to love God, it retained the moral obligation to love the neighbor. The central pillar of its vision of the good life was a universal beneficence transcending all boundaries of tribe or nation and extending to all human beings. True, this was an ideal that could not be immediately realized (and from which some groups, deemed inferior, were de facto exempt). But the goal toward which humanity was moving with a steady step was a state of human relations in which the flourishing of each was tied to the flourishing of all and the flourishing of all to the flourishing of each. Marx's vision of a Communist society, encapsulated in the phrase "from each according to his abilities, to each according to his need," was historically the most influential (and most problematic) version of this idea of human flourishing.[8]

In the late twentieth century another shift emerged. Increasingly, hu-

5. Augustine, *Trinity* 13.8.

6. Augustine, *City of God* 19.17.

7. Charles Taylor, *A Secular Age* (Cambridge, MA: Harvard University Press, 2007), p. 245.

8. Karl Marx, *Critique of the Gotha Program,* in *Essential Writings of Karl Marx* (St. Petersburg, FL: Red and Black, 2010), p. 243.

man flourishing came to be defined as experiential satisfaction (though, of course, other accounts of human flourishing remain robust as well, whether they derive from religious or secular interpretations of the world). Having lost earlier reference to "something higher which humans should reverence or love," it now lost reference to universal solidarity as well. What remained was concern for the self and the desire for the experience of satisfaction. It is not, of course, that individuals today simply seek pleasure on their own, isolated from society. It is also not that they don't care for others. Others are very much involved. But they matter mainly in that they serve an individual's experience of satisfaction. For religious people in this category, this applies to God no less than to human beings. Desire — the outer shell of love — has remained, but love itself, by being directed exclusively to the self, is lost.

Hope

One way to view these three phases in the conception of human flourishing — love of God and neighbor, universal beneficence, experiential satisfaction — is to see them as a history of the diminution of the object of love. From the vast expanse of the infinite God, love first tapered off to the boundaries of the universal human community, and then radically contracted to the narrowness of a single self — one's own self. A parallel contraction has also occurred with the scope of human hope.

In the book *The Real American Dream*, written at the turn of the millennium, Andrew Delbanco traced the diminution of American hope. I am interested in it here because America may be in this regard symptomatic: it would be possible to trace an analogous diminution of hope in most societies that are highly integrated into globalization processes. A glance at the book's table of contents reveals the main point of his analysis. The chapter headings read: "God," "Nation," "Self." The infinite God and the eternal life of enjoying God and one's neighbors (at least some of them!) was the hope of the Puritans who founded America. American nationalists of the nineteenth century, notably Abraham Lincoln, transformed this Christian imagery, in which God was at the center, into "the symbol of a redeemer nation." In the process, they created a "new symbol of hope."[9] The scope of hope was

9. Andrew Delbanco, *The Real American Dream: A Meditation on Hope* (Cambridge, MA: Harvard University Press, 1999), p. 77.

31

significantly reduced,[10] and yet there still remained something of immense importance to hope for: the prospering of the nation, which was itself a "chosen people," called upon to "bear the ark of the Liberties of the world," as Melville put it.[11] But then, in the aftermath of the 1960s and 1980s, as a result of the combined hippy and yuppie revolutions, "instant gratification" became "the hallmark of the good life." It is only a minor exaggeration to say that hope was reduced "to the scale of self-pampering."[12] Moving from the vastness of God down to the ideal of a redeemer nation, hope has narrowed, argues Delbanco, "to the vanishing point of the self alone."[13]

I observed above that when the scope of love diminishes, love itself disappears: benevolence and beneficence mutate into the pursuit of self-interest. Something similar happens to hope, which is understandable if hope is love stretching itself into the future of the beloved object, as I suggested at the beginning of this chapter. So when love shrinks to self-interest, and self-interest devolves into the experience of satisfaction, hope disappears as well. As Michael Oakeshott rightly insisted, hope depends on finding some "end to be pursued more extensive than a merely instant desire."[14]

Unsatisfying Satisfaction

Love and hope are not the only casualties when the experience of satisfaction becomes the center of human striving. As many have pointed out, sat-

10. The claim that the scope of hope was reduced when it was directed away from God and toward the nation has been contested. Delbanco himself maintains that the national ideal is lesser than God. In his review of Delbanco's book, Richard Rorty protests: "Why, one can imagine Whitman asking, should we Americans take God's word for it that he is more vast than the free, just, utopian nation of our dreams? Whitman famously called the United States of America 'the greatest poem.' He took narratives that featured God to be lesser poems — useful in their day, because suitable for the needs of a younger humanity. But now we are more grown up" (Richard Rorty, "I Hear America Sighing," *New York Times Book Review*, November 7, 1999, p. 16). The dispute about which dream is bigger — the dream of a nation or of God — must be decided in conjunction with the question of whether God in fact exists or not. For only under the assumption of God's nonexistence can God be declared lesser than the nation, however conceived.

11. Herman Melville, *White Jacket; or, The World in a Man-of-War* (New York: Plume, 1979 [first published 1850]), chap. 36.

12. Delbanco, *Real American Dream*, pp. 96, 103.

13. Delbanco, *Real American Dream*, p. 103.

14. Michael Oakeshott, "Political Education," in Michael Oakeshott, *Rationalism in Politics and Other Essays* (Indianapolis: Liberty, 1991), p. 48.

isfaction itself is threatened by the pursuit of pleasure. I don't mean simply that we spend a good deal of our lives dissatisfied. Clearly, we are dissatisfied until we experience satisfaction. Desire is aroused, and striving begins, goaded by a sense of discontentment and pulled by the expectation of fulfillment until satisfaction is reached. Dissatisfied and expectant striving is the overall state, and fulfillment is its interruption; desire is eternal, and satisfaction is fleetingly periodic.[15]

More importantly, almost paradoxically, we remain dissatisfied in the midst of experiencing satisfaction. We compare our "pleasures" to those of others — and begin to envy them. The fine new Honda of our modest dreams is a source of *dis-satisfaction* when we see a neighbor's new Mercedes Benz. But even when we win the game of comparisons — when we can park the best model of the most expensive car in front of our garage — our victory is hollow, melancholy. As Gratiano puts it in Shakespeare's *Merchant of Venice,* "All things that are, are with more spirit chased than enjoyed."[16] First, marked as we are by what philosophers call self-transcendence, in our imagination we are always already beyond any state we have reached. Whatever we have, we want more and different things, and when we have climbed to the top, a sense of disappointment clouds the triumph. Our striving can thus find proper rest only when we find joy in something infinite. For Christians, this something is God.

Second, we feel melancholy because our pleasure is truly human and hence truly pleasurable only if it has meaning beyond itself. So it is with sex, for instance. No matter how enticing and thrilling it may be, it leaves an aftertaste of dissatisfaction — maybe guilt, but certainly emptiness — if it does not somehow refer beyond itself, if it is not a sacrament of love between human beings. It is similar with many other pleasures.[17]

---

15. Offering a particularly bleak version of this point, Arthur Schopenhauer writes that in human existence, there is only "momentary gratification, fleeting pleasure conditioned by wants, much and long suffering, constant struggle, *bellum omnium,* everything a hunter and everything hunted, pressure, want, need and anxiety, shrieking and howling, and this goes on in *secula seculorum* or until once again the crust of the planet breaks." Arthur Schopenhauer, *The World as Will and Representation,* trans. E. F. J. Payne (Mineola, NY: Dover, 1969), 2:354.

16. Shakespeare, *Merchant of Venice,* 2.6.12-13.

17. This observation fits with one of the central conclusions of the Grant Study of well-adjusted Harvard sophomores that was begun in 1937, which, after more than seventy years of following its subjects, remains one of "the longest running, and probably most exhaustive, longitudinal studies of mental and physical well-being in history." In an interview in 2008, its longtime director, George Valliant, was asked, "What have you learned from

When we place pleasure at the center of the good life, when we decouple it from the love of God, the ultimate source of meaning, and when we sever it from love of neighbor and hope for a common future, we are left, in Delbanco's words, "with no way of organizing desire into a structure of meaning."[18] And for meaning-making animals as we humans ineradicably are, the desire to satisfy self-contained pleasures will always remain deeply unsatisfying.

Accounts of Reality, Conceptions of Flourishing

For the sake of the fulfillment of individuals, the thriving of communities, and our common global future, we need a better account of human flourishing than experiential satisfaction. The most robust alternative visions of human flourishing are embodied in the great faith traditions. It is to them — and the debates between them as to what human flourishing truly consists of — that we need to turn for resources to think anew about human flourishing. In what follows I will suggest contours of a vision of human flourishing as contained in the Christian faith (or rather, one strand of that faith). A vision of human flourishing — and resources to realize it — is the most important contribution of the Christian faith to the common good.

The Centrality of Human Flourishing

Concern with human flourishing is at the heart of the great faiths, including Christianity. True, you cannot always tell that from the way faiths are practiced. When surveying their history, it seems on occasion as if their goal were simply to dispatch people out of this world and into the next — out of the vale of tears into heavenly bliss (Christianity) or out of the world of craving into nirvana (Buddhism), to give just two examples. And yet, for great religious teachers, even for the representatives of highly ascetical and seemingly otherworldly forms of faith, human flourishing has always remained central.

Grant Study men?" His response was that "the only thing that really matters in life are your relationships with other people" (Joshua Wolf Shenk, "What Makes Us Happy?" *The Atlantic*, June 2009, p. 36). Applied to the question of satisfaction, this suggests that relationships give meaning to pleasure; pleasure hollows itself out without them.

18. Delbanco, *Real American Dream*, p. 103.

Take Abu Hamid Mohammad al-Ghazali, one of the greatest Muslim thinkers, as an example. "Know, O beloved, that man was not created in jest or at random, but marvelously made and for some great end," he begins one of his books. What is that great end for a being whose spirit is "lofty and divine," even if its body is "mean and earthly"? Here is how al-Ghazali describes it:

> When in the crucible of abstinence he [mankind] is purged from carnal passions he attains to the highest, and in place of being a slave to lust and anger becomes endued with angelic qualities. Attaining that state, he finds his heaven in the contemplation of Eternal Beauty, and no longer in fleshly delights.

These lines come from the introduction to al-Ghazali's book, which is all about "turning away from the world to God." That may make it sound as if the book is not about human flourishing at all. And yet its title is *The Alchemy of Happiness*.[19] Precisely by talking about turning away from the world to God and purging oneself from carnal passions, the book *is* about flourishing — in this world and the next.

Or take one of the greatest of Jewish religious thinkers, Moses Maimonides. At the beginning of *The Guide of the Perplexed*, he says that the image of God in human beings — that which distinguishes them from animals — is "the intellect which God made overflow into man."[20] To underscore this point, Maimonides ends his work by stating that intellect is "the bond between us and Him."[21] True human perfection consists

> in the acquisition of the rational virtues — I refer to the conception of intelligibles, which teach true opinions concerning divine things. This is in true reality the ultimate end; this is what gives the individual true perfection, a perfection belonging to him alone; and it gives him permanent perdurance; through it man is man.[22]

19. Abu Hamid Muhammad al-Ghazali, *The Alchemy of Happiness,* trans. Claud Field (Gloucester, MA: Dodo, 2008), p. xii.

20. Moses Maimonides, *The Guide of the Perplexed,* trans. Shlomo Pines (Chicago: University of Chicago Press, 1963), 1.2.

21. Maimonides, *The Guide of the Perplexed,* 3.51.

22. Maimonides, *The Guide of the Perplexed,* 3.54. Though prevalent, this "intellectualist" reading of Maimonides' account of human perfection has not remained unchallenged. For an alternative reading that emphasizes not just human apprehension of God but human love of God, as well as human "return" to the world as a being transformed by the

The nature of ultimate reality, the character of human beings, the meaning of their lives, and the most worthy of their pursuits — all these things cohere. The whole religious system is connected with human flourishing.

Contemporary fellow Muslims and Jews might quarrel with al-Ghazali's and Maimonides' accounts of human flourishing, most likely deeming them too ascetical or intellectual. Indeed, many internal debates within a religious tradition concern the question of just what it is that constitutes properly understood human flourishing. Christians might do so as well (though many Christian sages and saints have understood flourishing in strikingly similar ways[23]). Christians might also disagree about the best means to achieve it (noting especially the absence of Jesus Christ in these accounts). My point in invoking al-Ghazali and Maimonides is not to offer a Christian assessment of their thought, though a respectful critical conversation among great faiths about human flourishing is important. It is rather to illustrate that the concern for human flourishing is central to great religious traditions, indeed, one of their defining characteristics.

Not so long ago, human flourishing was also central to the institutions of higher learning in the West. They were largely about exploration of what it means to live well, to lead a meaningful life. They were less about how to be successful at this or that activity or vocation, but about how to be successful at *being human.* In my terms, they were about human flourishing. This is no longer so. In his book *Education's End,* Anthony Kronman tells a compelling story of how the ideal of a "research university" and fascination with "postmodernism" in culture and theory colluded in making colleges and universities give up on exploring the meaning of life.[24] Today, he writes, "if one wants organized assistance in answering the question of life's meaning, and not just the love of family and friends, it is to the churches that one must turn."[25]

---

knowledge of God "to participate in the governance of one's society according to the principles of loving-kindness, righteousness, and judgment," see Menachem Kellner, "Is Maimonides's Ideal Person Austerely Rationalist?" *American Catholic Philosophical Quarterly* 76 (2002): 125-43 (quotation on p. 134).

23. It has been a widespread Christian *critique* of Islam in the Middle Ages and Renaissance that it was "founded on pleasure," as Pope Pius II expresses in his letter to the Ottoman sultan Mehmed II. Aeneas Silvius Piccolomini, *Epistola ad Mahomatem II,* ed. and trans. Albert R. Baca (New York: Peter Lang, 1990), p. 91.

24. Anthony T. Kronman, *Education's End: Why Our Colleges and Universities Have Given Up on the Meaning of Life* (New Haven: Yale University Press, 2007).

25. Kronman, *Education's End,* p. 197.

As a self-confessed secularist, Kronman is critical of the way religious traditions go about giving answers to the meaning of life. He believes — wrongly, I think — that faiths are inherently inhospitable to responsible pluralism and always demand a sacrifice of intellect. As a person of faith, I think that a secular quest for the meaning of life is very likely to fail, and that the viable candidates for the meaning of life are all religiously based. But whatever position one takes in the debate between secular humanism and religious traditions, both share a concern for human flourishing and stand in contrast with a pervasive cultural preoccupation with experiential satisfaction in wide swaths of societies today — in the West and elsewhere.

Fit

Al-Ghazali's *The Alchemy of Happiness* and Maimonides' *The Guide of the Perplexed* not only illustrate the centrality of human flourishing to religious traditions; they also highlight one significant way in which religious accounts of human flourishing differ from the contemporary propensity to see flourishing as experiential satisfaction. The difference concerns a fit between how the world, including human beings, is constituted and what it means for human beings to flourish. The central chapters of al-Ghazali's book, for instance, deal with the knowledge of the self, of God, of this world, and of the next world.[26] To know what it means to reach happiness, you need to know who you are and what your place is in the larger household of reality — created and uncreated.

In this regard, al-Ghazali is not unusual. As illustrated by Maimonides, most religions and most significant philosophies operate with the idea that there is a fit — maybe a loose fit, but some kind of fit nonetheless — between an overarching account of reality and a proper conception of human flourishing. And most people in most places throughout human history have agreed that there should be such a fit. They have done so mainly because their lives were guided by religious traditions. Let me flesh out this notion of a fit by stepping away for a moment from religious figures such as Augustine and al-Ghazali and looking briefly at two philosophers, one ancient and one modern: Seneca and Nietzsche.

Seneca and the ancient Stoics (who have benefited from something of

26. See al-Ghazali, *Alchemy of Happiness,* pp. 1-26.

a comeback in recent years)[27] coordinated their convictions about the world, about human beings, about what it means to live well, and about the nature of happiness.[28] They believed that god is cosmic reason, spread throughout creation and directing its development completely. Human beings are primarily rational creatures; they live well when they align themselves with cosmic reason. They are happy when, in alignment with cosmic reason, they achieve tranquil self-sufficiency and are not subject to emotions such as fear, envy, or anger, no matter what the outward circumstances might be. Thus do Stoic accounts of the world and of human flourishing cohere.

My second example, Friedrich Nietzsche, was a modern thinker who was radically opposed not just to Christianity but also to the ancient Stoics.[29] Even he, an antirealist thinker suspicious of all systems, seems not to have been able to shake off the idea of a fit between an intellectually responsible understanding of the world and what it means for human beings to flourish within that world. The whole Western tradition of morality should be rejected, he believed, not just because it is to blame if "man, as a species, never reach[es] his highest potential power and splendor."[30] The Western tradition of morality is inappropriate primarily because it does not fit who human beings actually are. Contrary to the assumptions of Western moral traditions, human beings are (1) not free in their actions but governed by necessity; (2) not transparent to themselves and others in their motivations, but opaque; (3) not similar to each other and hence subject to the same moral code, but each different. Conversely, Nietzsche's own advocacy of the "will to power" of "higher humans" fits precisely these features of human beings and makes possible the maximization of the excellence of "higher humans."[31] His "will to power" is simply the ten-

27. See Katerina Ierodiakonou, "The Study of Stoicism: Its Decline and Revival," in Katerina Ierodiakonou, ed., *Topics in Stoic Philosophy* (Oxford: Oxford University Press, 1999), pp. 1-22.

28. For the purposes of this essay, I am following the discussion of Seneca and the Stoics in Nicholas Wolterstorff, *Justice: Right and Wrongs* (Princeton, NJ: Princeton University Press, 2008), pp. 146-79.

29. See Friedrich Nietzsche, *Beyond Good and Evil* (New York: Vintage, 1989), p. 15.

30. Friedrich Nietzsche, *On the Genealogy of Morality,* trans. Carol Diethe, ed. Keith Ansell-Pearson (Cambridge, UK: Cambridge University Press, 1994), p. 8.

31. This last point stands even if it is true that Nietzsche cannot give rational reasons for preferring his noble morality to Western slave morality, because he did not believe that there are objective facts about what is morally right and what is morally wrong. See Brian Leiter, "Nietzsche's Moral and Political Philosophy," *Stanford Encyclopedia of Philosophy,* April 24, 2010: http://plato.stanford.edu/entries/nietzsche-moral-political/.

dency of all beings (humans included) not just to survive but to enlarge and expand — to flourish, so to speak — even at the expense of others. In a way that is completely different from the Stoics, Nietzsche's account of human flourishing also fits his account of reality as a whole.

Absence of Fit

In contrast, those among our contemporaries who think that flourishing consists in experiential satisfaction tend not to care about how this notion of flourishing fits with the character of the world and of human beings. The reason is not simply that, for the most part, they are ordinary people rather than philosophers (such as Seneca or Nietzsche) or great religious thinkers (such as Augustine, al-Ghazali, or Maimonides). After all, over the centuries — and up to the present — many ordinary people have cared about aligning their lives with the character of the world and of ultimate reality. No, the primary reasons have to do with the nature of the contemporary account of flourishing and the general cultural milieu prevalent in today's Western world.

First, as I have noted above, satisfaction is central to how many contemporaries think of human flourishing. Satisfaction is a form of experience, and experiences are generally deemed to be matters of individual preference. Everyone is the best judge of his or her own experience of satisfaction. To examine whether a particular experience fits into a larger account of the world is already to risk relativizing its value as an experience.

As an illustration, consider a religious version of the account of human flourishing as experiential satisfaction. In such cases, faith will shed its power to orient people and will be reduced to a servant of experiential satisfaction, which is a major malfunction of faith. From being revered as the "Creator and the Master of the Universe," who by that very identity defines who human beings are and how they should live, God is then transformed into something like a combination of "Divine Butler" and "Cosmic Therapist."[32] Instead of faith framing and defining the experience of satisfaction, the experience of satisfaction defines faith.

This kind of transformation of faith is in line with the pervasively

---

32. On God as "Divine Butler" and "Cosmic Therapist" among American teenagers, see Christian Smith, *Soul Searching: The Religious and Spiritual Lives of American Teenagers* (Oxford: Oxford University Press, 2005), p. 165.

antimetaphysical tenor of contemporary Western culture. "In post-Nietzschean spirit," says Terry Eagleton, "the West appears to be busily undermining its own erstwhile metaphysical foundations with an unholy mélange of practical materialism, political pragmatism, moral and cultural relativism, and philosophical skepticism."[33] In his book *The Meaning of Life,* he notes that many contemporary intellectuals, unsurprisingly, tend to dismiss serious reflection on "human life as a whole as disreputably 'humanist' — or indeed as the kind of 'totalizing' theory which led straight to the death camps of the totalitarian state." In their view, there is "no such thing as humanity or human life to be contemplated"; there are only various culturally conditioned and individually inflected changing life projects.[34] If each person is an artist of her own life, aiming to achieve experiential satisfaction unconstrained by moral norms reflective of a common human nature, then it seems superfluous to ask how the stream of ever-new artistic self-creations aimed at experiential satisfaction fit within the larger account of reality.

My point is not that it would be impossible to offer a plausible interpretation of reality ("plausible," I say, not "true"!) into which an account of human flourishing as experiential satisfaction could be nestled comfortably. My point is that many today would not care whether they live with or against the grain of reality. They want what they want, and the fact that they want it is a sufficient justification for wanting it. Arguments about how their desires fit with a more encompassing account of reality — how they relate to "human nature," for instance — are simply beside the point.

Creator and Creatures

It is a mistake, a major mistake, not to worry about how well our notion of flourishing fits the nature of reality. If we live against the grain of reality, we will experience emotional highs, but we will not find lasting satisfaction, let alone be able to live fulfilled lives. That's what the Christian tradi-

33. Terry Eagleton, "Culture and Barbarism: Metaphysics in a Time of Terrorism," *Commonweal,* March 27, 2009, p. 9.

34. Terry Eagleton, *The Meaning of Life: A Very Short Introduction* (Oxford: Oxford University Press, 2007), p. 35. For a parallel critique of the impact of postmodernism on the engagement with the question of the meaning of life in educational institutions of higher learning, see Kronman, *Education's End,* pp. 180-94.

tion, along with other great religious and philosophical traditions, has always insisted. The great Christian saints, theologians, and lay leaders of the past believed that accounts of human flourishing had to cohere with ideas about God as the source and goal of all reality. But how should they be made to cohere?

At the very outset, we can eliminate one possible option. We cannot start with a preferred account of human flourishing and then construct a picture of God to go with it, designing the fit between God and human flourishing the way we might look for a jacket to match our slacks. We would then be consciously enacting Nietzsche's devastating critique of the emergence of Christian morality and Christian faith as a whole. According to Nietzsche, Christians designed false beliefs about God in order to legitimate their preferred values. If we were to start with an idea of human flourishing and then "build" God to match our values, then the only difference between Nietzsche's version and ours would be Nietzsche's dismissal of those values as being perverse, as opposed to our upholding of them as healthy. More importantly, by constructing a picture of God to fit already given notions of human flourishing, we would be enacting one of the most troubling malfunctions of faith: divesting faith of its own integrity and making it simply an instrument of our own interests and purposes.

Let's return once more to Augustine. We may sum up his convictions about God, the world, human beings, and human flourishing in four brief propositions, tailored to highlight the relationship of his position to that of Stoics, Nietzsche, and many of our contemporaries. First, he believed that God is not an impersonal Reason dispersed throughout the world, but a "person" who loves and can be loved in return. Second, to be human is to love; we can choose *what* to love but not *whether* to love. Third, we live well when we love both God and neighbor, aligning ourselves with the God who loves. Fourth, we will flourish and be truly happy when we discover joy in loving the infinite God and our neighbors in God.

For Augustine, convictions about God, human beings, and human flourishing all cohered. That's the positive side of the fit: it specifies what is in, so to speak, when it comes to human flourishing. But the fit also specifies what is out. If we share Augustine's convictions about God and human beings, we have to reject some interpretations of reality and some accounts of human flourishing. Consider once again, now from an Augustinian perspective, the Stoic, Nietzschean, and contemporary Western accounts of flourishing.

If we believe that God is love and that we are created for love, the Stoic ideal of tranquil self-sufficiency will not do. Instead of caring for our neighbor's well-being to the extent that we care about leading our lives well, as the Stoics did, we will care for our neighbors' well-being — including the neighbor's tranquility — for their own sake, not just ours.[35] Our concern will then be not just to lead life well ourselves. Instead, we will strive for life to go well for our neighbors and for them to lead their lives well, and we will acknowledge that their flourishing is tied deeply to our flourishing.[36]

Similarly, if we believe that God is love and that we are created for love, we will be disinclined to believe that the Nietzschean noble morality designed to further the excellence of the "higher humans" is a proper road to human flourishing. Compassion and help for those whose lives are not going well — the vulnerable, the weak — will then be an essential component of leading *our* lives well.

Finally, if we believe that God is love and that we are created for love, we will reject the notion that flourishing consists in being experientially satisfied. Instead, we will believe that we will be experientially satisfied when we truly flourish. When is it that we truly flourish? When is it that we lead our lives well, and our lives are going well? We lead our lives well when we love God with our whole being and when we love neighbors as we (properly) love ourselves. Life goes well for us when our basic needs are met and when we experience that we are loved by God and by neighbors, when we are loved as who we are, with our own specific character and history and notwithstanding our fragility and failures. Echoing Augustine's comment on the contrast between Epicurean and Christian visions of happiness, instead of our slogan being "Let us eat and drink" (or some more sophisticated version of the same that privileges "higher pleasures"), it should be, "Let us give and pray."[37]

Loving God, Loving Neighbor

What I have written about the relationship between God and human flourishing is but a theological echo of two central verses from the Chris-

---

35. On this line of interpretation of Augustine, see Oliver O'Donovan, *The Problem of Self-Love in St. Augustine* (New Haven: Yale University Press, 1980), and Wolterstorff, *Justice*, pp. 180-206.

36. I owe the idea that human flourishing consists formally in a combination of life being lived well and life going well to Wolterstorff, *Justice*, p. 221.

37. Augustine, *Sermon 100 (150)*, p. 7.

tian Scripture: "God is love" (1 John 4:8) and "You shall love the Lord your God with all your heart, and with all your soul, and with all your strength, and with all your mind; and your neighbor as yourself" (Luke 10:27). Each of these verses, in a different way and with a specific Christian inflection, repeats themes that are deeply rooted in the Hebrew Scriptures, themes of God's abiding love for Israel (Exod. 34:6) and God's command to love God and neighbor (Deut. 6:5; Lev. 19:18). In conclusion, let me apply this notion of human flourishing, together with its undergirding convictions about God, to the proper functions of faith in human life.

Every prophetic religion, including the Christian faith, has the following two fundamental movements: the ascent to God to receive the prophetic message, and the return to the world to bring the received message to bear on mundane realities. Both movements are essential. Without ascent, there is nothing to impart; without return, there is no one to impart it to.

Most malfunctions of faith are rooted in a failure to love the God of love or a failure to love the neighbor. Ascent malfunctions happen when we don't love God as we should. We either love our interests, purposes, and projects, and then use language about God to realize them (we might call this "functional reduction"); or we love the wrong God (we might call this "idolatrous substitution"). Return malfunctions happen when we love neither our neighbor nor ourselves properly; when faith either merely energizes or heals us but does not shape our lives so that we live them to our own and our neighbor's benefit, or when we impose our faith on our neighbors irrespective of their wishes.

The challenge facing Christians is ultimately very simple: Love God and neighbor rightly so that we may avoid malfunctions of faith as well as relating God positively to human flourishing. Yet the challenge is also complex and difficult. Let me highlight three aspects.

First, we need to *explicate* God's relationship to human flourishing with regard to many concrete issues we are facing today: from poverty to environmental degradation, from bioethical issues to international relations, from sex to governing. If they do not show how a Christian understanding of God and a vision of human flourishing apply to concrete issues, these notions will remain vague and inert, with little impact on the way we actually live.

Second, we need to *make plausible* the claim that the love of God and of neighbor is the key to human flourishing. For centuries, nonbelievers have not just called into question God's existence, but they have railed against God's nature, against the way God relates to the world, and consequently against theistic accounts of how humans ought to live in relationship to God. Sometimes it feels as though they would not have minded God existing if they could have just believed that God is good for us. And this just underscores how difficult it is to make plausible to nonbelievers the connection between God and human flourishing. For the notion of what is "good for us" — and not just the existence and character of God — is highly contested.

Finally, maybe the most difficult challenge for Christians is to actually *believe* that God is fundamental to human flourishing. Now it is not sufficient for us to believe it in the same way we might believe that there may be water on some distant planet. We must believe it as a rock-bottom conviction that shapes the way we think, preach, write, and live. Charles Taylor tells the story of hearing Mother Teresa speak about her motivation for working with the abandoned and the dying of Calcutta. She explained that she did the hard work of tending them because they were created in the image of God. Being a Catholic philosopher, Taylor thought to himself, "I could have said that, too!" And then, being an introspective person and a fine philosopher, he asked himself, "But could I have *meant* it?"

That, I think, is today's most fundamental challenge for theologians, priests, ministers, and Christian laypeople: to *really mean* that the presence and activity of the God of love, who can make us love our neighbors as ourselves, is our hope and the hope of the world — that this God is the secret of our flourishing as persons, cultures, and interdependent inhabitants of a single globe.

CHAPTER 3

Raised for Our Justification:
Christ's Spirit for Us and for All

Lois Malcolm

Maria is a lawyer in a prestigious law firm in the Twin Cities of Minnesota. She is also a single mother of two very bright children just entering their teens. A Latina, Maria was raised a Roman Catholic in inner-city Chicago, but she gradually stopped attending church in her late teens. The liturgy had little meaning for her; she felt that the church was not attending as much as it could to her concerns for racial and economic justice; and, in general, much that went on in the church seemed to her to be too moralistic and too hypocritical. Nonetheless, she had her children baptized in a Lutheran church in her neighborhood, though she rarely took them to church after that. She found the Lutheran church to be too Norwegian and not very welcoming to her as a Latina. Her children received almost no religious instruction in the home.

Therefore, it came as a surprise to her when her son, David, started asking profound questions about God in the fifth grade. He was writing book reports on religious figures for school, and through the invitation of some friends started attending the youth group in the Lutheran church where he had been baptized. (The leadership in that church was becoming more attentive to being hospitable to outsiders.) Soon he was not only involved in the youth group but also in many other aspects of church life and was developing friendships with members beyond simply those in his age group. At his insistence, his mother and his sister started attending the church and now they are, as a family, active members of that church. Maria's only explanation for this unexpected turn of events is that the Holy Spirit must somehow have been involved.

This story exemplifies two patterns sociologists have identified. The first is that of *secularism* — what many describe as our being a part of a "post-Christian" society. The second is that of a *resurgence* of interest in religion and spirituality — what many describe as our being a part of a "postsecular" society. Against the backdrop of these two trends, I seek to understand how we might discern the Spirit's work in our time. I do so by way of a genealogy that traces and analyzes biblical and historical strands for understanding the Spirit's work. Focusing on one strand — the Pauline, and its Lutheran interpretation — I contend that we live in an era in which the task of discerning the Spirit revolves not only around the reform of Christendom but also around the apostolic proclamation of the gospel in an era that is both post-Christian and postsecular.

Naming the Whirlwind[1]

Beyond Christendom

I begin with the recognition, presupposed in the missional literature that has emerged within the past couple decades, that Christendom — the fusion of Christianity with civil power that began with Emperor Constantine's conversion — can no longer be presupposed.[2] The decline of Christendom and the cultural dominance Christianity had traditionally enjoyed in the West is usually explained by some version of secularization theory, a theory of the process whereby a society transforms from being closely identified with religious institutions to being more separated from them. A range of social theorists, including Karl Marx, Sigmund Freud, Max Weber, and Emile Durkheim, have argued that the modernization of society would be accompanied by a decline in religiosity.[3] They presupposed that modern societies were based on rationality (in the development of

1. Cf. Langdon Gilkey's *Naming the Whirlwind: The Renewal of God-Language* (Indianapolis: Bobbs-Merrill, 1969), and *Reaping the Whirlwind: A Christian Interpretation of History* (San Francisco: HarperSanFrancisco, 1977).

2. See, e.g., Darrell L. Guder, ed., *Missional Church: A Vision for the Sending of the Church in North America* (Grand Rapids: Eerdmans, 1998); Lesslie Newbigin, *The Gospel in a Pluralist Society* (Grand Rapids: Eerdmans, 1989); and Richard H. Bliese and Craig Van Gelder, eds., *The Evangelizing Church: A Lutheran Contribution* (Minneapolis: Fortress, 2005).

3. See, e.g., Jose Casanova, *Public Religions in the Modern World* (Chicago: University of Chicago Press, 1994).

science, technology, and democratic institutions) and that such rationality would soon call for a decline in religious belief and practice — what Weber called the "disenchantment" of the world.[4]

There are three processes often identified with the secularization of a society.[5] (1) They undergo a process of *differentiation,* whereby the secular spheres in a society (e.g., politics, economics, and science) become functionally differentiated from the religious sphere, which in turn develops its own, more privatized, sphere. (2) This differentiation is often accompanied by an actual *decline in religious practice* (i.e., people no longer tend to believe in God and they stop going to church). And (3), as Charles Taylor has noted, a society that undergoes secularization experiences an actual shift in its *plausibility structures.* In such a society, belief in God is no longer "axiomatic"; it is "no longer unchallenged and, indeed, unproblematic." Now it is merely "understood to be one option among others, and frequently, not the easiest to embrace."[6] In Taylor's words, "We live in a condition where we cannot help but be aware that there are a number of different construals, views which intelligent, reasonably undeluded people of good will can and do disagree on."[7]

Beyond Secularization

Since the early books on missional theology, we have seen the emergence of literature on a range of new developments within world Christianity.[8] There are a range of new studies on global Pentecostalism (and its Neo-Pentecostal and charismatic variants).[9] Attention is now being paid to the importance of contemporary diasporas (such as the migration of Africans to Europe and the United States) — and people in transition from one cul-

4. Max Weber, *The Vocation Lectures: Science As a Vocation, Politics As a Vocation,* ed. David S. Owen, Tracy B. Strong, and Rodney Livingstone (Indianapolis: Hackett Publishing Company, 2004).

5. Charles Taylor, *A Secular Age* (Cambridge, MA: Harvard University Press, 2007).

6. Taylor, *A Secular Age,* p. 3.

7. Taylor, *A Secular Age,* p. 11.

8. See, e.g., Lamin Sanneh, *Disciples of All Nations: Pillars of World Christianity,* Oxford Studies in World Christianity (New York: Oxford University Press, 2008); see also Philip Jenkins, *The Next Christendom: The Coming of Global Christianity* (New York: Oxford University Press, 2007).

9. See, e.g., Donald Miller and Tetsunao Yamamori, *Global Pentecostalism: The New Face of Christian Social Engagement* (Berkeley: University of California Press, 2007).

ture to another — as sites for rethinking ecclesiology and missional theology.[10] And within the United States the phenomenon of the loosely defined "emergent church" (which also has a range of variants) has been gaining attention for its emphasis on personal authenticity and strong communal bonds.[11] In addition, there are studies of the tendency, among many, to claim to be spiritual (i.e., not secular) but not religious.[12]

Moreover, a narrow account of the secularization process, which couples modernization with secularization, has been questioned by a number of thinkers, such as the theologian Harvey Cox, the sociologist Peter Berger, and the philosopher Jürgen Habermas, among others. All of them had earlier espoused some form of secularization theory, but now have begun writing about the resurgence of religious phenomena. Cox has written about Pentecostalism;[13] Berger describes what he calls the process of "desecularization";[14] and Habermas has written about what it means to be a "post-secular" society.[15]

It appears that modernization has not been accompanied simply by secularization, but rather by *pluralism:* people can choose to be religious or not. As Berger has observed, religion is no longer inherited or taken for granted: adults make a choice to go to a synagogue, temple, church, or mosque. "Deciding not to go at all," a category that stretches from agnosticism to atheism, is part of this pluralism.[16] It appears, then, that the forces of modernization lead not only to secularization but also to the resurgence and emergence of a range of forms of religious practice. People yearn for community and some sense of a larger meaning in an increasingly atomized world. They yearn for a deeper ground of moral and spiritual certainty in the face of a plethora of choices. Religious practice provides a

10. See, e.g., Jehu Hanciles, *Beyond Christendom: Globalization, African Migration and the Transformation of the West* (Maryknoll, NY: Orbis, 2008).

11. See, e.g., Ray S. Anderson, *An Emergent Theology for Emerging Churches* (Downers Grove, IL: InterVarsity, 2006).

12. See, e.g., Paul Heelas and Linda Woodhead, *The Spiritual Revolution: Why Religion is Giving Way to Spirituality* (Oxford: Blackwell, 2005).

13. Harvey Cox, *Fire from Heaven: The Rise of Pentecostal Spirituality and the Reshaping of Religion in the Twenty-first Century* (Reading, MA: Addison-Wesley, 1996).

14. Peter Berger, *The Desecularization of the World: Resurgent Religion and World Politics* (Grand Rapids: Eerdmans, 1999).

15. Joseph Ratzinger and Jürgen Habermas, *The Dialectics of Secularization: On Reason and Religion* (San Francisco: Ignatius Press, 2006).

16. See John Micklethwait and Adrian Wooldridge, *God is Back: How the Global Revival of Faith is Changing the World* (New York: Penguin, 2008).

means for performing or enacting a sense of a larger whole in the midst of a highly chaotic and unpredictable world.[17]

And yet, what drives contemporary people to religious practice is not merely what they have inherited, a tradition they can take for granted, but what has personal and existential meaning for them.[18] People no longer simply go to church or believe in God because it is the socially acceptable thing to do. Whether defined with respect to the hierarchical structures of the medieval period or the bureaucratic structures of modernity, institutional Christianity appears to be on the wane. We seem to be in a "new age" in which Christianity has to be actually *experienced* or *practiced* in order for it to be viable for people.[19] The forms of Christianity that are flourishing throughout the world are those that have a strong experiential and practical impact on their adherents, though they vary in what they emphasize. Some define Christian membership with respect to more clearly defined patterns of communal practice or place greater emphasis on adherence to particular doctrines and particular kinds of ethical behavior. Others define Christian membership with respect to more profound charismatic or mystical experiences.

Amid this plethora of options, how do we discern the Spirit's work in our community and world? In order to address this question, I seek to examine some of the biblical and historical resources that inform our understanding of what it might mean to experience and discern the Spirit from a Christian perspective.

A Biblical and Historical Trajectory

Two Trajectories Stemming from Acts and John

Something happens after Jesus' death.[20] His disciples experience not only the risen Jesus, but they also experience the presence and power of the Spirit within and among them; they find themselves transferred into a new

17. Robert Wuthnow, *After Heaven: Spirituality in America Since the 1950s* (Berkeley: University of California Press, 1998).

18. See, e.g., Robert Wuthnow, *The Restructuring of American Religion* (Princeton: Princeton University Press, 1990).

19. See Sanneh, *Disciples of All Nations*, and Jenkins, *The Next Christendom*.

20. For a fuller description of the Holy Spirit in the Bible, see George Montague, *The Holy Spirit: Growth of a Biblical Tradition* (Eugene, OR: Wipf and Stock, 2006); see also Lois Malcolm, *Holy Spirit: Creative Power in Our Lives* (Minneapolis: Fortress, 2008).

world — a new age of life, new birth, and new creation.[21] In Luke's account in the book of Acts, the risen Jesus promises his disciples that they will receive power when the Holy Spirit comes upon them, enabling them to be his witnesses from Jerusalem to Judea, to Samaria, to the ends of the earth (Acts 1:8). The Spirit soon descends at Pentecost — with a violent wind and tongues of fire — and a new community emerges, gathering together for teaching, fellowship, the breaking of bread, and prayers. They experience many *charismatic* "signs and wonders"; they share all things in common, and God adds many to their number daily (Acts 2). As the good news is preached to new groups of people, the Spirit transforms the community itself from being a movement within Judaism to being a movement that includes Gentiles as well, as described in Peter's encounter with Cornelius (Acts 10) and the first Apostolic Council's decision regarding whether Gentile converts need to follow Jewish law (Acts 15).

In the Gospel of John's account, the risen Jesus sends the Spirit and commissions the disciples: "As the Father has sent me, so I send you" (John 20:21). Instead of describing charismatic "signs and wonders," the Gospel of John reads more like a *mystical* text, using words like "life," "loving," "knowing," and "believing" to describe how the Spirit will be Jesus' living presence among his disciples after he leaves.[22] In his farewell speech at the Last Supper, Jesus promises to send the Advocate, who will "abide" in them. Through this Advocate, they will "abide in" or "be" in Jesus — "you in me and I in you" (John 14:20) — even after he departs. Moreover, if, as Jesus says, "all that the Father has is mine," then what the Spirit discloses to the disciples is not merely Jesus' presence but all that Jesus shares with the Father (John 16:14-15). Indeed, Jesus' prayer is that his unity and intimacy with the Father will be reflected in the unity and intimacy that the disciples have with one another (John 17).

The trajectory stemming from Acts would recede in Christian history. Even in the New Testament we see that the emphasis on charismatic gifts and "signs and wonders" tends to fade (e.g., in Colossians, Ephesians, and the Pastoral Letters). Of course, there would be exceptions (e.g., the Montanists and the Donatists), but it would not be until the radical Franciscans in the medieval period that the theology of this trajectory would be

21. Arland Hultgren, *Christ and His Benefits: Christology and Redemption in the New Testament* (Philadelphia: Fortress, 1987), pp. 31-40.

22. James Dunn, *Jesus and the Spirit: A Study of the Religious and Charismatic Experience of Jesus and the First Christians as Reflected in the New Testament* (Grand Rapids: Eerdmans, 1997), p. 350.

formalized in Joachim de Fiore's vision of a time when the Spirit would fall on all people equally.[23] Moreover, it would not be until the emergence of the radical wing of the Reformation that the sense of the Spirit's falling on all people would begin to influence mass movements on a large scale. The Enlightenment, with its emphasis on freedom and equality for all people, would articulate a secularized version of this vision of an age of the Spirit.[24] Alongside the Enlightenment, there would also emerge revival movements on a massive scale both in the United States and in Europe.[25] Still later, what Henry Van Dusen describes as a "third force" within Christianity would emerge: the Pentecostal movement (with its later Neo-Pentecostal and charismatic variants) that is now is having such an impact on shaping world Christianity.[26]

By contrast, the trajectory stemming from John would have the greatest theological influence in the Christian West. In the theologies of Origen and Irenaeus — and on through Athanasius, the Cappadocians, and Augustine — the groundwork would be laid not only for the development of later Christological and Trinitarian doctrine but also for the importance of the church as an institutional mediation of the means of grace. Jesus is the incarnate Logos, the Father's word and wisdom, through whom we are not only reconciled to God but through the Spirit's power are also divinized through the sacraments and our participation in Christ's life. Athanasius would make the crucial arguments that established why Christ and the Spirit must also be divine. In the same way that the Son must be divine in order to redeem humanity (since only God can save), so the Spirit must also be divine in order to complete the Son's work by divinizing us (since only God can sanctify).[27]

23. See Jürgen Moltmann on Joachim de Fiore in *Trinity and the Kingdom* (Minneapolis: Fortress, 1993), pp. 202-9.

24. Paul Tillich, *A History of Christian Thought,* ed. Carl Braaten (New York: Touchstone, 1972), part 2.

25. See, e.g., Thomas S. Kidd, *The Great Awakening: The Roots of Evangelical Christianity in Colonial America* (New Haven: Yale University Press, 2007).

26. Henry P. Van Dusen, "The Third Force's Lesson for Others," *Life,* June 9, 1958, pp. 122-23.

27. See Lewis Ayres, *Nicaea and Its Legacy: An Approach to Fourth-Century Trinitarian Theology* (New York: Oxford University Press, 2004).

Luther's Critique of the Two Trajectories

As a reformer within a declining Christendom, Martin Luther was highly critical of both trajectories. Regin Prenter, in his classic *Spiritus Creator,* analyzes two phases in the development of Luther's concept of the Holy Spirit.[28] In the first phase, Luther criticized the Augustinian tradition he inherited for presenting the spiritual life as an ascent to what he called our "higher nature" above our "lower nature" (Prenter, part 1). Instead, he argued that it is precisely in "inner conflict" — where the sinner experiences the wrath of God in conscience and the very anguish of death and hell (and even experiences the desire for God to be someone else or that God not exist) — that the Spirit brings the crucified Christ to us as our victor over sin and death. In inner conflict, the Spirit conforms us to the crucified Christ. Inner conflicts are God's *opus alienum* (strange work), which prepares us for God's *opus propium* (proper work), which is to give the conscience peace. By means of the lowly signs of Word and sacrament, which we receive by faith (and not by sense experience or reason), the Spirit creates new life out of death amid our inner conflict. Linking the Spirit's groaning in our weakness (Rom. 8:26) with the Spirit's moving in the waters of the deep (Gen. 1:1), Luther describes how the Spirit creates new life within us, bringing to us the living presence of Christ, toward whom we move in faith — taking on Christ as our alien righteousness — and from whom we move toward our neighbor in the constant work of love.

In the second phase, Luther criticized the enthusiasts, who had taken his critique of the Roman sacramental system to mean that they could escape the "bodily effect" of the Spirit's outward means of grace in Word and the sacraments, and simply have an immediate inward experience of the Spirit and his gifts (Prenter, part 2). By contrast, Luther emphasized the public character of the means of grace, the Word's public promise of forgiveness in the body and blood of Christ in the Lord's Supper, the spiritual flesh *(Geistfleisch)* that gives life to the whole human being, body and soul. The Spirit's work, he argued, is hidden in the outward public signs of revelation. These signs are so public that they are available to all the people of God, both good and bad. The Spirit unites these signs with God's promises to forgive sins and give us eternal life. God has promised to be present in these signs; they are Christ's crucified and raised humanity for us.

---

28. Regin Prenter, *Spiritus Creator* (Eugene, OR: Wipf and Stock, 2001). Hereafter, chapter and page references to this work appear in parentheses in the text.

Through these public signs Christ is present as one who has received our life into himself. Through them the Spirit places our life in a real unity with Christ's death and resurrection, and we are reborn eternally. Through them the Spirit forgives and expels sin, freeing us to work on behalf of our neighbor in our particular stations and calling in the secular world (which includes unbelievers and evil people).

Prenter sharply contrasts developments in later Lutheran theology to the eschatological character of Luther's theology and its emphasis on how the creative Spirit makes the living Christ present in our lives (Prenter, p. 232). Later Lutheran theology, he observes, tended to move in either of two directions. On the one hand, it veered toward *nomism* (legalism), denying the Spirit by replacing the present and living Christ with an empirical righteousness. On the other hand, it veered toward an *antinomianism* (lawlessness), replacing the present and living Christ with a doctrine of the forgiveness of sin that results from Christ's work of satisfaction, but that separates it from the living Christ (thus giving us a message *about* Christ without the Spirit).

Later Lutheran orthodoxy would seek to be a compromise between these two tendencies: it became antinomian in its teaching on justification and nomistic in its teaching about sanctification. When this orthodox compromise fell apart, pietism evolved and "squandered the teaching on justification," thus becoming nomistic (Prenter, p. 232). In response, orthodoxy would become increasingly antinomian, with ethics becoming an insoluble problem (a difficulty that would became apparent during World War II, especially to Reformed critics like Karl Barth).[29]

Retrieving Paul

The Content of Paul's Missionary Theology

In order to grapple with these difficulties, Prenter urges a return to the "biblical realism" of Luther's theology, a realism that brings to the fore the eschatological character of the Spirit's work (Prenter, pp. 302-5). But when we turn to examine Luther's theology in light of recent biblical scholarship

29. See William Lazareth's discussion of Reformed criticisms of Lutheran ethics in Lazareth, *Christians in Society: Luther, the Bible, and Social Ethics* (Minneapolis: Fortress, 2001), chap. 1.

on Paul, we arrive at a difficulty. Since the Reformation, the doctrine of justification was the main lens for interpreting Paul's theology. However, biblical scholars since the nineteenth century have argued that there are, in fact, a range of themes that are central to Paul's theology. As James Dunn has pointed out, Paul "ransacks his vocabulary" to find a plethora of metaphors to speak about the "overwhelming experience of eschatological newness" that he found in the gospel of Jesus Christ. Thus, in Paul's letters

> we find metaphors drawn from the law court (justification), from the slave market (redemption), from warfare (reconciliation), from everyday life (salvation = wholeness, health; waking up, putting on new clothes, invitation to a banquet), from agriculture (sowing, watering, grafting, harvesting), from commerce and trade (seal, down payment, accounting, refining, building), from religion (circumcision, baptism, purification, consecration, anointing), and most significant of all, from the major events of life and world history (creation, birth, adoption, marriage, death, resurrection).[30]

In addition, biblical scholars have argued that Paul's theology needs to be interpreted against the backdrop of Old Testament messianic expectation and its developments in second-temple Judaism. N. T. Wright has argued that when Paul speaks of Jesus as the Christ or the Messiah, he presupposes two things: (1) He presupposes Israel's expectation that God's "single-plan-through-Israel-for-the-world" would culminate in the Messiah, who would "fight the glorious battle against the ultimate enemy, build the new temple, and inaugurate a worldwide rule of justice, peace, and prosperity."[31] (2) He presupposes that, as Messiah, Christ is the one in whom God's people are summed up — so that what is true of him is true of them. Thus, when Christians enter into Christ's life through baptism and faith, they are, in fact, *in him*. Christ is the "seed of Abraham" precisely because he "contains" the whole people of God in himself, making them a part of Abraham's family and thus heirs according to the promise.[32]

The context of messianic expectation and Paul's appropriation of it for understanding Christ's identity bring about a shift in our understanding of Paul's emphases. How are we to relate this new reading of Paul to a

---

30. Dunn, *Jesus and the Spirit*, p. 309; see also pp. 442-43.

31. N. T. Wright, *Justification: God's Plan and Paul's Vision* (Downers Grove, IL: InterVarsity, 2009), p. 105.

32. Wright, *Justification*, p. 105; see Gal. 2–4 for the whole argument.

lens for reading him based on the distinctive theological emphases of Reformation orthodoxy, which centered on the doctrine of justification? To begin to address this question, I turn to an argument Arland Hultgren made more than two decades ago in *Paul's Gospel and Mission*.[33] In that book Hultgren argues that Paul's theology needs to be understood in terms of his call to be an apostle to the Gentile nations. Paul had a world-embracing mission to proclaim the gospel of God's redemptive work in Christ to persons everywhere — Jew and Gentile alike. The new age of the Spirit, which has already dawned with Jesus' resurrection from the dead, is the messianic kingdom that is anticipated in the prophets' eschatological promises, which *in principle* includes all the nations in its scope. But for it to include all the nations *in fact* in this time before the *parousia*, a mission needs to be carried out among the nations: proclaiming the gospel and establishing congregations among them as the "first fruits" of the new creation.

In carrying out this mission, Paul speaks of justification in two contexts: (1) the justification of all humanity through Christ's "act of righteousness" (Rom. 5:8), which is known only through the gospel, and (2) the "realized" justification of believers through faith (Hultgren, p. 96). Both senses are rooted in the Scriptures. The first context (i.e., justification through Christ's act of righteousness) is rooted in the righteousness of God to be manifested in the coming of the Messiah or the messianic age. Here justification is theocentric and cosmic in scope. It presupposes an apocalyptic model that speaks of the revelation or manifestation of God's righteousness (Rom. 1:17; 3:21). God's righteousness has been revealed apart from the law in the death and resurrection of God's son, Jesus. The crucified Christ bears divine condemnation against sin and is the means — the "mercy seat" — that God has provided to reconcile the world to Godself, not counting human trespasses any longer and thereby demonstrating God's righteousness (Rom. 3:21-26). God's righteousness through this act is effective for all, bringing "justification in life for all" (Rom. 5:18). In the judgment following the *parousia*, God will certify this saving righteousness and complete the new creation in the age to come, be everything to everyone (1 Cor. 15:28), and have mercy on all (Rom. 11:32) (Hultgren, p. 96; see also chaps. 2 and 3).

The second context (i.e., justification by faith) is developed in the

33. Arland Hultgren, *Paul's Gospel and Mission* (Philadelphia: Fortress, 1985). Hereafter, chapter and page references to this work appear in parentheses in the text.

story of Abraham and the promise given that in him all the nations will be blessed (Gen. 12:3), a promise he accepted by faith apart from circumcision and observing the law (Rom. 4:9-25; Gal. 3:6-18). All people who hear this promise and believe that God's promises have been confirmed in Jesus become a part of the eschatological community. Justification in this context is *anthropocentric* and *personal* (or anthropological as opposed to cosmic in scope). It presupposes a forensic model: the believer lays claim to the righteousness and grace of God, freely given apart from the works of the law. There is no longer any condemnation (Rom. 8:21): the believer is already a "new creation" (2 Cor. 5:17) (Hultgren, pp. 96-97; chap. 4).

Hultgren maintains that these two ways of speaking about justification are rooted in Paul's missionary theology (p. 145). On the one hand, Paul is propelled by the conviction that the prophets' eschatological promises concerning the nations — that they, too, will know the Lord and participate in the messianic kingdom of peace and unity — have been confirmed in God's sending his Son to redeem the world. On the other hand, in this era between Christ's resurrection and the *parousia,* he has been commissioned as an apostle to usher in the first stage — the "first fruits" — of the gathering of all nations into the messianic kingdom. He proclaims the good news to the nations and establishes congregations among them so that even now, while living in the present age, all who accept this good news might enjoy the eschatological gift of justification already, become a part of the new creation (the age to come), and live in the certainty that nothing in all creation, or even in things to come, can separate them from God's love in Christ (Rom. 8) (Hultgren, pp. 143-45).

Paul's Differing Pastoral Responses

When we examine how this missionary theology emerges in Paul's pastoral practice, we see that he emphasizes different kinds of things in different contexts, depending on the problems he is addressing. For example, Paul writes his letter to the Galatians in order to address the question of what constitutes membership in the new Spirit-filled messianic communities he has started. In response to his opponents, who argue that Gentile converts need to follow Jewish law, he asks whether the Galatians received the Spirit by doing works of the law or by believing what they heard (Gal. 3:2-5). He answers his own question by saying that "Christ redeemed us from the curse of the law by becoming a curse for us" so that "in Christ Jesus" the "blessing of Abraham," which entails receiving the promise of the Spirit in the messianic age, might come to the Gentiles as well (Gal. 3:13-14).

God has sent his Son to redeem us from the law. Through faith and baptism, all people (male or female, Jew or Greek, slave or free) are clothed with Christ's identity (Gal. 3:28). They, too, like Paul, are crucified with Christ and now live their lives by faith in Christ, who lives within them (Gal. 2:20). God has sent his Son to redeem them from the law so that God can adopt them as children. And because they are children, God sends the Spirit of his Son into their hearts so that they, too, can cry out in intimacy, "Abba! Father!" (Gal. 4:6). Circumcision and uncircumcision — the distinctions that the law makes — no longer count in defining their identities. All that counts now is "faith working through love" (Gal. 5:6).

By contrast, Paul deals with a very different kind of problem in 1 Corinthians. This congregation was predominantly Gentile and probably mirrored the cultural diversity of the population of Corinth, a major urban center. There are serious conflicts in this community (e.g., factions vying for control, flagrant sexual immorality, questions about appropriate Christian conduct, neglect of poor members at the Lord's Supper). And it appears that those in the community who boast of having an elevated spiritual wisdom are, in fact, at the heart of many of these difficulties. In response to all their conflicts, Paul writes the letter in order to make an appeal for reconciliation (see 1 Cor. 1).

Paul's way of dealing with their conflict is to proclaim the crucified Christ, who calls forth a new humanity out of Jews and Greeks, choosing what is foolish and weak in the world's eyes in order to "reduce to nothing things that are" (1 Cor. 1:28). As apostle, Paul proclaims the message of the cross, which has a very different kind of logic than that used by the exemplars of his day (the Greek sage, the Roman rhetor, or the Jewish rabbi). Jesus' crucifixion — a stumbling block for Jews and foolishness to Greeks — reveals God's wisdom and power, the spiritual wisdom and power of the new messianic age, which the rulers of this age cannot understand (1 Cor. 2:6-8).

But it is wisdom, nonetheless, albeit secret and hidden — and thus a very different kind of wisdom from mere human wisdom (1 Cor. 2:7). We receive this wisdom only through God's Spirit, the Spirit who searches everything, even the depths of God. Indeed, through the Spirit, we are able to "discern all things" and are "subject to no one else's scrutiny" (1 Cor. 2:6-15). But this kind of spiritual wisdom is not a cause for arrogance. What distinguishes those who rely merely on their natural powers (the *psychikos)* from the truly spiritual *(pneumatikoi)* is that they are so filled with Christ's "life-giving spirit" (1 Cor. 15:45) that they need not succumb to "jealousy and quarreling" (1 Cor. 3:3), but can appreciate the varying contributions each one has to make to their "common purpose" (3:8). From the vantage point of Christ's life-giving Spirit, they need not boast of their various leaders or factions, since all is theirs: the leaders of their various factions, the world, life and death, the present or the future. All belongs to them, since they belong to Christ, who belongs to God (1 Cor. 3:22-23).

In fact, they have all been baptized into Christ's body. They all share the same Spirit, regardless of their prior status (1 Cor. 12:13). This does not mean a loss of individuality. There are a variety of gifts, services, and activities in this body because the Spirit gives to each member "a manifestation of the Spirit" to contribute to the body. But these individual gifts are for the "common good" and not simply for one's own personal aggrandizement (12:4-6). Thus, through the Spirit's life within them, they can become fully interdependent on one another, sharing in one another's joys and sufferings — even giving, after the pattern of the crucified Christ, more respect to those who are less honorable (1 Cor. 12).

Paul and a Postsecular Context

In its interpretation of Paul, the Reformation tradition has often interpreted Paul's pastoral response to the Galatians to be a critique of nomism, drawing a parallel with Luther's critique of the nomism of the Augustinian tradition. Likewise, it has interpreted Paul's pastoral response to the Corinthians to be a critique of antinomianism, drawing a parallel with Luther's critique of the antinomianism of the enthusiasts.[34] There are obvious parallels between these two different pairs of pastoral responses.

Nonetheless, there are important differences between these two pairs of responses as well, differences related to the very different contexts and vocations that defined Paul's and Luther's respective pastoral ministries. Within the context of a corrupt Christendom, Luther was a Reformer who faced two issues: (1) liberating the Augustinian tradition from the nomism it had inherited and, once he had started that reform, (2) dealing with en-

---

34. See, e.g., Gerhard Forde, "The Work of Christ," in *Christian Dogmatics*, vol. 2, ed. Carl Braaten and Robert Jenson (Philadelphia: Fortress, 1984).

thusiasts who had carried his argument for Christian freedom so far that they no longer relied on the public mediation of Word and sacraments (the problem of antinomianism).

By contrast, within the context of the Roman Empire, Paul was an apostle commissioned to proclaim the gospel to the Gentiles. Israel's expectation of a messianic age had culminated in the crucified Messiah, making the promise of the Spirit now available to Gentiles as well by faith. As an apostle to the Gentiles, Paul faced two questions. (1) How was the universal character of the promise of the Spirit to be appropriated by particular communities? (Thus, in Galatians he sets his critique of nomism within the larger question of what the particular means would be for appropriating God's universal promise of the Spirit: keeping Jewish law or faith in Jesus Christ.) (2) And once those communities were established, with people coming from diverse Gentile backgrounds, what were the grounds for their unity in spite of diversity, now that the basis for their participation in these new communities was not the Jewish law but solely the presence of Christ's Spirit among them by faith? (In 1 Corinthians, therefore, Paul's sets his critique of antinomianism within the larger question of how the Spirit creates unity amid diversity.)

As I observed above, our situation today is characterized by the decline of Christendom. We live in a pluralistic world in which people no longer presuppose the plausibility structures that Luther and his opponents would have shared. Our context, as Oswald Bayer has noted, is an inherently antinomian one, where particularity and diversity are taken as a given — not the universality and unity of truth.[35] This context (and the set of problems that emerge within it) has strong resonances with the context that Paul addressed.

Indeed, the contemporary philosopher Alain Badiou has argued that we read Paul as an original thinker whose thought weaves truth and subjectivity together in a way that continues to be relevant for us today.[36] In our day, we presuppose cultural and historical relativism. We thus find it difficult to speak truth in the face of the forces that define our age. On the one hand, our secular world is configured as a world market, which imposes an abstract homogenization on different cultural identities. On the

35. Oswald Bayer, *Martin Luther's Theology: A Contemporary Interpretation*, trans. Thomas H. Trapp (Grand Rapids: Eerdmans, 2003), pp. 65-66.

36. See Alain Badiou, *Saint Paul: The Foundation of Universalism*, trans. Ray Brassier (Stanford: Stanford University Press, 2003). Hereafter, chapter and page references to this work appear in parentheses in the text.

other hand, the thrust of an encroaching world market only fosters the cultivation of particular identities, creating even more fragmentation. How can we speak truth in the face of these forces?

Badiou argues that the apostle Paul has relevance to this question because, in his day, he mobilized a "universal singularity" in his proclamation of the particular gospel of Jesus Christ for all people — against "prevailing abstractions" (legal then, economic now) and against "communitarian or particularistic protest" (pp. 13-14). On the one hand, Paul sought to drag the good news of the gospel out from being restricted to the Jewish community. Yet he did not want it to be determined by the "statist generality" of Roman law and conditions for citizenship; rather, anyone could become a Christian subject — slaves, women, and people of every profession and nationality. And he also distanced himself from the "ideological generality" of Greek philosophical and moral discourse, the counterpoint to a conservative vision of Jewish law (Badiou, chap. 1).

Accordingly, Paul proclaimed a new way of being a subject who bears a universal truth that simultaneously shatters the strictures of Judaic law and the conventions of the Greek *logos*. What Paul presents is a new kind of law (the righteousness of God), which establishes a subject (the believer) whose only identity lies in having been declared a subject in an event of declaration (proclamation and believing in the gospel). By declaring that one has a new identity in Christ, the gospel provides a way of being a particular subject who bears universal truth beyond any kind of abstract law or communitarian boundary. We live now by faith in Christ. And yet, the gospel cannot be used solely to buttress one's own interests (or that of one's group) because it is something claimed in principle for all people. As a result, the gospel can only be lived in love for others (since all others in principle can lay claim to a new subjectivity in Christ by faith) and hope (from the standpoint of certainty in the "truth procedure's completed character") (Badiou, chap. 1).

In summary, Badiou helps us locate Paul's argument within our antinomian context, where particularity and diversity are the givens, and the primary problem we face is not the need for liberation from the nomism of inherited tradition but the problem of how to speak truth's universality and unity when we no longer share plausibility structures for speaking truth. Within such a context, Paul's apostolic proclamation of the gospel to all who trust in Jesus Christ has particular relevance, since it roots the gospel's claim to universality within God's particular promises to Israel that have now been fulfilled in Jesus' death and resurrection. Along with Hultgren, Badiou helps us set Paul's argument for our justification by faith in Jesus Christ and its relationship to the problems of nomism and antinomianism within a different context — not that of the reform of Christendom, but that of an apostolic proclamation within a post-Christian and a postsecular world.

Reaping the Whirlwind

In light of these arguments, we turn to address questions raised earlier in this chapter. How do we discern the Spirit's activity when, on the one hand, our very plausibility structures for believing in God have been eroded, and yet we find ourselves, on the other hand, with a yearning for a deeper sense of identity (a deeper sense of meaning and purpose) and a deeper sense of belonging to community? And how do we choose from among the plethora of options, both Christian and otherwise, that promise to address this deep yearning, from calls to return to the clearly defined beliefs and ethical practices of a previous era to calls to enter into more palpable charismatic and mystical ecstasies that we have yet to experience? How do we discern the Spirit's truth in such an age? I bring this discussion to a close by proposing that we attend to three crucial areas that need attention: (1) reclaiming the central thrust of Paul's missionary theology; (2) deepening and broadening our understanding of the Spirit's work in this age between the resurrection and the *parousia;* and (3) understanding what it means to discern the Spirit.

Reclaiming Paul's Missionary Theology

In this era after Christendom, we need to reclaim what lay at the heart of Paul's apostolic mission as the basis for all that we do as Christians. As Hultgren has argued, Paul's theology was essentially a missionary theology.[37] As the apostle to the Gentiles, Paul established a new plausibility structure for appropriating God's promises to the Jews. At the heart of his missionary work was the declaration that through Jesus' death and resurrection, God had ushered in a new messianic age of the Spirit for all people, and the implications were cosmic in scope. Regardless of our back-

---

37. Hultgren, *Paul's Gospel,* p. 145.

ground, we now can participate in that new age of the Spirit through faith in Jesus Christ. The Spirit's work in the public declaration of that promise — and our trust in that promise and baptism into Christ's death and life — constitutes the plausibility structure in which we, too, can participate in that new age. The promise is available for all — both good and bad. God makes no distinction. This is why Luther's emphasis on the *public* character of Word and sacrament (in response to the enthusiasts) remains as vital for our day as it did then. Moreover, the promise is not only for some isolated religious sphere of life; it has to do with what God has done for all of creation. Therefore, believing in this promise does not transport us out of this world. Rather, as Luther emphasized (in response to the Augustinian tradition), God became human precisely to free us to be fully human in the midst of our "secular" life. We are freed by the promise not to enter into some special spiritual or religious sphere but solely to serve our neighbors in love in our everyday lives.

This promise, which we appropriate by faith, actually involves our being transformed by the Spirit into the living image of Christ within us as individuals and communities. The *universal* promise actually addresses *particular* people. By faith in this promise, we now have a new identity in Christ, one that is established not by human laws or criteria for membership but solely by the Spirit, who creates faith. But this still leaves us with the question of what the basis is for our unity with others, especially those who are different from us, since the Christian community is in principle open to all humanity. In a pluralistic world, how do we enact "faith working through love" in actual communities shaped by the promise? How do we enact the new coherence of identity that we have in Christ amid the diversity of forces that impinge on and influence our lives?

Attending to the Depth and the Breadth of the Spirit's Work

The Depth of the Spirit's Work

Ironically, the loss of Christendom has meant that the Lukan understanding of the Spirit's activity propelling the Christian community in mission throughout the world with all its "signs and wonders" has now come to the fore once again as a major force within Christianity, after its long slumber within the hierarchical structures of Christendom. Here Paul, along with the Johannine tradition, provides more explicit insight into how we might understand the Spirit's work in transforming individuals and communities into their new identity in Christ. Here we must attend to the *depth* of the Spirit's work in transforming us into Christ's image, both as individuals and as communities. In a postsecular world, where shared presuppositions can no longer be presupposed, we need to attend to the ways the Spirit forms us in Christ's image in this messianic age between the resurrection and the *parousia.*

Paul makes it clear that we are baptized into a new identity. We are crucified with Christ; we now live our individual lives by faith in the Son of God. Through the Spirit we are "in Christ" and Christ is "in us." The same Spirit who raised Jesus from the dead will also give life to our mortal bodies. We now can live from the vantage point of the Spirit's new messianic age; we no longer need to live merely reacting to the chaotic forces of this passing age. As adopted children, we have received the Spirit of God's Son, who gives us the same intimacy Jesus had with his "Abba, Father." This resonates with how the Gospel of John emphasizes that the Spirit of truth is Jesus' living presence among us. Although no longer bodily present with us, Jesus is with us through the Spirit — "you in me and I in you" (John 14:20) — sharing with us all that he has from the Father (John 17).

All this spiritual power is not to be used for self-indulgence. Precisely because we are baptized into Christ's death, all that happens in our lives is a matter of discerning God's will (Rom. 12:1-2), which always sums up the law in loving our neighbors as ourselves (Gal. 5:14). While we live, we are "always being given up to death for Jesus' sake." But through the Spirit's power, the crucifixion of our sinful selves results in our being able to live in an abundant eschatological newness, which benefits not only us but others as well (2 Cor. 4).

Moreover, Paul makes clear that baptism pertains not only to our individual life but to our corporate life as communities. As people from diverse backgrounds, we now have a new basis for defining our identities (beyond gender, class, race, ethnicity, and even religious affiliation). Through baptism into Christ's intimacy with the Father, we now are formed as a unity in a corporate body — Christ's cruciform body — and now all share in the Spirit's life. Nonetheless, incorporation into this body does not mean a loss of individuality. And yet this diversity is rooted in the gifts the Spirit gives us for the common good and not according to any other criteria. Rooted in the Spirit's gifts, our differences need not lead to quarreling and wrangling (vying for control) because we all now share the abundance of the Spirit's life. Indeed, the Spirit gives us the freedom to be slaves to one another, seeking not only our own interests but the interests of others as well. This has resonance with the Gospel of John, which describes how the Spirit enables us to "dwell" in Jesus' unity with the Father — Jesus in the Father and the Father in Jesus — in an intimacy that enables us to truly live in unity with one another.

What this means is that the proclamation of the crucified Christ is directly linked with the creation of a corporate body, constituted by the diverse gifts the Spirit manifests among us for the common good. The assembly *(ekklesia)* is not merely the domain of the preacher, the apostle, or the teacher (as it had become in later tradition); rather, it is constituted by the full range of the Spirit's gifts, which includes everything from gifts of service and leadership to gifts of healing, miracles, speaking in tongues, prophecy, discernment of spirits, and special words of wisdom and revelation, to gifts of service, leadership, and so on (1 Cor. 12; Rom. 12:6-8).

The Breadth of the Spirit's Work

Nonetheless, this attention to depth in Christ's Spirit cannot be divorced from the attention to the *breadth* of the Spirit's work throughout the world. Here Paul's theology and the Lukan tradition, drawing on the prophetic tradition of messianic expectation, provide a corrective to any attempt to set strictures around the Spirit's activity by seeking to base Christian identity and membership in either a retrieval of Christendom or the erection of a new exclusive spiritual or religious community, which would be set apart from the rest of humanity for whom Christ died.

The decline of Christendom has meant that Christian communities can retrieve the missionary identity they had in the apostolic age. Our very identities — as the first installments of the Spirit's messianic age — are defined by our being "called, *gathered,* and sent" into the world. Our very *beings* are defined by God's mission in the world; we do not just *do* mission.[38] This means that we "have no power except what is given: the gospel and the Spirit." We have "no sense of an us/them way of thinking."[39] God's promise in Jesus Christ is always a promise for all people — both good and bad — until the time when God, in fact, will be "everything to everyone" (1 Cor. 15:28).

---

38. Patrick Keifert, *We Are Here Now: A New Missional Era* (Eagle, ID: Allelon, 2006), pp. 28-29.

39. Hultgren, *Christ and His Benefits,* p. 203.

Further, this means that Christian communities are always to be open communities, continually welcoming the newly baptized who will, in turn, transform communities by their very presence (as the baptism of Cornelius's household transformed not only Peter's self-understanding but that of the Jerusalem community as well). Moreover, it means that Christian communities are *in principle* always multicultural communities. They consist of people throughout the world — in Asia, Africa, Europe, and the Americas — whose only point of commonality is their baptism into Christ's crucified and raised body.

This means that the church itself must continually undergo the process of discerning the spirits and of distinguishing what is essential and what is peripheral to Christian belief and practice, as the early church did. They must continually discern how the universal promise in Jesus might best be enacted in each new particular context (as Paul did with the Galatian congregation or Peter did in his encounter with Cornelius). In so doing, they must continually distinguish between true and false uses of spiritual power (as Paul did with the Corinthian congregation). Lastly, there will continually be points of tension and conflict on this side of the *eschaton,* as different types of sinful people, coming from diverse backgrounds, receive the Spirit's gifts. Therefore, the need is ongoing for deep attention to the Spirit's activity in our midst.

Finally, our experience of the Spirit is but an advance pledge or foretaste of the coming kingdom of glory, when Christ's life-giving Spirit will bring about the rebirth of the entire cosmos.[40] As we see futility, injustice, and war around us, we groan with the rest of creation and cry out for a time when God's justice and mercy will prevail and the "'life-giving' Spirit will wake the dead to eternal life and drive the violence of death out of the whole creation."[41]

As we groan between the ages, our confession of Jesus as Lord of all relativizes all other temporal and spiritual authorities, including the "spirit" of any age. But we do not seek a "christocracy" over political, social, or economic spheres of life. Christ's kingship is "not of this world" (John 18:36; cf. Matt. 4:8-10; Luke 4:5-8). There is a place for lawful authority on earth (Rom. 13:1-7; 1 Tim. 2:1-3; 1 Pet. 2:13-17).[42] Here Reformation

40. See Jürgen Moltmann, *The Spirit of Life: A Universal Affirmation* (Minneapolis: Fortress, 2001).
41. Moltmann, *The Spirit of Life,* p. 74.
42. See Hultgren, *Christ and His Benefits,* p. 204.

theology has much to contribute to our understanding of how the gospel frees us to serve the secular world, which has a legitimate place as part of God's good creation, where believers and nonbelievers work alongside each other.[43]

Nonetheless, since God's promises in Christ are for the salvation of the entire world, they do also provide an implicit claim that God wills a just and lawful order, which believers will seek to discern. Though the New Testament does not spell out a robust social ethic or a specific political or economic program, it does provide a vision of the coming kingdom that points toward what we might align ourselves with even in this age: a vision of a future when God's justice and peace will prevail for all. Of course, we do so with an "eschatological reserve." The kingdom of God — redemption in its fullness — is a future hope and a divine gift, not a human achievement. But this "not yet" nature of the kingdom is not a call for resignation, but for a hope that gives vitality and force to our work for justice and peace, even as it relativizes any nation or society that "glories in its achievements while there are still persons who not share in them."[44]

Testing the Spirits

As we live between the ages, we seek discern God's purposes for us, confident that our groaning takes place within God's Trinitarian life, where the Spirit intercedes for us with sighs too deep for words, according to God's will (Rom. 8:26-27). By dying and rising with Christ, we are transformed by the Spirit. We now "walk" in the Spirit; that is, we live our lives led by the Spirit. This walk is not defined as a new set of commandments (beyond the two great commandments: to love God and to love one's neighbor as oneself). Rather, the working of the Spirit in our lives shows itself chiefly in testing *(dokimazein)* our judgments at each given moment to see whether they are in accord with the will of God.[45] We now share the mind of Christ with one another and are called not to attend merely to our own interests, but to the interests of others (Phil. 2:1-5). We are thus called to be

---

43. See Michael S. Horton, "The Time Between: Redefining the 'Secular' in Contemporary Debate," in Horton, *After Modernity? Secularity, Globalization, and the Reenchantment of the World* (Waco, TX: Baylor University Press, 2008), pp. 45-66.

44. Hultgren, *Christ and His Benefits,* pp. 204-5.

45. Oscar Cullmann, *Christ and Time: The Primitive Christian Conception of Time and History,* trans. Floyd V. Filson (Philadelphia: Westminster, 1964), p. 228.

transformed by renewing our outlook on life so that we can, in fact, discern God's will in specific circumstances (Rom. 12:2; see also Phil. 1:9; 2:13). We are not to quench the Spirit in this, but to test all things and hold fast to what is good (1 Thess. 5:19).

The biblical writers give us criteria for this testing process. In the Old Testament the charismatic endowment of the Spirit on prophets, leaders, and kings must always be tested against God's law and the prophetic witness to justice and mercy, especially for those who have the least power. Likewise, the Spirit of messianic expectation is always a Spirit of truth whose life-giving energies establish a reign of justice and harmony not only within all people, but also within the cosmos itself.

In the New Testament, the writers of the Synoptic Gospels, John, and Paul all affirm that the whole law (which is coterminous with God's will) is fulfilled by love: love of God, which can express itself only in love of neighbor (Matt. 22:40; Gal. 5:15; Rom. 13:8ff.).[46] For Paul, as we have seen, the law — with its distinction between circumcision and uncircumcision — no longer counts as a basis for our receiving the Spirit. All that counts now is "faith working through love" (Gal. 5:6). Nonetheless, Christ fulfills the law, and as the Spirit transforms us into Christ's image, we are given power to fulfill the law, which is summarized in the command to love.

In light of the criterion of love, Paul observes that "all things are lawful, but not all things are beneficial" (1 Cor. 10:23). He thus gives us two criteria for discerning *diverse* manifestations of the Spirit: affirming that "Christ is Lord" along with seeking the common good, what will build up the community as a whole (1 Cor. 12, 14). In a similar vein, 1 John gives these two criteria for testing the Spirits: that Christ came in the flesh and that we are to love our neighbor — indeed, to the point of caring for those brothers and sisters in need — because God first loved us.

In these various criteria, we see that the *particular* affirmation of what God has done in Christ always opens us up to the *universality* of God's love for all people. In turn, this particular affirmation also gives us a basis for seeking *unity* even amid our *diversity.* Hence, as we seek in our time to discern the Spirit's work in our midst, we need to attend to how the particular affirmation of Christ's lordship both (1) deepens our unity with one another amid our diversity, even as it also (2) continually expands our horizons since the promises of God in Jesus are always for all people — indeed, for the whole cosmos.

---

46. Note that this is a dominant motif in the Gospel of John.

Conclusion

If the secularizing forces of the modern age sought what was universal and diversifying (but with the demise of Christendom lost the particular affirmation of Christ's lordship with its unifying thrust), then in our postsecular age we yearn for some unity (or coherence) amid all our particularity and diversity. In light of this yearning, I have argued that we need to retrieve the apostolic thrust of Paul's missionary theology. Our challenge today is not the reform of Christendom. Rather, our challenge is to pray for the confidence that Paul had in the apostolic proclamation: God's promise to Israel of a Spirit-filled messianic age is now available for all people through Jesus Christ. As we proclaim this message — and hear it and place our trust in it — the Spirit enacts in our midst not only the plausibility of this new age but its reality in our lives as a foretaste, a first installment, of what is yet to come.

As we stand between the ages — groaning inwardly for a time when sin and injustice, and the death they perpetuate, will be no more — we have hope. We can be confident that our hope is not merely a futile exercise. Because of Jesus, we, too, have access to the Spirit, who not only helps us in our weakness but gives us access to God's own Trinitarian life by interceding for us. And, as the one we now can call "Abba, Father" hears the Spirit's intercessions, the Spirit transforms us into Christ's image in ways that not only give us hope, but also transform our very yearnings into lives that embody Christ's cruciform wisdom and power.

GLIMPSES OF THE
HOLY SPIRIT IN ACTION

Section II grounds church-planting initiatives in the generative soil of story. The chapters in this section narrate how specific congregations were created and led by the Spirit, providing the reader with hints for how history might lead to future expectations of the Holy Spirit *in action* planting congregations. They unearth the generative DNA from congregations in very different ways, one probing personal experience and the other probing local stories for common themes. Innovation abounds in missional church planting, but it is not without roots. These essays deepen the missional church discussion of church planting through their understanding, appreciation, and attentiveness to the Holy Spirit in action through the witness of history. Through these congregational stories, the reader glimpses the creative nature and power of the Holy Spirit, imaginative ways to view one's own ecclesiastical inheritance, and the potency of congregational histories to orient, open, and advance the Spirit-led potential for congregations as yet unborn.

The title of Leith Anderson's chapter, "New Churches for a New Millennium: The Holy Spirit Does It Again," hints at the spark, anticipation, and enthusiasm for church planting that ignite this kind of ministry. With faithful confidence in God's ongoing ecclesial creativity among us, Anderson traces his own unsuspecting journey into church planting as the senior pastor of Wooddale Church in Eagan, Minnesota. He provides several important elements for would-be church-planting congregations: historical perspectives on church planting; a theologically missional foundation for church planting; six "truisms" about church planting; and considerable practical experience through Wooddale's own planting of new congregations for twenty years. Several visionary what-ifs conclude the chapter, sparking an imagination for a growing rather than declining future for Christian churches in North America. Anderson invites congregations to follow the Spirit's lead into dedicated, informed, and adventurous church planting.

Every community and every congregation has a history of its own unique beginnings. In "Hints from the Past for the Present and Future: Five Congregations and Their Church Planting Stories," Susan Tjornehoj masterfully grounds church planting in stories that provide rich soil for new growth. From the biblical themes of wanderer and stranger, alien and neighbor, Tjornehoj explores the birth narratives of one metropolitan community and five vastly different congregations within it. As an experienced pastor and judicatory leader of missional efforts, she elegantly and eloquently creates a tapestry from these strands of history that illustrates how planting new congregations is deeply rooted in the contextual soil where past and future are held in the tension of the present. While using a Lutheran theological lens that is liturgical and sacramental, she offers glimpses and wisdom that evoke questions and curiosity, which might, in turn, unearth a church-planting Spirit in the fertile soil of any congregation's particular historical context.

CHAPTER 4

New Churches for a New Millennium:
The Holy Spirit Does It Again

Leith Anderson

We sat in two concentric circles of chairs centered in a church classroom in Eden Prairie, Minnesota. The purpose was to find out what local pastors thought about theological education. There was animated critique of the church and the academy. The Lily Endowment had underwritten a multiyear study on theological schools and the church for the Association of Theological Schools (ATS), the transdenominational accrediting association for North American seminaries. Our task force began in 2004 and met regularly for three years. We hosted experts, shared books, and explored the preparation for and practice of parish ministry in the three traditions of Roman Catholicism, mainline Protestantism, and evangelicalism. Everyone in the group either was at that time or previously had been a seminary president or professor.

The discussions were helpful and interesting. But I kept wondering how they connected to the local congregations that we all agreed were the primary objects and beneficiaries of theological higher education. I told the task force members about a group of local pastors with whom I regularly met in St. Paul and Minneapolis: a broad mix of Christian traditions, including pastors from Presbyterian, Lutheran, Baptist, Assemblies of God, independent, and Roman Catholic affiliations. Thinking that these local church leaders would offer a perspective different from that of professional educators, I invited the ATS task force to Minnesota to listen in on a wide-ranging discussion of churches, theological education, and pastoral leadership. We called the event a "fishbowl," and it became a prototype for similar listening events across the country.[1]

As I recall the hours of conversation, the focus was on missional leaders and missional churches; in truth, the focus was more on the shortage of both. Reflecting on their own theological education and their observations of seminary graduates coming after them, the participants bemoaned the epidemic shortage of a sense of mission, a theology of mission, and especially the leadership of mission in North American congregations. The message to theological educators was that they should equip current and future students to lead congregations in passionate and effective mission in new ways, so that the church could fulfill the divine call to be the people of God in our world and generation.

Missional church leadership is not a new idea, but it may not be migrating from academic papers to congregational ministry. So I propose that a most practical step to both be missional and to inject mission into the everyday life of more North American churches is through the starting of thousands of new congregations. In this chapter I will first explore the biblical, theological, and historical roots for planting churches. Second, I will create a framework for discussing new churches in general. Finally, I will argue for the particular methodology of churches planting other churches, using my personal experience as senior pastor of Wooddale Church, which has been planting churches since 1990.

Personal Persuasion

My personal journey in mission through starting new churches began in a seminary classroom that felt more like a college locker room. I was teaching a church leadership course at Bethel Theological Seminary in Arden Hills, Minnesota. My class wasn't scheduled to begin for half an hour, but I had arrived early to set up. The previous class had just left, and the room was short on fresh air and long on handmade posters with magic-marker writing that had been stuck to the walls with masking tape. My first reaction was to be irritated by the leftovers, but then one poster caught my at-

1. See the President's Report to the Biennial Meeting of the Association of Theological Schools, Atlanta, GA, June 2008, by Daniel O. Aleshire, "Making Haste Slowly: Celebrating the Future of Theological Schools": http://ats.edu/Resources/PublicationsPresentations/Documents/Aleshire/2008/Biennial-MakingHasteSlowly.pdf.

tention: THE MOST EFFECTIVE WAY TO REACH PEOPLE FOR JESUS CHRIST IN OUR GENERATION IS THROUGH NEW CHURCHES. As the pastor of a congregation that is older than I am, it was an annoying proposition. But I couldn't get the words out of my mind. I wondered if I was stuck in the perpetuation of an ineffective, antiquated institution while the Holy Spirit was doing something spectacular somewhere I had never gone.

After a few months of periodic reflection on the words from that poster, I introduced the idea to the elders of Wooddale Church. Our congregation was in a building program to erect a large worship center with thousands of seats and a world-class pipe organ. The price was moving toward 300 percent of the original budget, and church leaders were getting nervous. I proposed that we look beyond ourselves, that we focus on mission instead of masonry, and that we join with the Holy Spirit in advancing the kingdom of Jesus Christ. How to do all this? Invite hundreds of parishioners from Wooddale Church, I said, to launch a new congregation that would begin public services on the same Sunday that the congregation moved into its new worship center.

I love it when there is unanimity among leaders in the church. They all agreed that this was a bad idea.

But the seed began to take root over the following months, and eventually I presented a formal proposal to the membership of the church. We called a "new church pastor," to whom we gave permission to recruit people and spend money. And though the launch of Woodridge Church — with two services and more than 400 people — wasn't on the same Sunday as services commenced in the new building of the mother church, it occurred only a few months later. Over the following years, the daughter became a megachurch, and it now effectively starts other new churches in neighboring communities. The success and satisfaction from the first daughter church gave us permission to repeat the process most years since that time: Wooddale Church now seeks to begin a new church at least once every year. I will say more about how that is done later.

Revisiting the First Century

There weren't many followers of Jesus at the end of the Gospel stories: only 120 were counted in the postascension gathering that is reported in Acts

1:15.[2] But there was an explosive surge in size when the Holy Spirit added three thousand on the Day of Pentecost.[3] While the importance of individual faith continued through the book of Acts, the Spirit's strategy for fulfilling God's mission changed from individuals to churches. Paul became the itinerant missionary evangelist with a strategy that included:

- Targeting new places and people[4]
- Beginning at synagogues where there were Jews and God-fearers who accepted the authority of the Hebrew Scripture[5]
- Going to places of prayer[6]
- Engaging unbelievers at public venues[7]

While there are wonderful reports of individuals coming to Christian faith, the intent and effect was to organize new believers into local missional congregations that would continue to evangelize their communities after Paul and other founders moved on. As Paul wrote back to the churches he established, they were encouraged to continue the mission. Paul wrote to the church in Colossae that "all over the world this gospel is bearing fruit and growing, just as it has been doing among you since the day you heard it and understood God's grace in all its truth" (Col. 1:6 [NIV]).

The early church grew from a small Jerusalem cadre to millions across the empire through evangelism and through the multiplication of new churches. The church of the first, second, and third centuries was the foundation and prototype of living out the purposes of God. But exponential growth in churches and among Christians was only part of the story;

2. "In those days Peter stood up among the believers (a group numbering about a hundred and twenty)" (Acts 1:15 [New International Version Bible; hereafter NIV]).

3. "Those who accepted his message were baptized, and about three thousand were added to their number that day" (Acts 2:41 [NIV]).

4. "It has always been my ambition to preach the gospel where Christ was not known, so that I would not be building on someone else's foundation" (Rom. 15:20 [NIV]).

5. Acts 14:1 reports that "at Iconium, Paul and Barnabas went as usual into the Jewish synagogue." The "as usual" is demonstrated throughout Paul's missionary journeys.

6. Normally it was required to have ten Jewish men to officially be a synagogue; if there were fewer than ten it could not be formally organized as a synagogue. When there was no synagogue, they went to the place of prayer by a river on the Sabbath where Jewish women and men, God-fearers, and others who might be predisposed to the Jewish religion would gather (see Acts 16:11-15).

7. Acts 17:16-34 demonstrates the progression of Paul's strategy in Athens, where he begins at the synagogue and then moves to the marketplace and the Areopagus.

those early believers lived righteously and transformed the society around them.

Rodney Stark's *The Rise of Christianity* combines the academic disciplines of history and sociology to analyze and explain how an obscure sect became the legal religion of the empire.[8] Stark describes in some detail the bleak realities of the Roman world: filthy living conditions, short life expectancy, widespread practice of abortion that left women infertile or dead, infanticide of female newborns, shortage of marriage-age women, disrespect for women in the culture, plagues that decimated one-third to half of the population of major cities, forced repopulation by the government, and persecution of Christians. He then reports the response of the church. Christians opposed abortion, and thus there were more children born into Christian homes. Christians forbad female infanticide and rescued female babies outside their community who were left to die. The ones they rescued, of course, were raised in Christian homes.

When there was a shortage of marriage-age women, to the point of bride-snatching and the marrying of prepubescent girls, the church, having a more plentiful supply of females, somewhat "cornered" the market. Churches expected their women not to marry until they were eighteen or twenty years of age, and to be virgins at marriage. When suitors came to churches looking for wives, they were required to first become Christians, including being baptized and receiving catechetical training, before they were allowed to marry Christian women. When many Romans fled their homes to escape epidemics, leaving behind the young, elderly, and disabled, Christians stayed (often risking loss of life) to nurture in the church fellowship those who had been abandoned. As a result, many became believers. When their relatives returned weeks or months later, they too were drawn to the faith and the church community. The forced repopulation of cities after epidemics brought in tens of thousands who spoke foreign languages, had no jobs, and had no places to live. The churches provided food, shelter, and help with employment. Newcomers were attracted to churches that met their physical and financial needs — and often came to faith and church.

Stark argues that the missional beliefs and behavior of the early Christians and churches slowly compounded their numbers from statistically insignificant to a majority of the population of the Roman Empire by the beginning of the fourth century. While we may have thought that

8. Rodney Stark, *The Rise of Christianity* (Princeton, NJ: Princeton University Press, 1996).

Constantine's Edict of Milan (AD 313) was the reason that Christianity went from *religio illicita* (unlawful religion) to *religio licita* (lawful religion), it was probably more a political necessity for the emperor, since most of his subjects were by then Christians and part of the church.

The point here is that the church grew numerically and transformationally for hundreds of years. The church lived out faith with a consistent relevance through prosperity and persecution. Karl Barth says, "[I]n order to serve the community of today, theology itself must be rooted in the community of yesterday."[9]

In September 2009 I met with a Cuban pastor from a town about an hour's drive from Havana. He told me that his local church had grown dramatically, that everyone in his town of 20,000 had heard the gospel of Jesus Christ, and that his experience was repeated all over Cuba. This is consistent with a cover story about the Cuban church in the July 2009 issue of *Christianity Today:*

> Dramatically higher attendance at established worship services and explosive growth of new *casas cultos* ("house churches") are two impossible-to-ignore signs of the vibrancy of Cuban Christianity today. The Assemblies of God, Cuba's largest Protestant group at 3,000 churches (up from 90 in the previous decade), for years tracked new congregations on a large wall map at their headquarters. But when growth exploded, they stopped adding red dots because it became impossible to display all the new churches on a single map.
>
> The Eastern Baptists, Cuba's second-largest Protestant denomination and historically linked to the American Baptists, have grown from 6,000 adult members in 120 congregations in the 1990s to 27,800 adult members in 1,200 congregations. Its 3,100 baptisms in 2008 was the highest number in the denomination's 100-year history. Methodists, Western Baptists, and Los Pinos Nuevos, a leading indigenous denomination, have also enjoyed significant growth.
>
> Cuban Protestants represent 4 to 6 percent of the island's population (between 450,000 and 700,000 people). Growth has been most robust in urban areas among denominations actively planting casas cultos, legalized in the 1990s in response to a surge in attendance at established houses of worship.
>
> Such rapid church growth has forced Cuban pastors to abandon

---

9. Karl Barth, "Evangelical Theology," in Ray Anderson, ed., *Theological Foundations for Ministry* (London: Weidenfeld and Nicolson, 1968), p. 32.

traditional leadership models and delegate responsibilities to newly active lay leaders. "The church is growing because pastors have loosened power," said a 34-year-old pastor in central Cuba. Pastors in his rural network of nine house churches are allowing lay missionaries to plant churches and even conduct baptisms and weddings because the pastors can't travel enough to keep up with demand.

From west to east, Cuban evangelicals are testing new methods of outreach. A network of house churches in western Pinar del Rio sends young pastors on bicycles to new towns to find new believers and turn their homes into casas cultos.

A popular-level view about Cuban Christians is that these believers live out their faith trapped inside an isolation box due to Communist Party control of information and travel. But the Cuban church has a robust view of its role as a cross-cultural missionary-sending church. An intricate woodcarving on a seminary chapel wall captures this global perspective. The carving shows Cuba with arrows flying out from the island and planting a Christian cross on every continent — including Antarctica.

Pastors across denominations believe Cubans are well equipped to be missionaries. They know how to live on little, possess a well-honed apologetic theology, and would find greater welcome in nondemocratic or developing countries than Americans would. Given that many churches have a majority of members with advanced academic and professional degrees, the Cuban missions model would be a missionary who works by day as a doctor or engineer and plants churches at night.[10]

When I interviewed the Cuban pastor, he not only confirmed what I had read but explained what happened in Cuba. He reflected on government persecution of Christians from the 1960s through the 1980s, saying that believers were restricted from higher education and superior employment. Many were imprisoned — to be "reeducated" in a Communist perspective. He said that Christians often worked harder to be the best students, even though they could not go to a university; Christians often were considered the best employees, even though they could not advance in their careers; Christians were the best prisoners, even though they were incarcerated for their faith.

10. Jeremy Weber, "Cuba for Christ — Ahora!" *Christianity Today* 53, no. 7 (July 2009): 20-28. Reprinted by permission.

When the Soviet Union collapsed in 1991, Cuba lost its primary financial benefactor and entered a period of economic distress. According to the pastor, that became the time for significant spiritual and ecclesiastical growth. It was also a time of harvest for years of living Christianly under persecution. Tens of thousands turned to Christ and the church. The revival continues today.

The pastor's analysis reminded me of the description of the first three centuries of Christianity by Rodney Stark. It also made me wonder what may happen in Cuba when there is a regime change or when the United States ends its long economic embargo. Difficulty has been the catalyst for spiritual vitality. If difficulty is replaced by greater freedom and prosperity, will that vitality lessen? In multiple conversations with Christian university students from Havana, I was told that their campus meetings went from a handful to a hundred. They were told to no longer meet in groups larger than ten. At first they thought this would destroy the movement of the Holy Spirit on their campuses. Instead, they moved from a large-group strategy to a small-group strategy and tripled their numbers almost immediately. They essentially became *casas cultos* (house churches).

In the Roman Empire during the first to the fourth centuries — as in Cuba and elsewhere in the twenty-first century — there is a connection between the missional work of the Holy Spirit and the establishing of new churches. Some may argue that new churches are the *fruit* of the Spirit's work, while others see new churches as the *means* of the Spirit's work. Whatever the perspective, it seems clear that new churches are an integral part of the mission.

For God and for the World

Speaking out of a strong Christological perspective, Karl Barth portrays ministry as what Jesus Christ did and does for and on behalf of God the Father, and that Christians and the church do not initiate ministry but participate in the ministry of God the Son. He describes us as the provisional representatives of the new humanity who are privileged to be part of what Jesus is doing in the church and in the world.[11]

Ray Anderson summarizes this Barthian approach when he observes

11. Leith Anderson, "Wooddale Baptist Church: Five Year Plan for Growth in Fellowship, Discipleship, and Evangelism," unpublished DMin diss. (Pasadena, CA: Fuller Theological Seminary, 1978), pp. 1-23.

that Jesus Christ, as God incarnate, "ministered to God the Father for the sake of the world. In so doing he created and continues all ministry to God the Father."[12] Anderson thus sees the theology of ministry that serves as the framework for the ongoing ministry of the church today as a direct outgrowth of the ministry of God in the Old and New Testaments of the Bible. Lesslie Newbigin and others have spurred the late-twentieth- and early-twenty-first-century focus on a more Trinitarian theology of mission and ministry. Craig Van Gelder explains that "this shift was from an understanding of missions as flowing largely out of Christology, which emphasizes the obligation of churches to participate in fulfilling the Great Commission, to an understanding that a Trinitarian God is involved in mission in the world in which the church participates."[13] Yet, when the heads of evangelical denominations were asked about their motivating theology of ministry in general, and church planting in particular, they uniformly spoke in Christological terms.[14] In other words, American evangelical denominational leaders do "emphasize the obligation of churches to participate in fulfilling the Great Commission." This is not to say that evangelicals lack a holistic ministry. On the contrary, evangelicals are increasingly engaged in issues of social justice, alleviation of poverty, creation care, peace initiatives, and other missional causes. However, they often undertake even these as the fulfillment of the example and the commands of Jesus. Christology runs deep and strong.

Van Gelder cites Newbigin's Trinitarian theology of mission, as articulated in the latter's book *The Open Secret* (1978), for an understanding of the church and its mission. Van Gelder says that "central to [Newbigin's] understanding of mission is the work of the Triune God in calling and sending the church through the Spirit into the world to participate fully in God's mission within all of creation."[15] Van Gelder shows that, in Newbigin's theological ecclesiology, the church is the creation of the Spirit and functions as a sign, foretaste, and instrument of God's redemptive

12. Ray S. Anderson, "Theology of Ministry Tutorial," Fuller Theological Seminary, Pasadena, CA, August 7, 1977, in Leith Anderson, "Wooddale Baptist Church," p. 4.

13. Craig Van Gelder, ed., *The Missional Church in Context* (Grand Rapids: Eerdmans, 2007), p. 20.

14. The "heads of communion" of the American denominations affiliated with the National Association of Evangelicals met in Atlanta September 24-25, 2009. When specifically asked about a Trinitarian or Christological theology of mission, the responses all reflected a Christological theology of mission.

15. Van Gelder, *The Missional Church in Context*, p. 3.

reign in the world. This seems consistent with Barth's eschatological view of the church as "the provisional representative of the new humanity." And, while Barth writes more from a Christological view of mission and Newbigin more from a Trinitarian and pneumatological view of mission, there is congruence in their understanding that ministry and mission are divinely rather than humanly initiated and propagated. As Christians and as the church, we are privileged to be included in what God is doing in our world and specifically in our generation.

In an April 2009 article in *Connections,* the international journal of the World Evangelical Alliance Mission Commission, Mark A. Awabdy and David Livermore (of the Global Learning Center at Grand Rapids Theological Seminary) address how evangelicals aligned with the World Evangelical Alliance (WEA) may connect their passion for personal evangelism with the social implications of God's mission. They feel that a more holistic and scriptural sense of mission is emerging, and that it moves beyond the polarizing debates between conversion and social gospel with an understanding of God's mission and our participatory role of joining God in making all things new.[16]

Craig Van Gelder joins the conversation on these converging themes: "Rather than the church having a mission, it is God who has a mission in the world, and it is God who calls and sends the church to participate in this mission. This introduces the perspective that the church is missionary by nature."[17] The question is, Are all churches missional? Whether asked from a Christological theology of mission or a Trinitarian theology of mission, the practical observation is no. Not that God cannot be or is not present in seemingly nonmissional congregations, or that the Holy Spirit is not working in the most dysfunctional of churches. It's just too easy to find aging, tradition-bound, self-serving, internally focused, survival-minded congregations. This is not meant to be an indictment; rather, it is a diagnosis that local churches too often fall short of the theologian's ideal of the missional congregation.

There are many good prescriptions that can bless and help otherwise nonmissional churches grow. Pray for the Holy Spirit to renew tens of thousands of congregations. Educate and train missional leaders in our seminaries. Provide tools to churches that want to change. Popularize the other-

16. David Livermore and Mark Awabdy, "Counting Sheep?! How Do We Measure Missional Effectiveness?" *Connections* 8, no. 1 (April 2009): 32-33.

17. Van Gelder, *The Missional Church in Context,* p. 10.

wise academic understanding of mission. Expose nonmissional churches to missional churches that can be their mentors — perhaps the single most effective opportunity for renewal of local congregations. All of these are helpful and important strategies, but let us focus on one strategy that has promise for participating in the mission of God and renewing the church of Jesus Christ in North America. That is the strategy of starting new churches.

Framework for Discussion

Before considering specific proposals for starting new churches, I would like to start the conversation with a framework for thought and discussion.[18]

1. New Churches Tend to be Evangelistic and Entrepreneurial

Evangelistic is the sense of reaching those who are unbelieving, unchurched, or underchurched. *Entrepreneurial* is the sense of doing what needs to be done to move to a next level of development and effectiveness.

The primary reason new churches are evangelistic and entrepreneurial is that they must be or they will not survive. Older established congregations are more likely to have the people and resources to continue as self-sufficient social organizations. According to the National Congregations Study (NCS) of Duke University, in both 1998 and 2006-2007 "the average congregation has only seventy-five regular participants and an annual budget of $90,000."[19] These numbers are too low to support a building, pastor, and basic church program. There simply are not enough people and not enough money for outreach beyond their own faith community. This is not to say that house churches with fewer people and less money cannot be missional — because they can. The challenges arise when local congregations are highly institutionalized but poor in resources, whereas the house churches are usually not very institutionalized. The typical and traditional church is forced into a survival rather than a missional mode by size, age of constituency, and the burdens of institu-

18. I use the terms "church" and "congregation" interchangeably: they refer to the local assembly and not to the universal church or to a denomination.

19. Mark Chaves, Shawna Anderson, and Jason Byassee, "American Congregations at the Beginning of the 21st Century," in *National Congregations Study* (Durham: Duke University, 2007), p. 3; see also http://www.soc.Duke.edu/natcong/.

tionalization. The other exception is the new church that is growing through the $75-90,000 size, is not institutionalized, often has a younger constituency, and is evangelistic and entrepreneurial.

New churches are also experimental. They may be forced into experimentation by lack of resources, but they are often more aware of new ideas and methods being practiced by other congregations. They read and relate to the culture, and they are open to rapid change. Tim Keller, the pastor of Redeemer Presbyterian Church in New York City, has become a leading intellectual force for and practitioner of church planting. The congregation he founded is large, missional, and influential, even though it holds services at Hunter College in Manhattan and has not yet moved into a building of its own. More significantly, Keller and the church have been an important catalyst of church planting in New York. Keller maintains that church planting was built into the very nature of the first-century church in the book of Acts. People commonly object today, however, claiming that our present task should be to focus on the many congregations that already exist in North America and Europe. In answer to that, Keller argues:

> New churches are by far the best way to reach 1) new generations, 2) new residents, and 3) new people groups. Studies show that newer churches attract new groups about 6-10 times better and faster than older churches do. It is because when a church is new, younger and newer people can get into its leadership faster. It is because when a church is new it has no tradition and can experiment. It is because when a church is new its main goal each week is not to satisfy the desires of the long-time members (there are none!) but to reach new people. As a result new churches [are] enormously better [at] reaching new people.[20]

2. Established Churches Are Reluctant to Change

Perhaps this is a self-evident truism. Most older organizations and most older people have established and become comfortable with traditions and practices. If these traditions and practices are not already missional, they are less likely to become missional.

20. Tim Keller, "Advancing the Gospel into the 21st Century: Acts 13–19, Part 1," Lecture, Redeemer Presbyterian Church, New York, NY, October 2003.

Church analysts sometimes talk about the relationship between message and method in local congregations. Churches that change both are likely to become destabilized; however, churches may change one or the other and continue. Some local congregations and national denominations have retained liturgy and polity while altering their biblical interpretation and the content of their message. Other local congregations and national denominations have retained their hermeneutics and doctrine while contemporizing their polity and liturgy. New churches are less bound by tradition and are able to begin at their chosen point of message and method to relate to their local demographic and to the divine mission.

3. New Churches Influence Established Churches

When one church in a community changes, it changes other churches in the community. The reasons range from competition to permission. Churches in communities and denominations are influenced by other churches with which they perceive they compete for status and resources. When the competition is succeeding, there is a motivation to adopt some of what they are doing. A better reason is permission-giving. When another church changes to reach out, serve God, bless others, and grow internally, the church-that-wouldn't-change has permission to try initiatives that would have been otherwise forbidden by tradition.

As seminary interns and recent graduates venture into parish ministry, they could be well positioned for future ministry if their formative experience is in a new church rather than in an established church. They will tend to perpetuate what they experience. Another way of saying this is that new churches tend to be the research-and-development sector of the religious world.

4. New Churches Are Needed

While churches on average are larger at the beginning of the twenty-first century than they were at the beginning of the twentieth century, there still are not enough congregations to minister to a national population of over 300 million in the United States. If we had retained the ratio of churches to population that existed at the beginning of the twentieth century, there would be far more congregations in the country today.

Established churches tend to be less outreaching, inviting, and socially permeable than new churches. It is thus unlikely that established churches will double in size to minister to the current population. If churches are going to minister for God and for the world, we need many more churches.

5. *The Spirit Is Starting New Churches*

The missional church is always looking for the present initiatives of the Holy Spirit. Where is the Spirit evident? What is the Spirit doing? The Holy Spirit launched tens of thousands of new churches across North America during the westward expansion of the pioneer population of the 1700s and especially the second half of the 1800s. Then there was another wave of church planting following World War II. By the late 1960s and through the 1980s, fewer new churches were started, except in high-growth states such as Florida and Arizona, and in newly expanding suburbs. Denominations that previously started new churches for new immigrants from Europe no longer enjoyed growth from migration and immigration. New churches in the Sun Belt were often the product of internal migration (people moving from one state to another and seeking a church that matched their previous denominational affiliation). There was a broad emphasis on church renewal rather than church planting — and a sense that we had enough churches already. A growing notion of tolerance and diversity existed, supplanting a fervor for evangelism that was rooted in the doctrine of the exclusivity of Jesus Christ as the sole means of eternal salvation.

Over the past two decades there has been a resurgence of church planting, especially among evangelicals and nondenominational congregations. Some denominations precluded starting new churches because of comity and parish policies that restricted the founding of new congregations within a geographical proximity of already established congregations of the same denomination. Evangelicals and nondenominationalists didn't have these restrictions, and they rapidly moved to seize the opportunity. Many towns have new churches meeting in school auditoriums, theaters, public halls, and other rented facilities.

The NCS reports that "in 2006-2007, more congregations were unaffiliated than were affiliated with any specific denomination" and, compared to 1998, "the percent of congregations with no denominational affiliation increased from 18 to 20 percent. That is not a statistically significant increase, but the percent of people in congregations with no denominational affiliation increased from 10 to 14 percent, which is a statistically significant increase."[21]

It is not a question of whether to start more new churches. The Holy Spirit is already doing it — especially with nondenominational churches. The NCS reports that "a surprising number of congregations have been busy starting other congregations," explaining that "15 percent of congregations, containing 19 percent of attendees, said they helped start a new congregation in the last two years. Even if these numbers overstate the reality (perhaps our informants said yes to this question if they supported an overseas congregation rather than started a new congregation in the United States), we wonder if church planting is shifting from a primarily denominational effort toward a more congregational effort."[22]

6. The Future Belongs to Those Who Start New Churches

Denominations populated by older churches with high median age and shrinking membership are less likely to dominate or significantly influence North American culture. Too many are not missional, and too many resist the changes to make them missional. They are in the latter stages of their institutional life cycle. By contrast, new churches that are missional, evangelistic, and entrepreneurial may attract larger numbers and younger constituents. They tend to be less institutional, less risk-adverse, and are at the initial stages of their institutional life cycle.

A comparison may be made to countries with aging populations and below-replacement birth rates (e.g., Japan and multiple European nations). Economists express concern about their future viability, vitality, and economic prosperity. Stated most simply, the future belongs to those who have babies; or, more precisely, the future belongs to those babies. Likewise, the ecclesiastical future belongs to denominations that birth new churches; or, more precisely, the future belongs to the new churches. I anticipate that the most influential churches in North America twenty-five years from now have not yet been founded.

---

21. Chaves et al., "American Congregations," p. 13.
22. Chaves et al., "American Congregations," p. 19.

Churches Starting Churches

There are many ways to start new churches. Denominations start churches with central authority, significant funding, and propagation of the strategy of national leaders. Missionaries start churches "from scratch" in what some church planters call a "parachute church start," where the missionary parachutes into a community and looks for people to join a core group that will eventually become a local church. Then there are new churches that grow out of church conflicts. One denominational executive described those as churches that fuss and fight like cats and then produce new kittens out of the conflict.

Consider a natural and effective approach that is often superior to the above ways of starting new churches: churches starting churches. This is the deliberate and purposeful birthing of new churches out of established churches. Keller describes this as a win-win process that benefits both the mother church and the daughter church "when the new congregation is voluntarily 'birthed' by an older 'mother' congregation. The daughter church brings the mother church into contact with many new groups of people and pioneers new programs that the mother church may have been too traditional to try. Though there is some pain in seeing good friends and some leaders go away to form a new church, the mother church usually experiences a surge of high self-esteem and an influx of new enthusiastic leaders and members. Together the two churches *both* usually see a major increase in numbers, joy, and confidence."[23]

Fred Barnes wrote an article for *The Wall Street Journal* that describes his experience as a layman invited to join a new church birth:

> In 2007, my wife Barbara and I left The Falls Church, which we had happily attended from the time we became Christians a quarter-century ago. It's a 277-year-old church in northern Virginia well known for its popular preacher, the Rev. John Yates, its adherence to traditional biblical teachings and its withdrawal in 2005 from the national Episcopal Church. Our three grown daughters and their families stayed behind at The Falls Church.
>
> We didn't leave in anger. We didn't have political or theological anxieties. Rather, we left for a new church because our old church wanted us to. The Falls Church has become entrepreneurial as well as evangeli-

---

23. Keller, "Advancing the Gospel into the 21st Century."

cal. It's in the church-planting business. And we were encouraged by Mr. Yates to join Christ the King, the church "planted" near our home in Alexandria. We were a bit ambivalent about the move, but when Christ the King opened its doors in September 2007, we were there.

Well, not quite *its* doors. The church began with a monthly service in a 600-seat school auditorium. About 30 people showed up, mostly members of the seed group dispatched from The Falls Church. Soon Christ the King, which was launched with a grant of $100,000 from The Falls Church, rented an assembly hall, seating about 100, in a private school and started regular worship every Sunday. Now, with 130 adults and 40 kids, we meet Sunday mornings in another church, whose own service is held in the evening.

"It's a pretty amazing start," Mr. Yates told me. But it's not unusual. Church planting is a burgeoning movement among evangelicals who are conservative in doctrine (but not fundamentalist) and inclusive in their outreach to unbelievers and lapsed Christians. It's a growing missionary field.

There's a theory behind church planting. It rejects the idea of trying to fill up existing churches before building new ones. Old churches are often "closed clubs" that don't attract new residents or young people or "the lost," says the Rev. Johnny Kurcina, an assistant pastor of The Falls Church. This is especially true in cities.

As an Episcopal Church rector, Mr. Yates began thinking about planting churches 20 years ago. But the bishop of Virginia "wouldn't allow us to discuss it," he says, "fearing that new Episcopal churches would lure people from older ones."

Mr. Yates was strongly influenced by the Rev. Tim Keller of Redeemer Presbyterian Church in Manhattan. Mr. Keller has led in creating new churches — Redeemer has planted more than 100 churches in New York and other cities around the world. Innovative new churches, he has written, are "the research and development department" for Christianity, attract "venturesome people" as fresh leaders, and have the spillover effect of challenging existing churches to revitalize their ministry.[24]

24. Fred Barnes, "When the Pastor Says It's 'A Time to Sow,'" *The Wall Street Journal*, March 20, 2009. Reprinted by permission of *The Wall Street Journal*, © 2009 Dow Jones & Co., Inc. All rights reserved worldwide.

Wooddale Church

Now let's return to my church-planting experience at Wooddale Church in Eden Prairie, Minnesota. At the beginning of the process, Wooddale Church invites a church-planting pastor to join the pastoral staff for nine to twelve months. That pastor is chosen through a disciplined process of prayer, search, multiple interviews, reference-and-background checks, and an assessment by an industrial psychologist. The candidate for this position is normally expected to have a full theological education, proven church staff experience, a track record of evangelism initiative and entrepreneurship, compatibility with the beliefs and values of the mother church, and a spouse (if married) who is clearly committed to the challenging process of founding a new congregation.

While this new church pastor engages in the life and ministry of Wooddale Church, the assignment is not primarily to minister but to learn. The goal is to have the new church pastor grasp the DNA of the mother church and become familiar with her principles, practices, and faith. The new pastor attends weekly agenda-driven staff meetings, spends time with each of the staff pastors, visits the many ministries of Wooddale Church, learns the local culture (visiting area churches, attending concerts and sports events, and being tutored in the local culture by multiple mentors), preaches, and generally becomes part of the pastoral team.

At the same time, the new church pastor is preparing for the launch of the new congregation within a year. This includes selection of the target community, choosing a name for the new church, planning events, and recruiting staff. The expectation is that the new church will begin with a multiple-person staff that is matched to the makeup of the target audience and community. A typical staff mix includes full- and part-time employees ranging from the founding pastor to others in worship arts, children's ministry, and administration.

However, the central responsibility of the new church pastor is to recruit as many people as possible to leave Wooddale Church and help start the new congregation. Typically, the new church pastor asks for names, visits every social and ministry group in the church, and takes a lot of people out for lunch or dinner to share the vision and hear the invitation to step out and help start the new church. Early in this church-planting adventure, the leadership of Wooddale Church decided to be open-handed in allowing recruitment. The new church pastor not only needs a lot of people but needs high-quality people to get the church off to a strong and healthy start. One church planter asked me, as senior pastor of Wooddale Church, to send individually addressed and signed letters to "the top 300" Wooddalers asking them to leave Wooddale Church and join the new congregation. I wrote, signed, and sent them all.

The first fear of open recruitment was losing too many people, especially key leaders. But we quickly discovered that most people are content in their home church and not interested in going elsewhere. They have established personal and family relationships that are woven into the fabric of their congregation. The burden is more on the church planter to recruit than on the parenting congregation to retain. In some cases, Wooddale Church has recruited members to go with the new church for a specific period of time (usually at least one year). They give their time, money, and ministry skill to help the new church get started and then return to the parent church. Sometimes they are so pleased with the new church that they choose to stay; but most return at the end of the agreed-upon time. If specific individuals are particularly needed in the new church, but are still unwilling to leave Wooddale Church, they may be asked to participate in both churches for a year (e.g., attending the Saturday night service in the parent church and the Sunday morning service in the daughter church).

Some church-planting strategies call for extensive meetings of the members of the founding core group to build strong relationships. Wooddale Church has chosen a different hub-and-spoke model, in which there are fewer core group meetings, and the new members are primarily connected to the founding pastor. This keeps the social organization open to newcomers. If the members of the founding core group become close friends before the church begins, it will be more difficult for the next round of newcomers to permeate and attach to the social organization.

While it is ideal to recruit at least one hundred congregants from the mother church, the right mix is more important than the number. Leaders will pay attention to building a core group with individuals who have a variety of spiritual gifts (1 Cor. 12; Rom. 12; Eph. 4; 1 Pet. 4). New churches are benefited by a starting team of gifted teachers, administrators, evangelists, caregivers, helpers, generous donors, and others. Strange as it may sound, too many donors — with no teachers or helpers — would not make for a healthy start.

The daughter churches of Wooddale Church all began with multiple staff and with multiple services — usually two.[25] This strategy empowers

---

25. Westwood Church in Chanhassen, MN, was an exception. The church began with

the new church to jump over the problems and challenges that frequently accompany size thresholds of fifty, one hundred, one hundred fifty, and so forth. Some churches become conflicted over the decision to add a second service, but these new churches always have at least two services from the start, so that is built into the DNA of the congregation even before its first Sunday.

Because new churches may attract individuals from a broad variety of religious backgrounds, who desire to impose their history on the new congregation, Wooddale Church normally retains full governance of the new legal entity. The new church is incorporated and legally registered — with the elders of Wooddale Church as the only voting members. New-comers to the new church are welcome to become members of Wooddale Church and subsequently transfer their membership to the daughter church; otherwise, they hold no official status or vote. During the early months of the new church's life, a leadership team is recruited and tested under the supervision of the founding pastor and the Wooddale Church leadership. Within a year that leadership team develops its own governance structure and church constitution. Upon the approval of the elders of Wooddale Church, the leadership board, charter membership, and legal independence from Wooddale Church are established. The goal is to have full independence in twelve to eighteen months, though specific transitions have ranged from less than a year to as much as two years.

Wooddale Church provides funds to start each new church. Unlike more traditional strategies used by many denominations, the funding model is not one of descending support for three to five years. Instead, there is heavy funding for the first year and minimal if any funding after the first year. The assumption is that it is better to start with a critical mass of people, staff, and ministries, and then quickly become self-supporting rather than be incrementally dependent on outside money. New churches usually start meeting in a public school or a theater and have rented office space in a nearby office building. Wooddale Church does not give money for land or buildings. Believing that the church is people rather than build-ings, Wooddale Church focuses on parishioners and ministry. In most

---

three services and 850 in attendance on its first Sunday. This was unusual but not completely surprising, because the founding senior pastor, Joel Johnson, had been a popular staff pastor of Wooddale Church for nearly fifteen years, Wooddale Church had a large constituency in Chanhassen, and the new church was in close proximity to Wooddale Church. Today West-wood Church is a congregation of thousands on a campus of over sixty acres and has planted its own new churches in the area.

cases, the new churches purchase a site and build a building with their own resources within the first five years.

The denominational affiliation of the new church is decided by the people of that church. This is a part of a strategy that says the kingdom of Jesus Christ is larger than any particular denomination. The exception to this choose-your-own denomination approach has been when there are partnerships with specific denominations. To help denominations establish strong new churches in the area, Wooddale Church has agreed to start churches that are Congregational, Baptist, and Reformed. In these cases, where there is an advance agreement with a denomination, the affiliation is predetermined, and the new church pastor is affiliated with and credentialed by that denomination.

The congregations Wooddale Church has established with this program are primarily located in the city of Minneapolis and the suburbs of Minneapolis and St. Paul.[26] However, Timberwood Church in Nisswa, Minnesota, is a new congregation of 600 people in a rural town with a population of 1,953. Because it is 150 miles from Wooddale Church, the recruitment model was not possible for Timberwood. Instead, as senior pastor of Wooddale Church, I built personal relationships with summer cabin neighbors and started up a Sunday evening Bible study. The Bible study grew to over one hundred participants by the end of the summer and moved into the Nisswa Community Center. Wooddale Church provided video sermons and rotating pastoral leadership to the Bible study group, and then recruited a founding pastor and organized the group into a church with two services on the next Easter. The very beginning steps of this church plant were different from those described above; thereafter, however, the process was similar to that followed closer to the home area of Wooddale Church.

When Woodridge Church, the first daughter congregation, was started during a major building program, there was doubt among the leadership and the congregation of Wooddale Church. The initial success with the first church gave us permission to try again. Most encouraging was the

26. For more information on specific churches started by Wooddale Church (Wooddale.org), visit the following websites: Woodridge Church (http://www.woodridge church.org); Woodcrest Church (http://www.woodcrestchurch.org); Westwood Community Church (http://www.westwoodcc.org); Oakwood Community Church (http://www.oakwoodonline.org); Bridgewood Church (http://www.bridgewood.org); Northwood Community Church (http://www.northwoodcc.org); City Church (http://www.citychurch mpls.org.); Timberwood Church (http://www.timberwoodchurch.org); Brookwood Church (http://www.brookwood.net).

undeterred attendance and finances of the mother church when the new congregations began. There was — and continues to be — a sense of blessing from the Holy Spirit on this endeavor, because membership numbers do not go down when hundreds of people are recruited to leave. It has been like the story in 1 Kings 17, when Elijah told the widow that she could keep pouring oil from the jug and it would be supernaturally replenished.

These new missional churches are serving God, discipling Christians, reaching unbelievers, and engaging their communities in effective ways that would be impossible for one church to do. Many thousands of people who would have been excluded are included. And the daughter churches are increasingly starting granddaughter churches.

What If?

What if the movement of the Holy Spirit in America's early twenty-first century extends the church planting of the first three centuries of Christianity in the Roman Empire, the wave of new churches across the North American frontiers in the late 1800s and 1950s, and the strategies of Redeemer Presbyterian Church in New York, Falls Church in Virginia, and Wooddale Church in Minnesota? What might this look like?

1. Local Churches Starting Local Churches

Rather than national denominations or area judicatories starting and funding churches, move the opportunity and responsibility to local congregations. The denomination may provide encouragement, networking, training, and recognition — but expect churches to start churches.

2. Celebrating New Church Starts

Traditional measures of clergy success and status have often centered on the size and influence of the congregation. This may mitigate encouraging parishioners to leave their church to start another church. Veteran church consultant and prolific author Lyle Schaller once told me, "Denominations should change what they report in their annual statistics. Stop asking how many members, attendees, and dollars. Just ask and report the answers to two questions: How many new churches did you start this year and how many new churches will you start next year?" He said this tongue in cheek, but his point was that the recognition and reward system could be changed in favor of new churches.

The corollary is to encourage seminarians and other future clergy to plan to start a new church rather than seek a call to an established church. This could be enhanced by promoting internships in new congregations.

3. Modeling by Large Churches

The largest churches in denominations, though relatively few in number, have disproportionate influence. If the largest churches give priority to church parenting, then others will follow. Denominations that exert their influence and focus their resources on encouraging large congregations to start daughter churches frequently may shape the behavior of smaller churches and set the long-term direction of the whole denomination.

Senior pastors of these large churches are almost always the key to church parenting. If they are committed to birthing a new church, it will happen; if they are opposed to birthing a new church, it won't happen. The best of all outcomes would be a future in which the pastors of America's largest churches are in collaboration and even competition to start new churches.

4. Organizing Consortiums of Smaller Churches

Churches with average weekly worship attendance of under 200 do not have the independent resources available to large congregations. They may band together with a few other churches to launch a new congregation. This will build stronger relationships between the consortium churches, encourage cooperation over competition, and increase missional health in all the participating churches.

5. Using Multiple Models

There are many more models for church planting than described here. Some churches recruit families to sell their homes and move to another state to join a church-planting pastor in an area where there is particular need or potential. Live video streaming of church services on the Internet can build a nucleus in a distant locale that is developed into a core group for a new congregation in a distant city. Multiple campuses of one congregation is a hybrid approach to church planting in which there is one church in several venues.[27]

Conclusion

The mission of God takes different expressions, depending on the context. Church planting is a means for mission that should not be limited to any particular methodology. In this chapter I have explored the approach in which the Spirit has led Wooddale Church in Eden Prairie, Minnesota, since 1990: churches starting churches. Through the Wooddale story, complemented by several others, I have argued that this methodology has particularly powerful generative potential for the future of the Christian church. Therefore, I would like to conclude with this invitational question: *What if missional churches planted tens of thousands of new missional churches, and this movement became the Spirit's catalyst for the renewal of tens of thousands of established churches in the twenty-first century?*

27. Wooddale Church has campuses in Eden Prairie and Edina, Minnesota, using video sermons at the Edina campus. In the same Twin Cities metropolitan area, Mount Olivet Lutheran Church, Bethlehem Baptist Church, and Eaglebrook Church have multiple campuses. One of the largest multisite churches using video is Northland — A Church Distributed (Orlando, FL) with participants numbering in the hundreds of thousands.

CHAPTER 5

Hints from the Past for the Present and Future: Five Congregations and Their Church-Planting Stories

Susan Tjornehoj

Introduction

The seeds of this essay were first planted in a course I took at Luther Seminary entitled "Developing a Contextual Missiology." As the director of evangelical mission in the Minneapolis Area Synod (MAS) of the Evangelical Lutheran Church in America (ELCA), I was presented with a clear task and opportunity: to develop a contextual missiology for the MAS. But where to begin? What furrows lie open? What seeds are there to plant? What fields are there to plow in a community that has over 160 ELCA congregations, with an average membership of 1,300, in a seven-county area?[1]

    In the first section of this chapter I will discuss how the biblical themes of wanderer and stranger, alien and neighbor, shape a theological framework for exploring missional church planting. In the second section I will provide an overview of the history and context of the Twin Cities metropolitan area in light of these themes. In the third section I will describe the missional planting of five specific congregations in this area. In the fourth section I will offer a Lutheran theological lens for church planting that is situated within a liturgical and sacramental framework. Themes emerge in the final section from the birth narratives of the congregations and the biblical themes of wanderer and stranger, alien and neighbor, providing glimpses and wisdom for the planting of missional congregations.

---

1. "Our Synod," The Minneapolis Area Synod of the Evangelical Lutheran Church in America: http://www.mpls-synod.org/oursynod (accessed August 24, 2011).

The furrows of this essay are written out of my ELCA denominational and synodical experience, particularly the MAS and the five congregations. I trust that the process that produced this chapter — the curiosity, questions, and emerging themes — may be helpful to readers and practitioners from other denominations and traditions.

The Biblical Back Story for Planting Missional Congregations

> *All earth is hopeful, the Savior comes at last!*
> *Furrows lie open for God's creative task:*
> *this, the labor of people who struggle to see*
> *how God's truth and justice set ev'rybody free. . . .*
>
> *We first saw Jesus a baby in a crib.*
> *This same Lord Jesus today has come to live*
> *in our world; he is present, in neighbors we see*
> *our Jesus is with us, and ever sets us free.*[2]

A Community without Borders

Out of the wind, the breath, and the Spirit, God interrupted chaos and spoke. This wandering one knows no boundaries and no borders. In the first act of creation, God removes the barrier between heaven and earth. In the birth of the child Immanuel (God-with-us), Jesus, the incarnate one, takes on human flesh and removes the separation between humanity and God. The Gospel of John testifies that the Word became flesh and moved into the neighborhood. On the cross, this God-with-us Messiah removes the border between death and resurrection. This vision of the kingdom is barrier-free. The prophet Isaiah envisions a world in which crooked roads are made straight, mountains are made low, and valleys are filled. This is done in order that the apostle Paul might testify that nothing — neither life nor death, nor things present nor yet to come — can separate us from the love of God in Christ Jesus.

These are images of a God whose mission field, whose territory, is

---

2. Alberto Taulé, "All Earth Is Hopeful," trans. Madeleine Forrell Marshall (Portland, OR: Oregon Catholic Press Publications, 1993), verses 1 and 4. Reprinted by permission.

without limit or borders, and whose only boundary is the cosmos itself — the edge of God's own love and imagination. The prophet Isaiah shouts with the invitation of God: "Enlarge your tent, and let the curtains of your habitations be stretched out; do not hold back; lengthen your cords and strengthen your stakes. For you will spread out to the right and to the left" (Isa. 54:2-3a). This is a text rich with mission. This God, who knows no borders, invites a community to stretch out, lengthen, strengthen, and not hold back. Anyone who has ever camped out or slept overnight in a tent knows that unless there is tension, a tent will collapse in on itself. This is what it means to be a faithful missional community: to live in tension, always stretching and being stretched, enlarging the tent. It's a community shaped by this God, who is determined that no one be left outside the tent of this kingdom.

A Wandering Community

"A wandering Aramean was my ancestor" (Deut. 26:5). Planting missional communities based on an identity of wandering? It's a community shaped in the image of God, breathed into being out of the earth's dust, enslaved in the pharaohs' courts. The word "wander" occurs over fifty times in Scripture. Our inheritance and mission is one in which wandering is essential. God broke through heaven itself in order to enter this world, this world that God so loved. God first wandered in ahead of us. The people of God wandered in the wilderness and marched through seas. Cain received his identity as a marked wanderer (Gen. 4:11). This community is marked with the cross, restless, always in motion — wandering toward the promise of hope and salvation and justice while living in the promise of hope and salvation and justice that has already come.

A Community of Strangers and Aliens

God is the first wanderer, restlessly removing all boundaries and borders, stretching out that cosmic tent. We know this God as Jesus Christ, and the restless Spirit creates and shapes a community that is both stranger and alien. It is a community never quite at home: it is restless and moving toward the land of milk and honey, a land of justice and mercy, grace and hope. All earth is hopeful! Abraham rose up from the bedside of his 127-

year-old wife, Sarah, who had just died in the land of Canaan. Through tears of grief, Abraham pleads: "I am a *stranger* and an *alien* residing among you; give me property among you for a burying place . . ." (Gen. 23:4). As citizens of the United States, a country whose power is the source of global pain, violence, and unnatural disasters, we can only speak along with Abraham, as strangers and aliens, with humility and through tears.

In this borderless, God-created world, the identity of the missional community is as one of the strangers. The word "stranger" appears sixty-five times in Scripture. In Matthew 25, Jesus becomes the stranger: "I was a stranger and you welcomed me" (Matt. 25:35). A wandering God, the Messiah and a stranger, Jesus executes justice for the orphan and widow, and he loves the stranger. "You shall also love the stranger, for you were strangers in the land of Egypt" (Deut. 10:18-19). Ephesians describes the power of this stranger, Christ Jesus, to form and shape a new community: those who were once Gentiles, aliens, and strangers are made citizens with the saints and members of the household of God (Eph. 2:11-22).

This Godly missional community, wandering, without borders, and strange, is considered alien. It is a community created in the image of God, the Messiah, who was crucified as an outsider, a threat, and an alien. In a xenophobic country that is fearful of strangers and outsiders, publicly suspicious of aliens, and prone to erect borders with barriers, this identity runs counter to the culture. Yet it is clear that *alien* is central to God's identity and thus to the community shaped by this God and directed toward God's mission. Scripture boldly reminds its readers and interpreters of the significance of this alien identity 140 times! And not once is "alien" used pejoratively. God shapes the ministry of this community through the voice of Moses (Lev. 19:10, 33-34): "You shall not strip your vineyard bare, or gather the fallen grapes of your vineyard, you shall leave them for the poor and the alien . . . . [W]hen an alien resides with you in your land, you shall not oppress the alien. . . ." First Peter 2:11 describes Christian conduct in a country occupied by Rome in this way: "Beloved, I urge you as aliens and exiles to abstain from. . . ." This follows the description of community as a chosen race, a royal priesthood, a holy nation, God's own people.

Embedded in this wandering community of strangers and aliens, of Rachel weeping for her children, of a creation groaning — is hope. All earth is hopeful, the furrows lie open for God's creative task, and the Savior comes at last. It is a community that is unbounded and free because its citizenship is in the household of God, where there is no fear of deportation and no need for documentation. It is a community of the banquet —

a community sent to invite and a community invited — as it lives its life out on the margins as stranger and alien. The Song of Mary and Jesus' first sermon announce that the blind see, the poor are lifted up, and the oppressed go free. The boundaries have been torn down.

A Community Defined by Love of Neighbor

"You shall not watch your neighbor's ox or sheep straying away and ignore them; you shall take them back to their owner. You shall do the same with a neighbor's donkey. You may not withhold your help. You shall not see your neighbor's donkey fallen on the road and ignore it; you shall help to lift it up" (Deut. 22:1, 3-4). There is a tenderness, a connection, a responsibility written into the very fabric of the living Word of God. The word "neighbor," in its various forms, occurs over two hundred times in Scripture. Being a part of this emerging and chosen community of God gives us a new relationship with those around us. The wandering God who has removed all barriers has given us the gift of neighbor, the gift of community. Care of neighbor, love of neighbor, and social solidarity are core religious values — an identity, if you will. In this holiness codes in Deuteronomy, the neighbor becomes a bird's nest: "[I]n any tree or on the ground, with fledglings or eggs. You shall not take the mother with you. Let the mother go" (Deut. 22:6-7). This suggests that love of neighbor includes all of creation. Creation itself is our neighbor.

"You shall love your neighbor." This is an invitation, a given, an identity, an opportunity, a command, the posture of a community created in God's image. It incarnates the movement of the Trinity within the community of God's chosen people. Jesus himself enters the neighborhood as Word, as Immanuel, as Son of God. When his powers drown the demons in the flesh of pigs, the world begs him to leave their neighborhood (Matt. 8:34, Mark 5:17). We know the end of the story: the cross was that final attempt to throw him out of the neighborhood. The Catholic missiologist Louis Luzbetak weaves love of neighbor into a *spirituality of mission* that is centered in the love of neighbor and the love of God.[3]

Martin Luther shaped some of his theology and thoughts around the loving and serving of one's neighbor. From his work on Romans, to his

---

3. Louis J. Luzbetak, *The Church and Cultures: New Perspectives in Missiological Anthropology* (Maryknoll, NY: Orbis, 1988), p. 10.

homilies on the Sermon on the Mount, to the *Christian in Society,* and to the treatise *On Trade and Usury,* Luther found solace and simplicity in a Christian's relationship and responsibility to his or her neighbor. Even as Luther and his followers were under the ban of both the church and the empire in 1523, and the possession or reading of any of his books (even his German New Testament) was prohibited by Roman Catholic priests, Luther reflects on what it means to be a neighbor. He argues that temporal authority is of divine origin, instituted for the restraining of evildoers: the Christian has no need of it, but is subject to it out of love for the neighbor.

> Since a true Christian lives and labors on earth not for himself alone but for his neighbor, he does by the very nature of his spirit even what he himself has no need of, but is needful and useful to his neighbor. Because the sword is more beneficial and necessary for the whole world in order to preserve peace, punish sin, and restrain the wicked, the Christian submits most willingly to the rule of the sword, pays his taxes, honors those in authority, serves, helps, and does all he can to assist the governing authority, that it may continue to function and be held in honor and fear. Although he has no need of these things for himself — to him they are not essential — nevertheless, he concerns himself about what is serviceable and of benefit to others. . . .[4]

Or again, Luther says:

> [W]here you see that your neighbor needs it, there love constrains you to do as a matter of necessity that which would otherwise be optional and not necessary for you either to do or to leave undone.[5]

The constraint of love shapes an identity, a God-given border, a new relationship in community. Christ's "Go and do likewise" is an invitation into a mission field, an entry into the very heart of who and whose we are.

In the next section I will explore how these biblical themes of wanderer and stranger, alien and neighbor, begin to shape and plant missional congregations in the metropolitan area of Minnesota's Twin Cities.

---

4. Martin Luther, "Temporal Authority: To What Extent It Should Be Obeyed," in Timothy F. Lull, ed., *Martin Luther's Basic Theological Writings,* 2nd ed. (Minneapolis: Fortress, 2005), p. 438.

5. Luther, "Temporal Authority," p. 440.

Overview of the Context and History of the Twin Cities Metropolitan Area

The Context

We were at Williams Arena on the campus of the University of Minnesota. There was tension in the air. The St. Paul Central High School girls' basketball team was playing Roseville High School in the state basketball tournament: an urban high school versus a suburban high school. St. Paul Central had canceled classes for this event, and dozens of school buses were dropping off young people who were excited and a bit nervous. It was a gathering of the nations — not at the end of time, not the vision of Revelation, but perhaps close. There were children from Somalia and Ethiopia and Eritrea, young people from China and the mountains of Laos, children with roots in Vietnam and Russia, Slovakia and Belarus, teenagers from Mexico and El Salvador, Germany and Turkey.

These students were just kids from St. Paul Central High School who were cheering on their team, many of whom were third- and fourth-generation African-American kids from Rondo, a historic African-American neighborhood. Could this have been the vision of the early city planners of St. Paul and Minneapolis in the 1850s, when they gathered to set aside land for this, the oldest high school in the state? A Somali teenager perhaps best illustrated the new context of the Twin Cities, where the Spirit is moving and active. There she was in her long black dress, bright-red tennis shoes, and a red hijab. She was wearing her school colors, waving black and red pompoms, yet in traditional dress — fully Muslim, fully American, just another teenager cheering on her team.

What fibers hold these children together? What webs? What sinews hold the metropolitan area together? Will these dry bones rise in new forms, or are there any familiar songs sung in Babylon? Now listen to the voices of the wanderers and strangers entering this new land in the following birth narrative of the Twin Cities metropolitan area.

A Historical Overview

Even the earliest inhabitants of Minneapolis were migrants, immigrants, and wanderers. The Dakota and Ojibwa nations were the first people who came to this land of rivers and lakes from places further east. They hunted game and gathered food along the banks of the Minnesota and Mississippi rivers. Cloud Man Village, a Dakota Mdewakanton community, was located on the western shore of what is now known as Lake Calhoun in Minneapolis, Minnesota. It was established in the 1820s, with Cloud Man as its chief. Cloud Man Village was one of at least six other Mdewakanton communities in the area from the early 1800s to 1852.

A treaty that was signed in 1838 opened up land east of the Mississippi River to white settlement. Soon the logging of trees and the plowing of prairies depleted the populations of deer and bear and other animals, staples of those first inhabitants of the area. Whooping cough ravaged the communities, and hunger drove the Mdewakanton band to sign the Treaty of Traverse des Sious in 1851. This treaty opened up lands west of the Mississippi River to eventual white settlement. It meant the abandonment of hereditary lands and resulting exile of the Dakota nation. By 1862, a conflict between the Dakota nation and the settlers and the U.S. military led to the exile of the Dakota to Nebraska and South Dakota. A once-thriving community of over 2,000 people dwindled to seventy residents in Hennepin County by 1899. These exiles were the descendants of the Native American people who had welcomed Father Louis Hennepin and others upon their visit to the area in the 1680s.[6]

After the War of 1812, the U.S. government moved to establish control of the Northwest. It built Fort Snelling at the confluence of the Minnesota and Mississippi Rivers, completing the structure in 1825. The U.S. military moved immediately to build roads and a sawmill; they planted hundreds of acres of vegetables, wheat, and corn; and they cut down trees for firewood. They enforced the laws of the United States while establishing the location of Fort Snelling as a key to international trade. The completion of Fort Snelling and the signing of treaties that led to the subsequent displacement of the Mdewakanton band of the Dakota nation — the tension and blood of those years — develop the themes that permeate the soil of a discussion about planting missional congregations in the Twin Cities metropolitan area. Deeply rooted in the middle of the 1850s are today's needs for security and protection; the identification of who is welcome and who is not; the determining of who belongs and who does

6. "A History of Minneapolis: Mdewakanton Band of the Dakota Nation": http://204.169.52.42/history/ehl.asp (accessed October 5, 2009).

not. These dynamics impact how the metropolitan area continues to develop today.[7]

The establishment of Fort Snelling as an outpost of the U.S. government meant that immigrants and traders, settlers and pioneers, explorers and invaders began coming to this area from the north and the south and the east. Soon Fort Snelling became the hub of the French Canadian settlement and was a major center of the fur trade.[8] The first steamships came up the Mississippi River from New Orleans in 1823. Transportation from the East Coast became easier when the Erie Canal was completed just two years later. People could now travel from the east by boat all the way to Detroit, Chicago, and Milwaukee (Holmquist, p. 5). Railroads reached Chicago in 1852, and the Mississippi River at Galena, Illinois, by 1853. Most immigrants traveled to Galena by train and then to St. Paul and Minneapolis by boat. Two steamboats a day left for Minnesota during the summer, and they each carried up to 800 people (Holmquist, p. 6). Steamboats eventually were replaced by the railroad after the first train between Chicago and Minneapolis arrived in 1867.

Immigrants were being encouraged to come to Minnesota by 1855. The newly formed territory appointed a commission of immigration. Until 1875, policies continued to favor free admission of all needed workers. In fact, laws were enacted that encouraged ship owners to improve steerage conditions. However, the first federal law began restricting immigration in 1875. Virtually all Asians were excluded, particularly Japanese and Chinese (Holmquist, p. 9).

Why did all of these new residents board steamboats at a capacity of 800 to come to Minnesota? Increased population in their home countries, changes in farming practices, famine, unemployment, persecution, and avoidance of compulsory military service served as *push* factors. But there were also *pull* factors: land, work, higher wages, and the promise of social equality. Young states, railroad companies, and steamship companies sent promotional materials. Some even sent remittances: cash to Europe, Asia, the Middle East, and Mexico (Holmquist, p. 4).

As trade routes opened up, developers flocked to this new area in the 1850s and 1860s. Town site developers and timber speculators came, small

7. "Historic Fort Snelling: A Brief History of Fort Snelling," Minnesota Historical Society: http://www.mnhs.org/places/sites/hfs/ (accessed October 5, 2009).

8. June Drenning Holmquist, ed., *They Chose Minnesota: A Survey of the State's Ethnic Groups* (St. Paul: Minnesota Historical Society Press, 1981), p. 5. Hereafter, page references to this work appear in parentheses in the text.

businesses sprang up, and schools and churches were organized (Holm-quist, p. 1). Governor John Pillsbury described labor as "the prime neces-sity" for this young frontier state (Holmquist, p. 3). New England Yankees welcomed laborers and immigrants from the British Isles, Germany, and Scandinavia. Chinese laborers came as early as 1876, and free blacks arrived after the Civil War. Minneapolis and St. Paul soon became prominent trading centers. This influx of laborers and developers, speculators and new residents made Minneapolis the eighteenth largest city in the United States in 1890 (Holmquist, p. 8).

The first permanent white settlers, workers, and laborers lived near St. Anthony Falls (Holmquist, p. 3). The falls were necessary to run the mills that powered the economic engine of this new city. By 1871, the west bank of the Mississippi had twenty-three businesses: flour mills, woolen mills, iron works, and mills for cotton, paper, and sashes. The falls were considered "the greatest direct-drive center the world has ever seen."[9] There were seventeen sawmills and thirty-four flour mills in 1905. Ten per-cent of the country's flour was produced in Minneapolis; at the city's peak, twelve million loaves of bread were produced there daily.[10]

Most residential development remained close to these original settle-ments until the 1880s. Eventually higher-income households, people who had the means to own a private carriage, moved up onto the hills and formed more fashionable districts. Foreign-born residents lived in small frame dwellings and worked in the lumber mills on the river, the railroad yards, and flour mills.[11] Residential areas expanded quickly along the elec-tric street car lines, and these patterns of development continued as the streetcar network was extended.[12]

Automobiles arrived in the 1920s, and a freeway system was put into place in the 1940s.[13] In "Growth Patterns of Mainline Denominations," Craig Van Gelder says that streetcars linked residences, work, shopping, and entertainment.[14] The automobile destroyed this linkage — and the

9. *Wikipedia*, s.v. "The Minnesota Archaeologist" by Scott F. Anfinson: http://en.wikipedia.org/wiki/Minneapolis,_Minnesota (accessed October 6, 2008).

10. "The Elements of Geography," by Salisbury, Brown, and Tower, Mill City Mu-seum: http://www.millcitymuseum.org/history.html (accessed October 6, 2008).

11. Judith Martin and David A. Langegran, *Where We Live: The Residential Districts of Minneapolis and Saint Paul* (Minneapolis: University of Minnesota Press, 1983), p. 3.

12. Martin and Langegran, *Where We Live*, p. 4.

13. Martin and Langegran, *Where We Live*, p. 5.

14. Craig Van Gelder, "Growth Patterns of Mainline Denominations and Their

focus on downtown. It made residential suburbs independent, and new values such as freedom and individualism began to emerge. These values continue to shape any discussion and vision for planting missional congregations in this metropolitan area. The automobile led to a massive relocation of urban and rural people to the suburbs, resulting in decentralization and a greater fragmentation of different groups of people. Race and class diversity physically separated into distinct residential zones.[15]

Themes of displacement and exile, of wandering and migration, of arrival and new land, form the contextual soil for planting missional congregations. In the next section I will explore congregational stories of planting in the furrows that lie open for God's creative task.

The Missional Planting of Five Congregations in the Metropolitan Area of Minneapolis and St. Paul

"This is *not* my church. This isn't my church. You've taken away my church." This was the cry of a stately, elegant, and proud Norwegian Lutheran woman named Mildred. Mildred's parents were probably baptized at Christ Lutheran Church on Capitol Hill in the late 1890s. By then they were already the second generation of this immigrant congregation in the growing city of St. Paul. Their language of worship was Norwegian. By the time Mildred was born, in the early 1920s, this congregation had built a beautiful new structure across the street from the Minnesota state capitol. It had a grand entrance on University Avenue. Streetcars dropped off worshipers, confirmation students, choir members, and council leaders every day of the week.

After the Swedes and the Britons, Norwegians were the third largest foreign-born group in Minneapolis in 1880.[16] In 1914, Norwegians controlled four of the city's twenty-seven banks and thirteen of the twenty-six musical organizations, owned 110 hotels, and had twenty-three of the 195 churches. Minneapolis had replaced Chicago as the primary destination of these new arrivals from Norway (Gjerde and Qualey, p. 27). Recent re-

---

Churches: A Case Study of Jackson, Mississippi 1900-1980" (PhD diss., Southwestern Baptist Theological Seminary, 1982), p. 54.

15. Van Gelder, "Growth Patterns," p. 56.

16. Jon Gerde and Carlton C. Qualey, *Norwegians in Minnesota: The People of Minnesota* (St. Paul: Minnesota Historical Society Press, 2002), 27. Hereafter, page references to this work appear in parentheses in the text.

search indicates that members of the Norwegian community associated very little with members of other ethnic groups outside of school or work (p. 29). An editor of a Norwegian-language newspaper wrote in 1914 that "large and affluent Norwegian American families had only two children — politics and church" (p. 34). This explains the political power of Norwegian politicians in the state of Minnesota between 1850 and 1914. Six Norwegians from Minnesota had been elected to the U.S. Congress, 893 held city and county offices, and 259 had served in the Minnesota legislature (p. 43).

With this kind of powerful influence in the Minnesota legislative process, it is no wonder that land became available across the street from the site of the newly constructed state capitol building in 1908. This forty-year-old congregation purchased the land and built a brand-new structure right there. They had arrived! Who knows how many legislators and governors worshiped in the sanctuary when they were in town governing? Another observation of these early Norwegian immigrants in the city was that their class differences were more pronounced (p. 30). This congregation catered to the Norwegian educated class, but had Sunday Schools scattered across the city in storefronts for the working-class Norwegian children. Themes of class, wealth, and domain were important in this story, and they will continue to be part of a discussion of the Spirit and the planting of missional congregations in this context.

This is the community into which Mildred was born in the 1920s. Her pastors left to be presidents of colleges and seminaries, and one became the U.S. ambassador to Ethiopia. Now in her eighties, Mildred had lived to see her beloved congregation become home to new immigrants from Cambodia and East Africa. Drums accompanied the rhythms of liturgy, and incense greeted worshipers on All Saints Sunday. The interior walls had been torn down to open up a gathering space; Mildred had chosen the colors and the furniture just two years before. But it was the artwork of He Qi, a brilliant Chinese artist who depicts biblical stories in silks and oils with vibrant Japanese and Asian features, that reshaped the space and created an art gallery. This was the gallery's first exhibition.

Mildred wept at the sight of those paintings. She cried out from the very center of her identity: "This is *not* my church. This isn't my church. You've taken away my church." Her tears spoke of a movement away from something sacredly familiar into the uncertainty of this mission of God. Historically, worshipers in ELCA congregations have overwhelmingly been descendants of Northern European immigrants, but the Spirit has been at work changing this and challenging the ethnic nature of these communities. Gone are the streetcars that brought early immigrants to church and work. Gone are the languages of the Lutheran ancestors — Swedish and Danish, Norwegian and German. The new languages of Khmer and Tigrinya, Spanish and Oromo have replaced them. Has mission defined as finding those "like us" from fjords and countrysides in the old country served its purpose? Maybe — but maybe not so fast. "You've taken away my church" is the anguished cry of new birth and re-formation, where modern and postmodern clash and coexist, and where new models emerge. We are a faithful people seeking new ways and new paradigms of loving our neighbor, of proclaiming the gospel, and of sharing a meal together.

As an immigrant and ethnic community, part of a re-forming movement of grace, we may think we have never done this before. Or perhaps we've *always* done it this way before, being faithful to the Spirit who is leading and planting missional congregations. To explore this question, I chose to root this project in the life and mission of five different ELCA congregations and contexts in the Twin Cities: a recent immigrant community; a predominantly white, middle-class suburban congregation; a congregation among the poor; a megachurch (a congregation in which over 800 people worship each weekend); and an emerging new church start. These stories will give perspective, structure, and content to our discussion of what planting missional congregations might look like in the coming years.

1. A Recent Immigrant Congregation: Our Savior's East African Lutheran Church

The following is an excerpt from *Reports to the 55th Annual Convention of Hauge's Norwegian Evangelical Lutheran Synod in 1900:* "This is our first attempt at publishing our reports in the American language."[17] Secretary Lohre had a deep concern for the younger people of his synod. At its heart, this discussion of language and young people was an evangelical need to share the faith. Lohre continued: "If your preference is the American lan-

17. Rev. N. J. Lohre, "Reports to the 55th Annual Convention of Hauges Norwegian Evangelical Lutheran Synod" (paper presented at the Committee Reports and Results of Proceedings, Grafton, North Dakota, 1900), p. 3. Hereafter, page references to this work appear in parentheses in the text.

guagc while ours is Scandinavian, we want to feel that the question of language is no longer to serve as a barrier between us" (p. 3). The mission of the church was to remove barriers. The president's report declared that the "heathen and all the people outside of Israel are included in the mission of the people of Israel. They are to make known unto them God's great deeds" (p. 6). Lohre's report described their mission as great, the same as Israel's: to make known God's deeds among the people. God had always led this small group of Haugeans onward, and in 1900 they had a great opportunity for work in the Lord's vineyard (p. 6).

Enthusiasm for mission and bearing witness were central to their mission. Loving God and loving neighbor meant striving to save those precious souls (p. 7). Home mission was to have the first priority for this small immigrant synod, whose roots were in the revival and awakening that swept Norway in the early 1800s. As they defined it, their mission was testimony that God's Spirit was still active in their congregations. Pastors were expected to give detailed reports of the activity of their congregations to document the history of God's kingdom (p. 9). Even in 1900 they had some idea of contextualized mission, of what it meant to plant missional congregations: "As members of the Hauges [*sic*] Synod we are called to work for the advancement of God's Kingdom according to the mission *peculiar* to our synod" (p. 9; italics added).

Home missions was the "life-power" of the Synod (p. 42), and it motivated change. In 1901, just one year later, this group of Lutherans held their first English-speaking synodical convention. Since they no longer lived in the country of their fathers, they determined not to build a replica of Norway in America. Within this pietistic movement are seeds of wisdom for us today. Their concern at the turn of the century for their children, their understanding of mission (that no interest in mission is a symptom of death), and their ability to remove barriers can be helpful to us as we construct a framework for planting missional congregations.

This love of children and desire for the planting of a church was the beginning of Our Savior's Lutheran Church in Minneapolis nearly one hundred years ago. They were planted by another congregation of the Hauge Synod at a Women's Missionary Society meeting. The women saw a mission field from their front porch, and they worked to provide for its birth. By 1950, Our Savior's had 600 young people in Sunday School. It was a flourishing congregation, and out of the very heart of the Hauge Pietists new visions continued to spring. They called their first woman pastor in the 1980s. And in January 2008 they stepped aside for a radically new mission: they *donated* their church building to the East African Lutheran Church. The remnant of Our Savior's joined another ELCA congregation while this new church moved in. The East African Lutheran Church of Minneapolis is now, outside of Ethiopia, the fastest-growing Oromo congregation in the world.

The Oromo church had its roots in the Ethiopian Evangelical Church Mekane Yesus. A group of Oromo students, some immigrants and some refugees, began meeting for Bible study at Augsburg College in 1987. Their numbers increased as more Oromo immigrants and refugees came to the Twin Cities. The community began to include more than students, and their need for space and a regular gathering time meant that they needed to move. Another migration! They were registered as a congregation in 1993 and became a member of the ELCA in 1995, the year their pastor and his family immigrated to this country; he was installed as their first pastor in 1998. The Oromo church moved from Augsburg College to Bethany Lutheran Church in the Cedar-Riverside-Franklin neighborhood. Once again, they outgrew those facilities and then moved into the donated Our Savior's facility in 2008. The tensions of identity, of being open to the foreign, of missional growth, of knowing that we can't afford to stay "like this" (meaning ethnic specific) — all these tensions are probably similar to those felt by the first immigrants who had a vision to start a new church from the front porch of the Women's Missionary Society meeting.

2. A Predominantly White, Middle-Class Suburban Congregation: God With Us Lutheran Church

The roots of this community are a combined revival, "inner mission," and folk church (Grundtvig) tradition in Denmark. These immigrants struggled to form a church in this new land. They first organized themselves into a mission society in 1872, but they still considered themselves members of the mother church in Denmark. As a mission society, they worked for a renewal of the spiritual life in the congregation and to preach the gospel among the countrymen whom the synod had not yet been able to reach. Home mission work was carried out through evangelistic and revival meetings held two or more times a year for four to six days. They did not consider the regular church life as the best way to build the church; the revival meetings were what led to the conversion of sinners. What was important was the answer to the question, "Are you saved?" H. Skov Nielsen, editor of a Danish newspaper, asked this question in 1933, "If we have a special mission to perform and minister to others than the Danish, is not our Danish heritage a handicap?"[18] This is a question central to a discussion of planting missional congregations. What are the barriers to this plant?

The preservation and perpetuation of the Danish heritage and a tendency to equate the Christian gospel with ethnic and cultural traditions caused many urban congregations to close after World War I and World War II. H. Richard Niebuhr charged that most immigrant churches "became moral, racial and cultural traditions in the new World, intent on maintaining their distinction."[19] As these distinct communities readied themselves for merger, the Danes asked themselves what dowry they brought to the new church — what unique contribution they made. Their response: a relaxed and evangelical spirit, baptismal regeneration and toleration, repentance and conversion, the spirit of freedom and democracy, pulsating gladness, a sweet and simple faith, joyous song, and laughter bubbling forth from the smiling roots of the Danish countryside.[20]

Is this dowry, these unique contributions, helpful to a discussion of planting missional congregations? A relaxed and evangelical spirit moved this congregation in the Seward neighborhood to start a new congregation in Edina in the 1940s, and in 1961 the congregation sold its urban church building and birthed itself a week later on the prairies of Eden Prairie. It is now a thriving suburban congregation in Eden Prairie, and the congregation in Edina is one that carries on the tradition of freedom and toleration as a Reconciling in Christ (RIC) congregation.[21]

They shed much of their Danish heritage when they purchased ten acres on the edge of the prairie more than fifty years ago. (Even today, however, this suburban congregation hosts an annual *smorgasbord*, a Scandinavian-style supper or luncheon buffet.) They quickly became the largest church in a small town and, while Eden Prairie is no longer growing significantly, this congregation continues to see steady growth. Five hun-

18. John M. Jensen, *The United Evangelical Lutheran Church: An Interpretation* (Minneapolis: Augsburg Publishing House, 1964), pp. 106, 115, 122, 174.

19. H. Richard Niebuhr, *The Social Sources of Denominationalism* (New York and Cleveland: The World Publishing Co., 1929), p. 223.

20. Jensen, *The United Evangelical Lutheran Church*, p. 267.

21. RIC is a designation some denominations use for congregations that publicly and intentionally welcome gay, lesbian, bisexual, and transgendered individuals into their community.

dred to seven hundred fifty people worship here each week in a worship space that was part of their fourth building project. Their pastor intends to retire and has a vision for at least the next six years. They partner with other ELCA congregations in Eden Prairie and worship at Thanksgiving with other faith communities — Jewish, Muslim, and Hindu — in the area. They have an active relationship with Amextra in Mexico.[22] Is it time for them to plant another missional congregation out of their earlier evangelical roots?

3. A Congregation among the Poor:
St. Timothy's of the City Lutheran Church

The Swedish church, unlike the Norwegians, Danes, or Germans, did not splinter in the early years of immigration. Church leaders taught immigrants that they not only belonged to an ethnic group but also to a larger church that had a role in the world.[23] Every conference of the Augustana Synod worked for the awakening of a Christian spirit and mission zeal in congregations and also introduced an ordered system for the gathering of means for mission and other charitable institutions. They had an early passion for ecumenism. The Minnesota Conference of the Augustana Synod, which included the current Minneapolis Area Synod, was a very vocal and powerful conference in the denomination.

St. Timothy's of the City (STC), in the Phillips neighborhood of Minneapolis, was started in the late 1800s. Its birth speaks to the evangelical spirit of the Swedish tradition: STC was a daughter (a church plant) of Augustana Lutheran Church. In turn, STC gave birth to another congregation, Calvary, on Chicago Avenue in south Minneapolis, and together they later started Diamond Lake Lutheran. But the early years of this congregation were times of struggle. An economic depression put many immigrants out of work, especially among the Swedish community who worshiped at this emerging congregation. As part of a larger community, they appealed to their leaders for help. These are the very same cries that sound from this congregation and their neighborhood today. An interim pastor

---

22. The Mexican Association for Rural and Urban Transformation (Amextra) is a nonprofit organization that operates its own community-development projects in Mexico.

23. Maria Erling and Mark Granquist, *The Augustana Story: Shaping Lutheran Identity in North America* (Minneapolis: Augsburg Fortress, 2008), p. 4.

was sent to close down the congregation in 2006; but what emerged was a vision that this congregation is in a prime location for mission. According to data on the Twin Cities, this is the most diverse neighborhood in the country, with over one hundred languages spoken in it.[24]

This old Swedish congregation is a beacon of light to undocumented families who live in the shadows of this country, this city, and this neighborhood. A clergy couple, fluent in Spanish, now serves not just this congregation but the neighborhood. They have planted a community garden and have a campaign to replace graffiti with the artwork of the neighborhood's children. Each Advent season this congregation partners with In the Heart of the Beast puppet theater to present La Natividad, an outdoor reenactment of the first Christmas, including the flight of the first family into Egypt. Herod represents the powerful ICE (Immigration and Customs Enforcement) agent, and the characters are members of this congregation; the place of safety is not Egypt but this ethnically diverse community of faith. That diversity can be seen along the neighborhood's streets: the Mercado Central, a lively Latino marketplace, is across the street from Ingebretsen's, a Scandinavian grocery store that was founded (in 1921) by one of the first immigrant Swedes who settled in this neighborhood; down the street is the Durdur bakery, which specializes in Somali delicacies, and next door to that is a Chinese grocery. This is a community that in some cases is still wondering about its next meal, but it is proclaiming the gospel among the vulnerable new residents of this land. Is this the same song of the first mission planters or a new one?

4. A Mega Congregation: Thanksgiving for Grace Lutheran Church

A leader in the Lutheran Church in America (LCA, a predecessor church body to the ELCA) — and a child of the Augustana tradition — began knocking on doors in Maple Grove, Minnesota, in July 1978. It was "a great site," according to the contemporaneous area pastors. The young families moving in were Lutheran, had grown up Lutheran, and wanted to "make their own mark." Thanksgiving for Grace Lutheran, Maple Grove, still has the distinction of having the largest number of charter members in a new

---

24. John A. Mayer, "CityView Report Twin Cities 2008: Strategic Data for Effective Ministry" (Minneapolis: City Vision, 2008), p. 26.

church start: 412 people signed the charter in 1979. "The timing was just right," their pastors said. "We have no division here; we work consensus." The truth of this statement was reflected in 2001, when the entire congregation moved to a brand-new site with virtually no loss in membership. Like the congregation in Eden Prairie, Thanksgiving for Grace is served by a long-term pastor whose vision is to retire from this congregation. The church's mission is to grow their congregation from cradle to grave and to support the life of the MAS through their offerings. Between 2001 and 2008, the baptized membership of this congregation grew by 32 percent (from 6,234 to 8,232). Every weekend more than 1,600 people worship at this community of faith. Their mission statement reads: "Gather joyfully, Grow spiritually, Go faithfully so that all may have LIFE and have it abundantly in Jesus Christ." As they celebrate their thirtieth birthday, could they be poised to plant a new missional congregation?

5. An Emerging New Church Start: Credit River Lutheran Church

The ELCA Constitution declares that in order to participate in God's mission, the church shall establish congregations.[25] Credit River Lutheran is a new start of the ELCA. It stands with a theological, historical, and missiological heritage rooted in the immigrant background of the Danes and Swedes, Norwegians and Germans, but with a distinctly *American* flavor. What does a missional church plant look like in the first decade of the twenty-first century?

Out of a vision of three congregations, a pastor developer was called to start a new community in the midst of the growth in Elko New Market and Scott County. A year ago they established weekly worship in a school building in Lydia, Minnesota. They are determined to be a faithful people doing service without being bound by a building. It has been slow going, with pastoral transitions in the three partner congregations. There is little sense of community in the housing developments scattered in this once-rural southern margin of the Twin Cities metropolitan area. Perhaps Credit River Lutheran Church will become that center, that community, where people find hope and joy. Their Web-site presence describes an

25. ELCA, *Constitutions of the Evangelical Lutheran Church in America: Constitutions, Bylaws, and Continuing Resolutions of the Evangelical Lutheran Church in America* (Chicago: ELCA, 1986), p. 23.

identity and theology: under the heading *Vision* is "thy kingdom come," and under *Mission,* "thy will be done." Their pastor has a column entitled "Thoughts on living into the *missio Dei* . . ." and writes, "If we seek this kingdom of God to come to us and through us in the world, we know that our actions need to align with the trajectory of this Christ-formed kingdom." This emerging community of faith seeks to shape a community in which this realignment is central to its identity.

A Lutheran Theological Lens for Missional Church Planting

On a Thursday evening a few years ago, I gathered with leaders from Celebrate! Lutheran Church in St. Michael, Minnesota, which is a growing and developing area northwest of the Twin Cities. They had gathered for worship in schools for ten years, and their pastor had an office in a strip mall next to a Subway sandwich shop. A few years ago earlier, they had organized as a congregation, and now they were negotiating a loan to build their first church building. Jared, the vice president of the congregation, was a young financial advisor new to the community. Jared commutes to Minnetonka (western suburb of Minneapolis) for work, his wife to Roseville (first-ring suburb of St. Paul), while their children attend school in St. Michael. The family has no ties to this burgeoning new city along I-94 other than this congregation. "Celebrate! is my only connection to the community. I know I'm not Catholic, I'm not evangelical, and I'm not Missouri Synod [Lutheran]. Celebrate! is where I belong."

Jared is one of the contemporary immigrants. Everyone at Celebrate! speaks English, and this new community of faith is drawn together by their children, a common education and economic background, and their identity as households that are new to the community. Other postmodern emerging congregations in the MAS have communities that are of similar background — in theology, income, interest, age, and educational background. New ethnic-specific congregations — Liberians and Sudanese, Hmong and Lao, Oromo and Latino — imitate their Swedish, Danish, and Norwegian predecessors. Large and small congregations gather like-minded worshipers — regarding class, education, theology, political persuasion, and so on — as tribes who speak a common language. Strangers and aliens, foreigners and wanderers, seek by nature to find what is familiar and to *come home.*

Two small volumes on Chinese and African Americans in Minnesota suggest that Minneapolis has always been ethnically diverse. Several anecdotal facts illustrate this. Norwegian and Swedish immigrants were neighbors to Chinese owners of laundromats and restaurants in the late 1800s. Over one hundred African Americans served in the Minnesota regiment in the Civil War. Freed slaves traveled up the Mississippi River and settled. Like their European immigrant neighbors, African Americans came to Minnesota looking for jobs and land, and they became barbers and cooks. St. Paul had its first African-American police officer in 1881. By 1895, black people lived in every ward in the city of Minneapolis.[26] Single male Chinese first arrived in Minnesota in the mid-1870s.[27]

These simple facts suggest that faith communities, unlike the neighborhoods in which they reside, have been segregated communities. Northern European Lutherans have coexisted with a diverse community since their first arrival. Home mission has focused attention on cultural, ethnic, and familial similarity. It reveals the desire of immigrants to stop wandering, shed an alien or foreign identity, and at last be home and settled. Is there something distinctive within the Lutheran heritage, the sacraments, and an order of liturgy that could shape another structure and provide another lens for a discussion of missional church planting? In this next section I will explore emergent themes through the structure of liturgy, the ELCA constitution, and the sacraments of font and table (baptism and Eucharist).

Water-Baptism-Identity

Mississippi, Minnehaha, Shakopee, and *Minnesota* are all Dakota names or variations on Dakota words. They stand today as indigenous reminders of the native peoples. Chaska, a town in the western metropolitan area, is the name of one of the Dakota leaders hanged by the U.S. government as a result of the Dakota conflict. The Mississippi, this river of life, was the source of power and international trade, a barrier and a conduit. It is across another river, the Jordan, that this new prophet John the Baptist bellows: "I

---

26. David Vassar Taylor, *African Americans in Minnesota: The People of Minnesota* (St. Paul: Minnesota Historical Society Press, 2002), pp. 5, 3, 22. 17.

27. J. J. Hill's Northern Pacific Steamship Company was transporting more than 44,000 tons of flour per year to Hong Kong, China, and Japan in 1901. Hill needed Chinese agents working to establish this important trade. Sherri Gebert Fuller, *Chinese in Minnesota,* The People of Minnesota series (St. Paul: Minnesota Historical Society Press, 2004), p. 3.

am the voice of one crying out in the wilderness. Make straight the way of the Lord" (John 1:23).

Water and rivers give an identity to a people. For the 214,000 ELCA Lutherans who worship in 162 congregations of the MAS, it is baptism that first gives a person a new identity, a missional identity.[28] It is ordinary tap water — from this river, its aquifers, its tributaries, lakes, and ponds, its source in Lake Itasca, or from rain and snow — that stops by to fill a baptismal font on its way to New Orleans and the Gulf of Mexico. "Child of God, you have been sealed by the Holy Spirit and marked with the cross of Christ forever."[29] The gathered community welcomes the newly washed one with these words, "We welcome you into the body of Christ and into the mission we share: join us in giving thanks and praise to God and bearing God's creative and redeeming word to all the world."[30] This expresses their identity.

The ELCA Constitution carefully articulates an identity as well. This constitution, written in 1987, declares under its statement of purpose: "The Church is a people created by God in Christ, empowered by the Holy Spirit, called and sent to bear witness to God's creative, redeeming, and sanctifying activity in the world. To participate in God's mission, this church shall: Proclaim, carry out Christ's Great Commission, and serve in response to God's love to meet human needs. To fulfill these purposes, this church shall establish congregations." The constitution goes on to shape how it will be organized under representational principles — "male/female, clergy/lay, persons of color and/or person whose primary language is other than English."[31]

We are a people rooted in and shaped by an identity of Christ crucified and Christ risen; a theology of the cross is simply in our bones. Douglas John Hall says in *The Cross in Our Context:*

> [B]eing Christian is one of profound world commitment. Discipleship of the crucified Christ is characterized by a faith that drives its adherents into the world with a relentlessness and a daring they could not manage on the basis of human volition alone. It could be said of the theology of the cross that its chief *end* is the genesis of a community

28. "Our Synod," The Minneapolis Area Synod of the Evangelical Lutheran Church in America: http://www.mpls-synod.org/oursynod (accessed August 24, 2011).

29. ELCA, *Evangelical Lutheran Worship*, p. 23.

30. ELCA, *Evangelical Lutheran Worship*, p. 23.

31. ELCA, *Constitutions*, pp. 20-21, 23-24.

impelled (pushed!) toward the world; that it is a theology of worldly engagement and therefore an inherently contextual theology, an incarnational theology; that it necessarily translates itself into an *ecclesiology* of the cross.[32]

Confession

The ritual of "Individual Confession and Forgiveness" from *Evangelical Lutheran Worship* begins this way: "Washed in water and marked with the cross, the baptized children of God are united with Christ and, through him, with other believers who together form a living community of faith. Although we are set free to live in love and faithfulness, we continue to turn away from God and from one another. Confessing our sin involves a continuing return to our baptism. You have come to make confession before God." Then the following instructions are printed in red lettering: "The penitent may use the following form or pray in her/his own words." After that, the confession itself begins, "Merciful God, I confess. . . ."[33]

There are many voices that invite confession from the church at large as well — from the Danes who wondered in 1933 whether their cultural trappings were a hindrance to mission, to Niebuhr's scathing critique of the caste system of denominationalism, to Martin Marty's understanding of ethnicity and its tribalism as "the skeleton of religion in America,"[34] to Gibson Winter's assertion in *The Suburban Captivity of the Churches* that "the metropolis is a religiously fragmented cluster of insular pockets estranged from one another. Its religious life is split through the middle by schism, and its religious organization upholds social class identities rather than the universal identity of those who are interdependent in Christ."[35] We confess our captivity and fear, our racism, classism, and ageism. We confess paralysis, denominationalism, blindness, even oblivion. Confessing gives voice to the Spirit's relentlessly creating soil in which missional congregations can be planted.

32. Douglas John Hall, *The Cross in Our Context: Jesus and the Suffering World* (Minneapolis: Fortress, 2003), p. 183 (italics in original).

33. ELCA, *Evangelical Lutheran Worship*, p. 244.

34. Quoted in Russell E. Richey, ed., *Denominationalism* (Nashville: Abingdon, 1977), p. 250.

35. Gibson Winter, *The Suburban Captivity of the Churches* (New York: Macmillan, 1962), p. 203.

This particular metropolitan area is unique in that it is considered one of the most segregated in the country, in which, for example, poverty is concentrated primarily in certain neighborhoods and communities — not distributed throughout the area. One African-American Lutheran pastor said, "Lutheranism, especially in the Midwest, is both culturally and ethnically defined." The pastor at the Oromo church in Minneapolis said, "We are reminded almost every day that we are foreigners." As legal residents holding a green card, their designation is still "resident alien." "Even when we become citizens," he said, "we are naturalized citizens." When asked what the biblical narrative for his congregation was, he went to the story of Jacob without hesitation: the story of a journey to a foreign land (Egypt) because of famine, and a deep longing to bring the bones back, always thinking of their old country, their land, their songs, and their prayers. Asked about a vision for the MAS, the Oromo pastor replied, "We must see and think and act as Jesus sees us from his prayer in John 17, that we are *one*." Our confession acknowledges that we have kept ourselves separate from one another and have not lived the reality of our oneness in Christ.

The hymn "You Have Come Down to the Lakeshore" gives voice to our confession:

> O loving Friend, you have come to call me . . .
> you've called out my name.
> On the sand I have abandoned my small boat;
> now with you, I will seek other seas.[36]

Because of our sin and our brokenness, we have not abandoned our small boats of tribalism, ethnicity, classism, and racism. Brooklyn Center, a metro suburb, was 96 percent white when Ronald Reagan was president of the United States. Now people of color make up 49 percent of the city. Between 2000 and 2007, the percentage of immigrants rose 20 percent, and poverty went up by 11 percent. Two-thirds of the 25,000 Liberians who live in Minnesota live in Brooklyn Park, Brooklyn Center, and Robbinsdale, Minnesota.[37] ELCA congregations in those same towns are predominantly white, older, experiencing decline and economic hardship, and they con-

36. Cesáreo Gabaráin, "You Have Come Down to the Lakeshore," trans. Madeleine Forell Marshall (Portland, OR: Oregon Catholic Press Publications, 1979), excerpts from verse 4 and refrain. Used by permission.

37. David Peterson, "Truly Diverse 'Burb," *Minneapolis Star Tribune*, December 9, 2008, B1.

fess, "We don't know what to do." The Spirit of creation and leading invites initial confession and humility as new missional congregations are planted on soil that is simultaneously holy and unholy — sacred and broken.

The Peace/The Meal

In worship the community of faith comes into the presence of the Living Word, Jesus Christ, and becomes a missional community planted in the waters of new life, in community, and nourished at the table set by Christ. Lutherans, like all Christians, are a people of the Word, called into life in the waters of baptism, and nourished to participate in God's mission at the Lord's table. Worship, the coming together as the people of God, is a defining, decentering, and recentering activity in which those who were once separate, alien, wandering, and strange are brought together by the power of the Spirit, and we become *neighbors.*

During the worship service, confession and absolution are often followed by the sharing of peace. It is a moment of incarnation in which the broken are reconciled and made whole, made one, re-formed into a new community. As this newly shaped community, we then gather at the table for the meal. In this event, this community is transformed and reminded of its true identity as citizens of the household of God: members of that community become bearers of the gospel, the good news, into the world God loves. It is a community in which strangers and aliens, created in the image of God, are at work setting free the oppressed, giving sight to the blind, removing all walls of injustice, a community that is incarnate on the margins, among the suffering and hopeless. It proclaims a world redeemed, a world without boundaries.

The Word convicts, kills, transforms, redeems, and gives life. In worship, the opportunities abound for lament, confession, telling stories, sharing failings and sin, naming prejudices, and truthtelling. In the world, this community discovers the God who is already at work there, bringing about hope and justice and life. Worship is the time when we hear the words of the angel and of the women at the empty tomb, "He is not here!" It is a missional call to get out of here and go find this risen one among the wanderers, strangers, and aliens — among *you.*

Lutheran theology understands that life's challenges and tensions do not disappear for people of faith, but are held in dialectical tension. The Lutheran dialectic may be helpful in imagining these newly planted communities — saint/sinner communities proclaiming both law and gospel, always forming and re-forming, living in God's kingdom now but not yet, always fallen but always risen, holding all things in tension and always a community of joy. The fact that it is not we who proclaim, but the one who sent us, means that the mission, the church, and the world never cease to be God's. We are part of a priesthood shared by all, but until all of the invited are seated at the banquet table, we are a community that is wounded, broken, and incomplete; a community longing and yearning to be one with God's vision and mission; a community free to admit failings and prejudices because it feasts on the Word, which gives life.

From a Trail of Tears to a River of Joy: What Five Congregations Might Tell Us about Planting Missional Congregations

"Behold I am doing a new thing" (Isa. 43:19). For the five congregations in this study, their missional identities — shaped by their missional histories — are shaping new ones. They have a common identity of being part of the ELCA and part of the MAS. Each is also a community with other aspects of a shared identity — perhaps economic status, cultural background, geographic location, or ethnic background. To plant missional congregations is to take seriously the historical and contextual soil in which they are to be planted. Soil is made up of decayed material, and from those dying things springs life. A vision for planting, at least in the Minneapolis Area Synod, claims an identity of stranger and alien, wanderer and neighbor, baptized, moving, and confessing. In the confessing, the Spirit convicts, re-forms, and gives us courage to become a new people freed from old ways.

The unity of a missional community can only be given through the one who makes us one. God's mission invites congregations to enter into deeper relationships, to become transparent with one another, and to share deeply what it means to be one and to see one another as Christ does. A new missional community will emerge when leaders from these communities prayerfully and intentionally seek God's wisdom and become neighbor and alien, stranger and wanderer, through one another.

We follow God into the world he loves. In the Twin Cities, living our oneness with God might mean congregations would do such things as invite discussions with members of the First People, the Mdewakanton, in order to explore what it means to do justice and shed ethnic and denominational heritage and domain. Planted missional congregations recognize that they are only one part of a greater community rooted in the restlessness of the Holy Spirit, who holds all things together. What would it look like, then, to become like that first Christian community and "hold all things in common"? In this Spirit of unity, we can freely discern hints from the past, address the present, and live into a future that turns a hidden trail of tears into a river of joy.

NEW APPEARANCES ON THE SCENE

There are important new phenomena appearing on the ecclesial landscape through the creative leading of the Holy Spirit. The three chapters in this third section contribute new scholarship and theological reflection in the area of congregational studies on emerging churches, multiculturalism, and postmodern organizational possibilities. Apostolic impulses and cultural contexts converge in the missional church conversation, creating theological openness to new adventures and developments. The three areas discussed in this section are anecdotal, but they are representative of the new visions and horizons stretching before the church in this new era of mission. In these chapters, Trinitarian theology provides a valuable missional framework for interpreting this creative and constitutive work of the Holy Spirit.

Daniel Anderson confronts a situation that many find distressing and many others find hopeful: new churches look different. In "Church Emerging: A Missional View," Anderson reflects on churches emerging on the landscape of Lutheranism based on his research into twenty of these new ministries. Thumbnail sketches of six emerging churches create an instructive descriptive backdrop for his observations. He notes three distinguishing areas of emphasis: new approaches to context; indigenous leadership, service, and worship; and transformative transcultural relationships. An experienced Lutheran pastor with a PhD in congregational mission and leadership, Anderson provides a five-tiered process for discerning missional identity that is usable in non-Lutheran contexts as well as Lutheran ones.

Harvey Kwiyani, a Malawi-born African doing mission work in St. Paul, offers Western Christians an African-influenced understanding of the Holy Spirit's power and presence in "Multicultural Church Planting: African Pneumatology in Western Context." Noting the lack of robust pneumatology in the current missional church conversation, Kwiyani both proposes and then demonstrates the use of missional theology that *begins* with the Holy Spirit as he tells the background story of a church plant in St. Paul. Through prayer and listening, a discernment team ascertained three warrants for a pneumatological missiology for St. Paul, but that is also applicable to other settings: postmodern spirituality; diversity; and hospitality to the needy. Through these warrants, Kwiyani issues an invitation to boldly venture into multicultural church planting, believing that the Holy Spirit not only calls, equips, and sends the church on this venture, but that the Holy Spirit actually *does* multicultural mission.

New organizational forms are appearing in churches just as they are in businesses today, while shifts in our understanding of the doctrine of the Trinity provide new theological frameworks for interpreting congregational life. In "Postbureaucratic Churches: Emerging Forms of Organization and Leadership," Todd Hobart explores four churches that are embracing different aspects of postmodern organizational forms. Extant scholarship on modern and postmodern organizations cites "dedifferentiation" and radical decentralization as helpful organizational principles, while Hobart's own research contributes the notions of interdependence (through networks and relational leadership) and openness to new organizational possibilities. Hobart, who has earned a PhD in congregational mission and leadership, interprets the experimental connections and cooperation he observed within the postbureaucratic churches that he researched in light of the doctrine of the Trinity and a missional ecclesiology. Through these interpreted glimpses of emerging postmodern organizational forms, which were demonstrated by real congregations, he offers innovative organizational possibilities for church planters to consider.

CHAPTER SIX

Church Emerging: A Missional View

Daniel Anderson

> *The church of Christ, in every age,*
> *beset by change, but Spirit led,*
> *must claim and test its heritage*
> *and keep on rising from the dead.*[1]

The Lutheran ministry arising down the street may appear to be quite different from its parent or elder sibling congregations in your community. New ministries are emerging on the cultural margins of the Evangelical Lutheran Church in America (ELCA) among hip, urban, culture-creative young adults; in communities of intentional diversity; in ethnic-specific communities; and in first- and second-generation immigrant communities from the global South and East.[2] Leaders and those who gather in these ministries are exploring ways to be church with a Lutheran understanding of the gospel, but an understanding that gets expressed in contexts and cultures not typically thought of as Lutheran.[3]

---

1. Fred Pratt Green, "The Church of Christ, in Every Age" (Carol Stream, IL: Hope Publishing Company, 1972), verse 1. Reprinted by permission.

2. The focus of this chapter — and the research it reflects — is on emerging ministry new starts in the ELCA. It addresses a particular Lutheran response to the twenty-first-century context and draws on Lutheran tradition, history, and confession to reflect on those missional efforts. My hope is that there is enough universal in the particular to be helpful for others.

3. Demographics of the baptized membership of the ELCA have consistently been reflective of its northern European heritage: at least 96 percent white, declining in numbers,

There has been a flourish of new mission developments within the ELCA in the past ten to fifteen years that have taken different tacks in sailing the turbulent waters of our times. They have developed under the label of "emerging ministry new starts" with support from the leadership of the ELCA responsible for new mission development. This chapter is grounded in observations from my research of twenty of those emerging ministries, with extended site visits in six of those ministries.[4] It is further grounded in the unique story of Lutheranism as it continues to emerge in America and in a missional perspective of lessons to be learned from and shared with emerging ministries.

Emerging Ministries in the ELCA

What follows are brief descriptions of the six emerging ministry sites visited by my research team in the fall of 2008. I have based these mini-sketches on interviews, field notes, and researcher observations, and they are intended to highlight particular aspects of these ministries that are significant for this conversation.

The first site is located in an artsy area of a major U.S. city. An old church building has been purchased and converted into a worship space and arts center. The language of abbey/abbot/abbess is used, and the ministry combines Lutheran and Anglican traditions, affiliation, and support. Those participating in the ministry are primarily urban, culture-creative young adults, many of them artists, professionals, and seminary or college students. The ministry has houses for communal living and is engaging in practices of "new monasticism."[5]

A second emerging ministry is also located in an urban neighborhood of a major U.S. city. It shares space rented from a neighborhood church with other ministries. Participants are also primarily urban,

---

and increasing in average age. Information about the membership of the ELCA is available at: http.//www.elca.org. New ministries are emerging among significantly different demographics and populations.

4. I will not use the names of particular emerging ministries and their leaders in this chapter per agreements made in the research process for my forthcoming PhD dissertation, "A Doxological Hermeneutic of Mission in Emerging Ministries in the ELCA."

5. Jonathan Wilson-Hartgrove, *New Monasticism: What It Has to Say to Today's Church* (Grand Rapids: Brazos, 2008). Wilson-Hartgrove is one of the authors writing about this movement within the emerging church movement and its influence on the church.

culture-creative young adults and professionals. Participants in the ministry have composed ten settings of the traditional liturgy in a variety of musical genres that they use in their worship. Indigenous liturgies and edgy preaching are hallmarks of the worship life of this community.

A third emerging ministry is located in a multicultural urban neighborhood in a major U.S. city in a church building owned by the ministry. Participants are primarily African Americans. The lay pastor is in the process of becoming ordained in the ELCA. The culture of worship draws from the African-American church tradition and Lutheran praxis and theology. Spoken word (poetry recitation), dance, and jazz and gospel music are regular parts of worship. This congregation emerged from a ministry to urban youth, which continues to be an important part of its ministry.

A fourth emerging ministry is located in a mid-sized vacation community in a scenic part of the country. The ministry meets away from the tourist center of town in a storefront property that functions as a youth drop-in center during the week and a gathering place on Sunday evenings for a free community meal, followed by adult study groups. These activities serve as the primary functions of this ministry, though the community also gathers occasionally for worship.

A fifth emerging ministry, located in a major U.S. city, is already twelve years old, making it one of the oldest of the twenty emerging ministries in the study. They meet in a rented theater in a neighborhood filled with apartments, condos, and ethnic restaurants. The participants in this ministry are primarily urban, culture-creative young adults and young families. Worship in this community includes significant amounts of alternative music composed by participants in the community, prayer, sacraments, and preaching. Earphones are available in the lobby. This is one of the few emerging ministries in this study that have experienced a transition of leadership from the founding pastors.

A sixth emerging ministry is located in a suburban neighborhood of a major U.S. city, a neighborhood that is in transition from primarily white residents to a multiethnic demographic. Participants in this congregation include older people, original members of a predominately white Lutheran congregation that engaged in an intentional transformational ministry process to better reflect their context. The result is this study's most diverse community in terms of age, race, ethnicity, and sexuality. Their mantra is that God welcomes all people. The only people not welcome are those who are unwilling to welcome "the other." A traditional Lutheran liturgy serves as common ground for the diverse cultures present among the participants. This emerging ministry focuses on engagement with its context through community events. The lay pastor of this ministry is also involved in a process to become ordained.

These six descriptions are cursory but serve as background for several significant areas of observation that follow. Three areas of focus and emphasis emerge from these ministries: *context;* the *indigenous* nature of these ministries; and the understanding of mission as *transcultural.* Emerging ministries tend to be small communities of people who are gathered in and shaped by a particular context, with ministry that grows from the giftedness of the community and draws the various cultures present in a community into a common, shared culture that is uniquely their own.

Context

Each of these postmodern ministries is highly contextual — but in very different ways from their modern counterparts. The modern approach to context asked how the church could be in ministry *to* the context. Demographic studies of neighborhoods led to defining target audiences, identifying the needs of those audiences, and developing programs and ministries to meet those needs. The modern approach to context is attractional, market/consumer driven, and needs-based. One of the twenty emerging ministries studied is making an intentional and effective use of this approach to context by targeting young adults with young families and addressing their needs; it has already expanded its ministry to a second site. However, most of the other emerging ministries are taking different approaches to context.

Many emerging ministries grow from their contexts, are shaped by their contexts, and engage in and with their contexts. In some cases that engagement with community means getting involved in community organizations such as chambers of commerce and arts councils. Some describe their relationship with the community in monastic terms that are reminiscent of a Benedictine commitment to place. Others use incarnational images of being the body of Christ in their neighborhoods. Several of the emerging ministries studied are involved in faith-based or broad-based community organizing. These emerging ministries hold what is essentially a subject-to-subject rather than a subject-to-object relationship of engagement with their community.

Each of the ministries studied looks very different from the others in worship, organization, and mission. This is due in large part to their commitment to contextual engagement with their neighborhoods. They reflect their contexts, and they also reflect the indigenous nature of their contexts in their ministries.

Indigenous Church

The missions of an indigenous church are shaped not only by the context but also by the gifts and callings of the participants in the ministry. Ephesians 4:11-16 was mentioned in interviews regarding the gifting and equipping of the church for the work of ministry. The indigenous nature of church shows up in several significant ways in emerging ministries, including leadership, service, and worship.

Ordained Leadership

Clergy members have served as primary leaders in modern and traditional expressions of Lutheranism. In the history of our faith tradition, persons who have felt called to be pastors ordinarily left their homes, went to seminary for four years to earn a master of divinity (MDiv) degree, and then agreed to be sent wherever the church might need them to serve. That is not so much the case in emerging ministries. Several of the leaders serving as mission developers in their emerging ministries are not yet ordained. Nearly all of the emerging ministries studied are developing leaders from within their community who will become future leaders in that community or similar contexts. One of the concerns of emerging ministries, given their highly contextual and culturally specific nature, is the question of where future leaders will come from. The answer is: from within.

The cultural shifts that have given rise to emerging communities have also affected the seminaries of the ELCA. Not long ago, people called to be clergy were required to travel to one of eight ELCA seminaries for four years of training that removed them from the very contexts where they might have been called to serve. Recognizing the need for ordained leaders in urban, rural, and ethnic ministry settings, where pastors were typically hesitant to serve and the limited numbers of clergy made filling those calls difficult, the ELCA developed a program to equip indigenous leaders from those communities to serve as ordained pastors. A three-year

TEEM (Theological Education for Emerging Ministry) program prepares lay leaders for ordination through seminary education with mentors and intensive class sessions on campus — without requiring an MDiv degree. Most of these leaders remain in their contexts and serve as lay pastors while they are being equipped to be ordained.

A recently developed second option for alternative seminary education is a Distributive Learning (DL) MDiv, in which students remain in their ministry contexts while earning an MDiv degree over the course of six years of cohort-based online learning, with occasional intensive courses on a seminary campus. Both the TEEM and DL programs of theological education were represented among the mission developers involved in this study. Additional alternative paths to ordained leadership in the ELCA were also represented. Some emerging leaders were ordained in another denomination and are transferring ordination to the ELCA. Others completed part of their theological education in non-ELCA seminaries and are completing a year of study at a Lutheran seminary for ordination in the ELCA. Nearly half of the twenty mission developers involved in this study have taken routes to ordination other than the traditional MDiv. Six were not yet ordained in the ELCA at the time of this study. All of this is to say that emerging ministries are developing indigenous leaders and that the seminaries of the ELCA are working in various ways to equip those leaders for ordination as pastors in the church. The ELCA remains committed to ordained leadership, but it is developing alternatives in the path to ordination.

Service

Serving within the emerging community and serving the surrounding community both rely on indigenous leadership. Most of these emerging communities spoke of their expectation that God will call forth people to serve, and when that happens, ministry will happen. This is quite different from typical Lutheran congregations that are structured with standing committees, including a committee whose task it is to find volunteers to fill the standing committees. Those constitutionally mandated structures don't exist in emerging ministries. The most common scenario identified leaders as participants who felt passionate about a need in the community or in the ministry and who would be supported by that emerging ministry to gather some folks and go for it. Ministry within the community and to the community surrounding the emerging ministries studied was dependent on the gifts and passions of the participants in the ministries. Of course, most of the ministries in the larger study are in the first three years of their mission development. Structures may emerge as ministries grow in size and mission, though even the more established emerging ministries draw on indigenous leadership. "Organic ministry" — ministry that grows naturally from the community — was another term used to describe this process.

Worship

Leaders in these emerging ministries draw on the gifts of participants in planning and leading worship experiences. What was most striking in the emerging ministries studied was the extent to which the music and liturgies being used in worship were composed and developed by participants in the ministry. Worship is an expression of the community that emerges from the gifts present in the community. Worship is different in each emerging ministry from other emerging ministries in part because of the indigenous nature of the gifts of the participants and the context in which they gather. Worship is also unique in each setting because each ministry has a distinct cultural identity that shapes the languages of worship. Worship resources, music, liturgy, and planning draw on the indigenous resources of the community.

Transcultural Mission

As of 2007, the membership of the ELCA (4,709,956 members gathered in over 10,000 congregations) was 96.8 percent white.[6] While there is diversity within that demographic in location (urban, suburban, rural, small town), age, worship formats (traditional, contemporary, blended, alternative), and acceptance or nonacceptance of LGBT clergy, the ELCA still reflects its northern European heritage and the monocultural focus of its Common Service era (more about the Common Service in the section that follows concerning the American Lutheran story). Despite the intentional efforts of the ELCA in the past twenty years to become more ethnically diverse, we are not. Efforts to be more hospitable to the "stranger" still label the other as *stranger*. The invitation to come and join us, no matter how

---

6. "Research and Evaluation," Evangelical Lutheran Church in America: http://www .elca.org (accessed October 25, 2009).

sincere, ignores the rigidity of our own traditions and culture and ignores the inclination of "other" folks to worship and pray in their own culture and languages.

The emerging church provides insight into this dilemma: it is a transcultural phenomenon.[7] Transculturation in this context is the phenomenon by which the Lutheran tradition meets the cultures of emerging communities; in that process, both cultures are transformed and a new culture emerges. Emerging ministries in the ELCA are emerging in cultures distinctly different from the ELCA's cultural roots. A Lutheran expression of the gospel is taking root and beginning to flourish in settings that are not traditionally Lutheran — among people in the twenty- and thirty-something age group who would never find their way into a traditional church. In those settings Lutheran meets hipster, and a new culture of Lutheran community is forming.

Nontraditional Lutheran settings include first- and second-generation Hispanic, Chinese, Hmong, Ethiopian, Tanzanian, and other immigrant communities who are encountering a Lutheran expression of the gospel in their own cultural languages. Those settings include ethnic-specific communities such as African-American and Native-American communities that meld a Lutheran expression of the gospel with traditions from their cultural heritages. Among the congregations in my research, there was at least one intentionally diverse community in which a culture that celebrates diversity is given priority over the personal cultures of the participants in the context of a Lutheran expression of the gospel. In all of these emerging settings in the ELCA that I researched, a Lutheran expression of the gospel is being translated into the cultural languages of people who are praying in their own cultural languages and with indigenous leadership.[8]

This is a new era of leadership development in the Lutheran tradi-

---

7. Fernando Ortiz, *Cuban Counterpoint, Tobacco and Sugar* (Durham, NC: Duke University Press, 1995). Ortiz introduced the term "transculturation" in 1940. He referred to a process of transition from one culture to another that is not one culture taking on the culture of another (as implied in acculturation) but that the interaction of cultures involves *deculturation* and the consequent creation of new cultural phenomena, *neoculturation*. In other words, when cultures meet, both are changed and something new emerges.

8. Lamin Sanneh, *Translating the Message: The Missionary Impact on Culture,* American Society of Missiology series (Maryknoll, NY: Orbis, 1989). Sanneh provides groundbreaking work on the translation of the gospel into global cultures and the impacts of such translation on culture. The idea that the gospel can be translated from one cultural expression to another is significant.

tion. In cross-cultural mission, leaders from the church are *sent to* cultures that are not their own to learn the receiving culture and share the gospel in that context. In the emerging church, indigenous leaders are rising up *from within* emerging cultures for leadership within their own communities. In some cases they are working as mission developers while they are being equipped and trained for ordination.[9] The onus of translating the gospel into emerging cultures is transferred to emerging leaders who are known in their contexts, already respected as leaders, know their cultural context, and are able to translate a Lutheran expression of the gospel into their own languages.

It would seem from this that the missional task is twofold: to continue to translate the gospel into the languages of the microcultures that abound in our society and to equip indigenous leaders for that work; and to find ways to unite those diverse multicultural and microcultural voices for the sake of God's mission in the world.

What Is God Up to in Emerging Ministries?

This was a guiding question in this research project. Answers to this question include the incarnational approach to context, the indigenous nature of ministry and leadership, and the transcultural relationship with the gospel that I have just discussed. There are two more bits of background information that further develop answers to this question. First, each of these emerging ministries was decidedly Lutheran in its expression of the gospel (though Lutherans raised in the traditional Common Service era of American Lutheranism may not recognize that expression as Lutheran). For Lutherans, ecclesiology, missiology, and doxology derive from confessional roots. (I will explore those roots as expressed and developed in emerging ministries below.) Second, what is emerging in the ELCA has significant connections to what has come before. We will visit the story of Lutherans in America in order to provide the context for the stories of newly emerging ministries in the Lutheran tradition and to consider the possibilities beyond current expressions.

9. ELCA Conference of Bishops, "Seamless Mission Leadership: Enhancing Mission Development and Equipping Mission Developers" (Chicago: Evangelical Lutheran Church in America, 2008). The Conference of Bishops provides guidelines for the involvement of lay mission developers in candidacy processes that lead to ordination.

Confessio

The Lutheran tradition is a confessional tradition. There are statements of faith that mark and define who we are as a church. There are four principles drawn from the Lutheran confessions that place emerging ministries within the Lutheran confessional tradition and help to further develop that tradition for missional expression in the world. The Augsburg Confession, published in 1531, was a mission statement of sorts for the emerging Reformation churches, and it is a founding document in the Lutheran tradition. Article VII of the Augsburg Confession defines the church:

> It is also taught that at all times there must be and remain one, holy, Christian church. It is the *assembly of believers* among whom the *gospel is purely preached,* and the *holy sacraments are administered* according to the gospel. For this is enough for the true unity of the Christian church that there the gospel is preached harmoniously according to a pure understanding and the sacraments are administered in conformity with the divine Word.[10]

In this section I will discuss four principles drawn from the Lutheran confessions that place emerging ministries within the Lutheran confessional tradition and help to further develop that tradition for missional expression in the world.

The first principle is a definition of church from a Lutheran confessional perspective that includes emerging ministries. Lutheran ecclesiology is built on assembly, Word, and sacrament. It becomes a missional ecclesiology when the assembly is both gathered and sent; when the gospel purely preached calls the church to join in God's mission in the world; and when the sacraments gather all people at a table of forgiveness and reconciliation, ordain in baptism, and send the baptized into God's mission in the world. The emerging ministries studied in this project are all communities assembled in Word and sacrament, and thus they are Lutheran in ecclesiology. I will later explore the extent to which they are also missional.

The very next line of Article VII of the Augsburg Confession states a second principle regarding Lutheran worship: "It is not necessary for the true unity of the Christian church that uniform ceremonies, instituted by

10. Robert Kolb and Timothy J. Wengert, eds., *The Book of Concord: The Confessions of the Evangelical Lutheran Church* (Minneapolis: Fortress, 2000), p. 42 (italics added).

human beings, be observed everywhere."[11] The ceremonies with which each emerging ministry gathers in Word and sacrament are unique in each context. There are similarities: most have weekly communion; most use the Revised Common Lectionary to some extent; most include elements of worship recognizable from the *ordo* of worship that includes gathering, Word, sacrament, and sending. Many include elements familiar to the Common Service, including confession, prayers of the church, sharing of the peace, and benediction. But worship in each setting is indigenous, rising from the gifts, passions, languages, and cultures of the people present. Worship in each context is unique, when compared with other sites, and most often changes from week to week in each site, within recognizable frameworks. Freedom in worship expression is a key principle in the Lutheran confessions for emerging ministries and is an instructive principle regarding possibilities for more traditional congregations.

And yet, drawing on a third principle found in the Apology of the Augsburg Confession related to Article VII, the Reformers affirm: "[I]n our churches we willingly observe the order of the Mass, the Lord's day, and other more important festival days."[12] Such "useful and ancient ordinances" were kept for the sake of those for whom such rites were familiar — and thus useful. Several of the emerging ministries studied have chosen to "observe the order of the Mass." In one context the texts of the traditional liturgy have been set in ten different musical settings, ranging from contemplative to alternative rock. These are indigenous settings of the traditional liturgy composed by musicians who are a part of that community. Continuity with the ancient church motivates the continued use of the liturgy, yet in the musical languages of the community.

Another community uses settings of the traditional liturgy because Hispanic immigrants, for whom the Catholic liturgical traditions of their homelands have significance, form that community. In another site, the most diverse of the sites studied, the traditional liturgy provides a common ground on which their many cultures can gather in worship. In yet another site, a Lutheran-Anglican ministry, the traditions of the Book of Common Prayer shape worship but are expressed in the cultural languages of the participants in the community.

A fourth principle emerged in the worship practices of Luther and the early Reformers: the Bible was translated into German, and settings of

---

11. Kolb and Wengert, *The Book of Concord*, p. 42.
12. Kolb and Wengert, *The Book of Concord*, p. 180.

the Mass were newly composed in German. In fact, Luther said, "I also wish that we had as many songs as possible in the vernacular which the people could sing during mass."[13] Luther, who had himself translated the Bible, created a setting of the German Mass and composed hymns that continue to be used in the church today. The experience of worship and faith were thus put into the language of the people, and as the Reformation expanded to neighboring countries, the languages of worship also expanded. The parallels between the worship life that emerged in the Reformation and the worship life that is emerging in the church today are significant and are founded on the same Lutheran confessions. Emerging ministries in the ELCA are an expression of and development within the Lutheran confessional tradition and also an expression of a logical next step in the historical development of American Lutheranism.

An American Lutheran Story

The story of Lutheranism in America is a story of immigration and the interactions of cultures. The first Lutherans to come to America came from the Netherlands and Sweden in 1620. Waves of immigrants followed from Germany and the Scandinavian countries, where Lutheranism was most often the established state church. In this new world Lutherans were just one of many minorities. As northern European Lutherans settled in particular regions in America, they gathered in their own churches and worshiped in the languages, liturgies, and traditions of their home countries. They were able to pray in their own language while living in the midst of languages and cultures very different from their own. Each of these Lutheran ethnic groups formed congregations and collectively formed synods based on ethnicity and language. Between 1840 and 1875, fifty-eight different Lutheran synods were formed in the United States.[14] And immigration to the United States from traditionally Lutheran northern European countries continued through the first two decades of the twentieth century.

At first, pastors and worship resources were supplied from home

---

13. Martin Luther, *Luther's Works: Liturgy and Hymns,* ed. Ulrich S. Leupold, vol. 53, *Luther's Works,* ed. Helmut T. Lehmann (Philadelphia: Fortress, 1965), p. 36.

14. Eric W. Gritsch, *Fortress Introduction to Lutheranism* (Minneapolis: Fortress, 1994), p. 57.

countries. But eventually second- and third-generation families of immigrants transitioned to English as their primary language. A need for English-language resources, liturgies, and theological training for clergy emerged, and Lutheran synods began to work together to develop those resources. Then, in 1888, the Common Service was published, and Lutheranism experienced a paradigm shift that transformed the face of Lutheranism in the United States for nearly a century.

The Common Service was in English, and it was the object of great debate between, on the one hand, those who held out for worshiping in traditional languages and retaining the unique liturgies from each ethnic tradition and, on the other hand, those who desired a common liturgy in English that could be shared by the many Lutheran synods present in the United States.[15] The publication of the Common Service in 1888 coincided with the merger of several Lutheran synods into the United Lutheran Church in America. The use of the Common Service liturgy facilitated a century of mergers that culminated in the merger of the American Lutheran Church (ALC), the Lutheran Church in America (LCA), and the American Evangelical Lutheran Church (AELC) into the Evangelical Lutheran Church in America (ELCA) in 1988.[16]

The many cultural and ethnic languages, liturgies, hymnodies, and traditions of Lutheran worship passed through the melting pot of American culture and emerged in the Common Service of 1888.[17] My grandfather was a part of the early-twentieth-century immigration from Norway. He arrived and learned English, and he did not allow any of his five children to learn or speak Norwegian. The strong desire and pressure to become a part of the American culture that immigrants experienced was also reflected in the practices of their faith.

In 1917 the Common Service Book was published: it included occasional services and hymns in English in addition to the Common Service liturgy. The Service Book and Hymnal (SBH) replaced the Common Service Book in 1958, and was the culmination of the Common Service tradi-

15. The Common Service Debate, as it is now called, took place during the 1880s, leading up to 1888, primarily in articles, editorials, and letters to the editor in *The Lutheran Church Review* (now published as *The Lutheran Quarterly*).

16. Currently there is only a handful of Lutheran synods, or denominations, in the United States, with the ELCA being the largest.

17. The term "melting pot" came into use in 1908, though the value of merging immigrant cultures and traditions into one American culture was a part of the ethos of this country in both the eighteenth and nineteenth centuries.

tion. Later Lutheran hymnals, including the Lutheran Book of Worship (LBW, 1978) and the Evangelical Lutheran Worship (ELW, 2006), have moved away from the Common Service to the use of ecumenically developed texts and liturgies. These more recently published hymnals reflect the diversification of worship expressions, ecumenical influences, and musical cultures that developed in the last quarter of the twentieth century with the inclusion of multiple settings of the liturgy and hymnody drawn from many ethnic traditions and musical genres.

The Common Service era — from 1888 through the publication of SBH in 1958 — ensconced American Lutheranism in an essentially monocultural expression of Lutheranism. It was a point of pride among Lutherans in the 1950s that one could enter nearly any Lutheran church in America on a Sunday morning and experience a common liturgy and a sermon preached on a Common Lectionary reading. The development of a common service in the 1880s felt like the coming together of diverse cultures and traditions to those involved, and what emerged was the expression of a common Americanized northern European culture of liturgy and hymnody. That common cultural tradition was a significant factor in the reality that the ELCA, at its foundation in 1988, was nearly entirely formed by people of northern European ethnic heritage.

Common Service–era Lutheranism was a reflection of the early-twentieth-century industrial culture of America in its day: standardized, assembly-lined, franchised, and name-branded — with interchangeable parts. You could walk into any Lutheran church and you would know what to expect. Theological schools trained pastors to fulfill those common roles and, to put it crassly, clergy members were interchangeable, generic parts in the church system. The Lutheran Church of the Common Service era was essentially monocultural with a common language, a common liturgy, a common lectionary, and a common eighteenth- and nineteenth-century northern European hymnody.[18]

At the end of the nineteenth century, the giving up of worship in the language and cultural heritage of their homelands for the sake of a common language, liturgy, and worship life was a sacrificial but highly missional move. It enabled the mergers of numerous ethnic-based synods into a handful of powerful denominations with emerging global and ecu-

18. The development of the electronic organ in the twentieth century further standardized the musical accompaniment for congregational liturgy and song, as organs became readily available and ubiquitous in Lutheran congregations.

menical impact. The Common Service and Common Lectionary formed a common identity for Lutheranism in the United States at a time when the many immigrant cultures were melding into an American mainstream culture. Lutherans found a niche identity within that culture, and within those narrow cultural boundaries Lutheranism grew to five million members in the ELCA at its founding in 1988, along with several million Lutherans in other Lutheran synods and denominations. The Common Service era of American Lutheranism found its place within the modern Christendom era of twentieth-century American history.

The changes and paradigm shifts that occurred in the United States during the last half of the twentieth century — and continue to occur — have been astounding. Technological advances that have resulted in cultural and economic globalization have affected nearly every aspect of life. The modern, functional Christendom-era and Common Service–era church has struggled faithfully to find ways to be more effective in its twenty-first-century context. The missional church movement has sought to redefine church and understand different ways of being church and understanding God in light of contextual realities. The emerging church is organically sending up shoots in the soil of these cultural realities. American Lutheranism faces new contextual realities that provide an epochal opportunity to "claim and test its heritage and keep on rising from the dead," as it says in the hymn "The Church of Christ, in Every Age."

The church that is emerging among new ministry starts within the ELCA is coming out amid a swirl of labels and movements. Ways of doing/being church are indeed testing our heritage and rising up in surprising contexts. Ministries struggle with issues that have been labeled modern or postmodern, in contexts that reflect both functional Christendom and functional post-Christendom realities, and with cultures that draw upon traditional, contemporary, emerging, and alternative sources. The debates these struggles engender have pointed to our experiences of change; to shifts in cultural, social, and global realities; to unclear, changing, and controversial roles and influences of religion in civil society; and to concerns about aging and declines in the memberships of many Christian denominations in the United States.

The church emerging within the ELCA comes out of a narrative of change and the sincere attempts to grow and strengthen the church that are represented by a series of movements in the church of the late twentieth century. The church-renewal movement of the 1960s-70s led to the church-growth movement of the 1970s-80s; the church-effectiveness movement of the 1980s-90s blended into the church health movement of the 1990s-2000s.[19] The ELCA and other church bodies continue to work with these movements with resources such as Natural Church Development, which uses assessment tools and coaches to improve the strategic focus and ministries of congregations.[20]

The various renewal movements in the last half of the twentieth century were responses of churches to their changed contexts. Churches faced with decline and a perception of irrelevance sought resources for renewal, growth, effectiveness, and health through programs, workshops, books, networks, conferences, continuing education for clergy, contemporary worship models, contemporary business and leadership models, and so forth. The role of the pastor evolved from an earlier chaplain-counselor model to a CEO-leader model. These movements brought about significant — but for the most part incremental and instrumental — change to the modern church as it faithfully sought ways to better fulfill its role.

Alternative movements, developed alongside these strategic movements, continue to arise in the church and have significant impact on the ELCA. *Missional* church, *transforming* church, *emerging* church, and *community organizing* are some of the movements that are raising and answering questions about what it means to be church in the twenty-first century.[21]

19. Elmer L. Towns and Gary McIntosh, *Evaluating the Church Growth Movement: Five Views* (Grand Rapids: Zondervan, 2004), pp. 75-120. Five authors, including Craig Van Gelder, who writes representing the perspective of the Gospel and Our Culture Network, give their perspectives of the church-growth movement and write responses to each other's perspectives.

20. For a description of Natural Church Development and its applications within the ELCA, see "Natural Church Development," Evangelical Lutheran Church in America: http://www.elca.org/Growing-In-Faith/Discipleship/Natural-Church-Development.aspx (accessed October 19, 2009).

21. The four movements mentioned here are movements that have influenced the particular ministries involved in this research project. In addition to these broader movements, Evangelism and Book of Faith initiatives are having an impact as programmatic movements developed within the ELCA. The *missional church* movement is at the core of the Congregational Mission and Leadership initiative of Luther Seminary and guides the work of its Center for Missional Leadership; see www.discerningmission.org. Definitions of and expressions about the *transforming church* can be accessed at: http://www.transformingchurch.com, and at: http://www.elca.org/Growing-in-Faith/Discipleship/Renewing-Congregations.aspx. The most common understanding of *emerging church* is reflected in networks of emerging churches, such as Emergent Village (www.emergentvillage.org). There is a Lutheran network of emerging leaders at: http.//www.luthermergent.ning.com. The ELCA is involved in *congregation-based organizing;* see www.elca.org/Our-Faith-in-Action/Justice/Congregation-based-Organizing.aspx.

Emerging ministry new starts in the ELCA are taking those questions seriously and are attempting to form answers of their own to those questions.

In summary, the story of Lutheranism in America began in ethnic, liturgical, and cultural diversity that served generations of immigrants who came to this country from northern European homelands. Churches provided community and the opportunity for people to pray in the vernacular of their own traditions, liturgies, and musical languages. The Common Service era served the church with a common identity and a common language in which to pray. What was diverse but separate was then united in a common church culture. In that unity was a common identity and strength for mission in a modern, early-twentieth-century North American culture of Christendom. What has emerged since then is the rise of microcultures within the nation and a growing number of people who must once again — yet for the first time — learn to pray in their own languages. The Lutheran story in America has gone from a diversity of ethnic cultures and expressions of Lutheranism through a common, monocultural era of Lutheran identity to the current encounter with a multi- and microcultured environment in which mission is transcultural. People of various cultures are encountering the culture of the Lutheran tradition, and that encounter changes both.

"I Need to Pray in My Own Language"

Each of the congregations I have served as pastor has had outreach ministries that provided food, clothing, and household necessities to those in need. A man who had recently emigrated from Mexico brought his family to collect some needed items, and in conversation he was invited to join us in worship that coming weekend. He expressed his gratitude both for the items received and for the invitation to worship, but he responded, "I need to pray in my own language." It was a conviction of the Reformers five hundred years ago and continues to be true today. God speaks with us, and we speak with God in our own language.

Today, however, we are a part of and are surrounded by numerous microcultures, each with its own language. Those languages encompass much more than the vernacular languages that we speak. We have differing musical languages, ritual languages, technical languages, gender languages, ethnic languages, socioeconomic languages, languages of sexual expression, languages of faith expression, generational languages, and regional

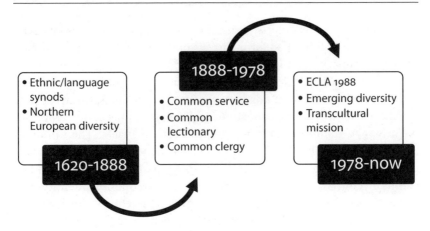

languages. People living within the same geographical context may well live in different worlds. My daughter, who is fourteen, lives in my house, and our worlds intersect in significant ways; but I do not live in her middle-school world, nor she in my professional one. My wife, who shares much of my world and history, is a physician who has spent much of her life in a world that I can only visit as a patient of one of her colleagues. My wife and my daughter are, of course, both female, which is another world foreign to my male comprehension. There are languages that we share, but there are even more that are unique to the cultures of which we are a part. What does it mean for us to pray in our own languages? How can we be church in a multicultural, many-languaged context? What might be a missional answer to those questions?

Lex Orandi, Lex Credendi, Lex Movendi

Lex supplicandi statuat lex credendi ("the law of prayer constitutes the law of belief") is an ancient motto of the church, credited to Prosper of Aquitaine, who was the secretary to Leo the Great from about 435 CE, and was defending Augustine's arguments "for the necessity of grace prior to faith."[22] In its original conception, doctrine is subordinate to worship. This ecclesiastical mantra appears most often among liturgical theologians as

22. E. Byron Anderson, *Worship and Christian Identity: Practicing Ourselves,* The Virgil Michel series (Collegeville, MN: Liturgical Press, 2003), pp. 24-29. Anderson traces the development and use of this mantra from its origins to current usage.

lex orandi, lex credendi, and it raises questions about the relationship between the worship and faith of the church. Most argue for a reciprocal relationship between *lex orandi* and *lex credenda:* worship shapes faith, and faith shapes worship.

Expanded forms of this motto have emerged in the history of the church to reflect the engagement of the church with the world. *Lex orandi, lex credendi, lex vivendi* (the law of living) connects worship and doctrine with the lived practice of faith. *Lex orandi, lex credendi, lex agendi* (the law of ethical action) connects worship and doctrine to the public agenda of the church. I propose *lex orandi, lex credendi, lex movendi* (the law of moving) as an expression of a missional perspective. Worship and faith are connected in reciprocal relationships with the movement of God and the church in the world.

Movendi is a form of the Latin word *moveo,* which has similar meanings and connotations as the English word "move." It means "to move or set in motion," but it can also mean "to disturb, to change, to dislodge, to begin." It can mean "to affect, to influence, to provoke." In a reflexive form it can mean "to dance."[23] In an imperative form it can be simply translated, "Go!" which has echoes of the Great Commission in Matthew 28.[24] A missional church — co-missioned with God — moves with God into the world to disturb, change, dislodge, begin, affect, influence, and provoke to redemption and reconciliation. As a church created by the Spirit's *imago Trinitatis* (in the image of the perichoretic Trinity), we move with God, with one another, and with the other for the sake of God's mission in the world. It is our worship and faith that shape the church as we go into the world, even as our going shapes our worship and faith.

The relationships of *lex orandi, lex credendi,* and *lex movendi* provide lenses for reflection on the emerging church movement and its relationships with the larger church's history and traditions. Earlier in this essay I argued that emerging ministries in the ELCA are confessionally Lutheran by virtue of their ecclesiology and doxology as communities gathered in Word and sacrament. I wondered to what extent they could be considered missional. The extent to which emerging ministries are missional depends on the extent to which their *lex orandi* and *lex credendi* result in *lex*

---

23. Catherine Mowry LaCugna, *God for Us: The Trinity and Christian Life* (San Francisco, CA: HarperSanFrancisco, 1991), pp. 271-72. LaCugna draws heavily on the metaphor of dance to describe a perichoretic Trinity and the relationship of God with creation.

24. *Collins Concise Latin Dictionary,* ed. Lorna Sinclair (Glasgow: HarperCollins, 1997), p. 136.

movendi, and the extent to which *lex movendi* shapes their *lex orandi* and *lex credendi.* One must ask how worship, faith, and mission influence and shape each other in each context.

A Missional View of the Church Emerging

The missional church movement provides lenses with which to view the role of the church in the world and to view certain theological and missiological assertions about the identity and purpose of the church. The story of the missional church movement is grounded in theological developments of the late twentieth century and their implications for the church.

Missio Dei

The Latin word *missio* means "sending." *Missio Dei* is *missio Trinitatis:* that is, the doctrine of *missio Dei* arises from Trinitarian theology. The Western understanding of Trinity as sending and the Eastern understanding of Trinity as perichoretic ground the missional understanding on the sending of the church into the world and the relational nature of that sending. These concepts are explored more fully in other documents from this and previous consultations, and the doctrine is at the heart of a missional-church theology.[25] The development of the missional church movement, while concurrent with the modern movements of the late twentieth century, is distinct from those movements and is the result of a missiological paradigm shift that quietly occurred in the midst of the twentieth century.

Karl Barth was one of the first theologians to articulate the idea that *mission is an activity of God* (in a paper presented to the Brandenburg Missionary Conference in 1932). He said: "The term *missio* was in the ancient Church an expression of the doctrine of the Trinity — namely the expression of the divine sending forth of the self, the sending of the Son and the Holy Spirit to the world."[26] This concept of *missio Dei* emerged clearly in 1952 at the Willingen Conference of the International Missionary Council

25. See, e.g., Craig Van Gelder, *The Missional Church and Denominations: Helping Congregations Develop a Missional Identity,* Missional Church series (Grand Rapids: Eerdmans, 2008), pp. 167-69.

26. Karl Barth, *Classic Texts in Mission and World Christianity,* ed. Norman E. Thomas, American Society of Missiology series no. 20 (Maryknoll, NY: Orbis, 1995), p. 104.

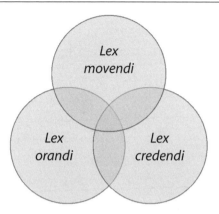

(IMC), even though the actual term did not emerge until later. Influenced by Barthian theology, mission was understood to be the very nature and activity of God. This language of mission as *missio Dei* was formulated following the conference at Willingen by Karl Hartenstein[27] and was further developed by Johannes Blauw in his 1962 publication, *The Missionary Nature of the Church*.[28]

A missional view — with a Lutheran spin — holds that God is a missional God who "calls, gathers, enlightens, makes holy, and keeps in faith" a church for the sake of God's mission in the world.[29] The missions of the churches *(missiones ecclesiae)* participate in the mission of God *(missio Dei)*. Fundamental questions for the missional church are: What is God up to in our context (locally and globally)? How are we called to join in that mission?

A Process for Missional Discernment in the Emerging Church

Whether or not any church is missional depends on its relationship with *missio Dei*. There is no single way to join God in God's mission in the world; each church in its own context is called to discern what God is up to

27. H. H. Rosin, *'Missio Dei': An Examination of the Origin, Contents, and Function of the Term in Protestant Missiological Discussion* (Leiden, Germany: Interuniversity Institute for Missiological and Ecumenical Research, Department of Missiology, 1972).

28. Johannes Blauw, *The Missionary Nature of the Church: A Survey of the Biblical Theology of Mission*, Foundations of the Christian Mission (New York: McGraw-Hill, 1962).

29. Kolb, *The Book of Concord*, p. 355.

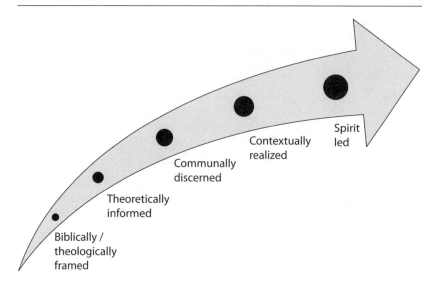

in that context and be a part of that mission. A missional hermeneutic provides a process of discernment for missional communities to enter into *missio Dei*.[30] This version of a missional hermeneutic will be used to draw the church — emerging and missional — into conversation with God's mission in the world: *missiones ecclesiae* (the missions of the church) are biblically and theologically framed, theoretically informed, communally discerned, contextually realized, and led by the Spirit for the sake of *missio Dei*.

Biblically and Theologically Framed

The confessions in the Lutheran tradition are the biblical and theological framework[31] that defined the positions of the Reformers in their argu-

---

30. Craig Van Gelder, *The Ministry of the Missional Church: A Community Led by the Spirit* (Grand Rapids: Baker, 2007), pp. 95-120. In a chapter entitled "Spirit-led Discernment and Decision-Making," Van Gelder describes a missional hermeneutic for leading in mission. A missional hermeneutic of leadership leads to "biblically-theologically framed, theoretically informed, communally discerned, strategic action." His formulation, along with variations introduced by Gary Simpson, serve as the basis for my own missional hermeneutic of leadership that I have developed in this chapter.

31. Lutherans may add "confessionally" to this framework because the Lutheran confessions are biblically and theologically framed. Others may add "tradition" as a norm for the church.

ments with the Roman Church. They are, in one sense, highly contextual arguments. Yet, because the confessions of the Reformers were biblically grounded and proclaimed a gospel of grace revealed in a theology of the cross, the confessions continue to have relevance for the church. A missional understanding of the church is itself biblically and theologically framed and argues that the *missiones ecclesiae* must begin in a biblical and theological framework as well.

Missional theology draws on *sending* and *perichoretic* understandings of the Trinity to shape a theology of *missio Dei* that informs the *missiones ecclesiae*. Missional theology draws on biblical proclamation of the already-but-not-yet kingdom of God, as well as God's story of redemption and reconciliation, as frameworks for understanding what God is up to in the world. A missional biblical and theological framework challenges the church — established and emerging — to understand itself to be not just an assembly gathered in Word and sacrament, but to understand that it gathers and is then sent for the sake of God's mission in the world.

Again, it remains to be seen to what extent emerging (and established) churches will be missional. The attractional DNA of the modern church and the relational DNA of the emerging church could both work *against* a missional DNA, which suggests that the church exists not for itself or the sake of its members, but for the sake of the other and to join with God in God's work in the world.

Theoretically Informed

A biblical and theological framework for the mission of God in the world is theoretically informed. The social sciences and related fields have much to contribute to our understanding of the world in which God calls us to join in mission. The modern church drew heavily on writings about leadership, demographic studies, and marketing and business models in its efforts to be more effective in ministry. The emerging church draws more heavily on writings about culture and ethnography, ritual studies, and church history (its ancient-future emphasis) as it develops its identity. The missional church conversation has been informed by ecclesiology and studies of the church, as well as by social science resources and methods that help us understand context and culture. All of these resources and others can be useful in understanding God's world and the contexts in which God calls us into mission.

Communally Discerned

Acts 15:28 begins with these words: "For it has seemed good to the Holy Spirit and to us. . . ." Missional questions (such as, What is God up to in the world? How can we join God in God's mission?) are questions of discernment. Discernment requires paying a great deal of attention to the presence of the Holy Spirit in the world and the leading of the Holy Spirit in one's community. Discernment is a communal process. Missional leadership is spiritual leadership. The missional church seeks to act on what "seem[s] good to the Holy Spirit and to us."

Communal discernment, at its best, involves a communicative process in which all who are affected by a decision are included in conversations that lead to discernment in an environment where all have a voice, speak freely, and listen attentively to the other and to the Holy Spirit.[32] A missional leader is one who gathers the appropriate people at the table and protects the sanctity of the conversation.

In the modern church, business leadership models of decision-making and strategic-planning processes were used to determine mission statements, visions, and goals. Pastors served as leaders in the processes and communicators of the vision. Emerging ministries tend to use leadership teams or elders for discernment of mission and decision-making. Modern pastors function much like CEOs. Emerging leaders function somewhat like community organizers within the ministry. The missional movement would challenge us to be communal and to use communicative practices of discernment as the Spirit creates and leads the church in community. Missional leadership is spiritual leadership.

Contextually Realized

The missional church is contextual: it becomes real in a particular moment, in a particular place, in particular rituals and actions, surrounded by a particular community, led by people with particular agendas, among people with particular joys and sorrows. Mission may be local or global, but it is always contextual. Earlier I contrasted the modern and emerging churches as having different approaches to context: the modern church

---

32. Jürgen Habermas, *The Theory of Communicative Action*, 2 vols. (Boston: Beacon Press, 1984). Habermas describes an *ideal speech situation* as part of his theory of communicative action that is useful in creating a just space for communal discernment.

tended to be in ministry *to* a context, and emerging ministries tend to emerge *from* their context. Both seem to emphasize the singularity of context. A missional perspective might suggest that we engage as missional churches and as missional people of God in *multiple* contexts — local, national, global, personal, relational, social, communal, virtual, and cultural. God is in mission in all contexts, and we realize our missions in particular but multiple contexts.

Led by the Spirit

It is the Holy Spirit who "calls, gathers, enlightens, and makes holy the whole Christian church on earth and keeps it with Jesus Christ in the one common, true faith."[33] It is the Holy Spirit who reveals God's Word to the church through the reading of the Bible and the proclamation of the gospel. It is the Holy Spirit who opens our eyes to the world around us to see as God sees so that our hearts might break with the things that break the heart of God. It is the Holy Spirit present with us whenever we gather in Christ's name who draws us into perichoretic communion with God, one another, and the world. It is the Holy Spirit, in the name of Christ Jesus, to the glory of God the Father, who creates the church, sends it, and leads it in mission for the sake of God's mission in the world.

The Church Emerging

The church emerging within the ELCA has much to teach us about engagement with context, an indigenous and organic understanding of ministry and leadership, and a transcultural embrace of cultures unfamiliar in the Lutheran/Christian tradition. Emerging ministries in the ELCA, by virtue of their otherness, are in a transcultural relationship with the ELCA, and both will be transformed as we grow in relationship with and learn from one another.

The ELCA is itself a church emerging. In good Lutheran confessional fashion, it continues to be in a constant state of forming and reforming. The ELCA's 2009 adoption of a social statement on human sexuality was a transcultural reform in which the place of the LGBT community in the church and the culture of the ELCA both experienced transformation. The

---

33. Kolb, *The Book of Concord*, pp. 355-56.

ELCA that has emerged in the wake of the 2009 assembly decision is changed in structure, perception, and mission in the world. Personally, I would argue that the ELCA, particularly as recently restructured, is becoming intentionally more missional, as is reflected in the subtitle of the ELCA's logo: "Evangelical Lutheran Church in America: God's Work. Our Hands."[34] The adoption of the social statement on human sexuality is but one example: the assembly's decision was biblically and theologically framed, theoretically informed, communally discerned, contextually realized, and Spirit-led for the sake of God's mission in the world. *Lex orandi* and *lex credendi* are increasingly shaped by *lex movendi.*

The emerging missional church offers a way of being church in the world in the twenty-first century, and that church understands God's mission in the world as its reason for being. The emerging missional church finds its life in serving that mission.

> We have no mission but to serve
> in full obedience to our Lord;
> to care for all, without reserve,
> and spread his liberating Word.[35]

Soli Deo Gloria!

---

34. The new structure of the ELCA adopted in October 2010 has three areas of focus that shape the organization of the denomination: Congregational and Synodical Mission, Global Mission, and Mission Advancement. The structure and staffing of the churchwide expression of the ELCA reflect those priorities.

35. Green, "The Church of Christ, in Every Age," verse 5.

CHAPTER 7

Multicultural Church Planting: African Pneumatology in Western Context

Harvey Kwiyani

Starting with the Spirit

In his essay contribution to Stephen Pickard and Gordon Preece's *Starting with the Spirit*, D. Lyle Dabney makes an argument for what he calls "a church that acts its age." Such a church, says Dabney, is one that seeks to embody its calling in its specific cultural context in a relevant way. He then articulates carefully that a church that acts its age in this postmodern context will be one that is shaped primarily by the theology of the Holy Spirit.[1] This is a long-awaited answer to Karl Barth's dream "of a new theology that would begin with the third article of the creed."[2] My contribution to this volume, which is in agreement with Dabney, was born out of an attempt to envision a contextual missiology that starts with the Spirit — a missiology beginning with the third article of the Apostles' Creed — in the particular context of St. Paul, Minnesota, at this particular time in the early twenty-first century.

A recent process of discernment for a church plant in St. Paul, which I had the privilege to lead, has led me to a firm conviction that not only will an emphasis on the work of the Holy Spirit make a significant difference on how the church takes shape, but also that any form of contextual missiology, anywhere in this postmodern world, must be faithfully grounded in a con-

---

1. D. Lyle Dabney, "Starting with the Spirit: Why the Last Should Now Be First," in *Starting with the Spirit*, ed. Stephen K. Pickard and Gordon R. Preece (Hindmarsh: Australian Theological Forum, 2001), pp. 11-12, 22-27.

2. Jürgen Moltmann, *The Spirit of Life: A Universal Affirmation* (Minneapolis: Fortress, 1992), p. 1.

textually relevant theology of the Holy Spirit. Having a particular interest in the place of the Holy Spirit in the missional church conversation, I will briefly survey what has been said so far by several of its major voices. After that, I will turn to the discernment process for the church plant that became the St. Paul Vineyard Church. I will explore the theological warrants that led to my assertion that, for mission to be faithfully rooted in a Trinitarian theology, it must have a sound pneumatological grounding.

A Stranger's Voice

In this chapter I take advantage of my foreign experience with Christianity in order to offer a stranger's voice to the Western conversation on the church and mission. I am an African. Most of my colleagues politely call me an African-African, to correctly underscore the fact that I am not an African-American. I am an African immigrant now living in Minnesota. I was born and raised in Africa, in rural Malawi, and spent the best of my formative years in a charismatic African village church in the 1980s.[3]

The forms and practices of the contextualized Christianity that I experienced growing up in that village greatly shaped my understanding of Christianity in its localized sense, which later informed my understanding of Christianity as a global phenomenon.[4] For instance, like many other African cultures, my culture continues to believe in a cosmology that allows for close interactions between the spirits and humans; therefore, I never questioned what the Holy Spirit would do *with* and *in* a community. My culture believes that the Holy Spirit is just one of the many spirits active in our community, and just like the other spirits, it is expected to perform extraordinary spiritual things. Actually, bearing in mind the exclusive monotheistic claims of Christianity, the Spirit was really expected — if not re-

3. The local forms of Christianity were shaped by the denominational foundations laid by the Western missionaries that had been elsewhere in the country earlier in the century. However, at this point, apart from the translated Bible and hymns, one could not see any Western influences. In addition, from the early 1980s, a series of Pentecostal/charismatic movements have swept across the country, unexpectedly and permanently changing the landscape of Christianity in Malawi.

4. When I have talked to my African friends, it has become apparent to me that most of them are only remotely aware of these categorical denominational distinctions that characterize Western Christianity. They do not think of themselves as Pentecostals or as charismatic Christians. They simply think of themselves as Christians.

quired — to do for the many African converts the numerous things they got from the other spirits before conversion.

As a result, I could not help wondering, at an early age, what made the Pentecostal and charismatic mission and evangelism efforts extremely successful in my home area.[5] While there may be many factors leading to this success, it was clear to me that there was a connection between their emphasis on the Spirit and mission. Consequently, the question of the role of the Holy Spirit in the Christian life in general, and in mission in particular, has always fascinated me. I write this chapter after serving on the mission field in Europe for seven years, and in Minnesota for an additional two years. These years on the Western mission field have crystallized the question further in me. The dying Christendom church in Europe and functional Christendom church in the United States stand in sharp contrast to the fast-growing church in Africa. I have thus always wondered, Could non-Western pneumatologies make a difference to Western missions? Could the missional church conversation benefit from a fresh emphasis on the ministry of the Holy Spirit through listening and learning from the rest of the world?

I look around at this functional post-Christendon West, and I realize that my story is in fact representative of the larger contemporary Christian story. Grandchildren and great-grandchildren of the early missionaries' converts in Africa — and in the rest of the world! — are coming back as missionaries to the West. Many of them, especially those from Africa, have known Christianity only in its enthusiastic forms, and they struggle to imagine it without that enthusiasm. My own story begins with my great-great-grandfather, who was converted in the 1860s when David Livingstone and the first missionaries lived in his village of Magomero in southern Malawi.[6] A hundred years later, the contextual-

---

5. Paul Pomerville has argued that this spirit-centered culture in Africa, and most of the non-Western world, accounts for the rapid spread of Pentecostalism in the world. See Paul Anthony Pomerville, *The Third Force in Missions: A Pentecostal Contribution to Contemporary Mission Theology* (Peabody, MA: Hendrickson, 1985), pp. 74-78.

6. David Livingstone (1813-1873) was a Scottish missionary/explorer who spent some time in the 1850s and 1860s in Malawi, long before it was declared a British protectorate in 1891. Livingstone's speech campaigns at Oxford and Cambridge initiated the University's Mission to Central Africa (UMCA), which sent missionaries from Britain to Central Africa. Their very first mission station was at Magomero, which is still today my paternal family's home. Within one hundred years of the arrival of the UMCA, Malawi had grown to become a Christian nation.

ized Christianity of the Pentecostal/charismatic movement overshad-owed the Presbyterianism that the Scottish missionaries brought to the area. My generation of Christians from the area is more likely to have been influenced by local independent Pentecostal churches than any-thing else. Certainly, quite a few of that generation will find their way to cross-cultural ministry. Living in St. Paul, Minnesota, I realize that I rep-resent a generation of Christians from the majority world who find themselves doing mission in the West. Some have called this particular aspect of missions *reverse missions,* and in this day it is an inevitable re-sult of the polycentric nature of the church and the migratory nature of God's mission.[7] Jehu Hanciles, in *Beyond Christendom,* suggests that Western mission in the twenty-first century will be shaped more by mi-gration than anything else, with many Christian immigrants moving from the South and East to the West.[8] The hope is that when the cultures and theologies come together, there will be mutual critiquing, which will then enrich both sides of the conversation.

The missional church conversation would be greatly enriched through an engagement with these strangers. It was started as a Western conversation among Western theologians and missiologists who were thinking about what they considered a Western problem. Unfortunately, proximity can usually blind us to the many cultural issues that would be obvious to a stranger. A well-known Chewa proverb from Malawi says that the stranger often comes with a sharp pocketknife, and as such, he is usu-ally better equipped for a community's long-standing problems than are his hosts.[9] Among the Chewa, it is believed that a stranger may have just the right knowledge or perspective needed to solve some old difficult problems, which implies the wisdom of listening to and learning from the stranger.

In his book *Welcoming the Stranger,* Patrick Keifert articulates well the "missional" need to be not only welcoming *to,* but also to be eager to

7. See Andrew F. Walls and Cathy Ross, *Mission in the Twenty-First Century: Exploring the Five Marks of Global Mission* (Maryknoll, NY: Orbis, 2008).

8. See Jehu Hanciles, *Beyond Christendom: Globalization, African Migration, and the Transformation of the West* (Maryknoll, NY: Orbis Books, 2008).

9. In Chichewa, "*mlendo ndi uyo abwera ndi kalumo kakuthwa.*" Knives are extremely important multipurpose tools in that part of the world. The proverb talks about a sharp knife, even sharper than those of the local leaders, because it has to be able to do something that has not been done before. It is a pocketknife because it is hidden, and you never know there is one until you ask.

learn *from,* the stranger.[10] Hospitality to the stranger is not just good for the stranger; it is also good for the host. There is a sense of vulnerability and humility that goes with being a host who learns from the stranger for, as Keifert suggests, not all strangers are safe.[11] However, these strangers are God's gift to the church. They bring with them many experiences, gifts, and talents that could be of great benefit to the Western church. Actually, in my opinion, at the center of the missional church movement is the voice of one stranger, Lesslie Newbigin. He returned to England after thirty years in India only to discover that the Christian West, which he had left thirty years earlier, had become secular while the church had not changed. In a sense, he was a stranger in India; but he was also a stranger in Britain after his return. The critical distance that had come out of his thirty years in India enabled him to see Britain in a different light. It is little surprise, then, that he says this of non-Western Christians:

> We need their witness to correct ours, as indeed they need ours to correct theirs. At this moment our need is greater, for they have been far more aware of the danger of syncretism, of an illegitimate alliance with the false elements in their culture, than we have been. But . . . we imperatively need one another if we are to be faithful witnesses to Christ.[12]

Newbigin was thus privileged to see what others who had been in the Western context all along could not see. If we can make use of my foreigner's eyes, let us now turn to the issue of the Spirit and mission, especially within the missional church movement.

The Spirit and Mission

Even though mission makes good use of many other disciplines of discourse, such as sociology and cultural anthropology, to make sense of the world is a primarily and inherently spiritual endeavor. It is a work of the Holy Spirit. Indeed, at the very least, mission is a pneumatological agenda. The Scriptures may actually suggest that mission and the Spirit are insepa-

---

10. Patrick R. Keifert, *Welcoming the Stranger: A Public Theology of Worship and Evangelism* (Minneapolis: Fortress, 1992).

11. Keifert, *Welcoming the Stranger,* p. 8.

12. Lesslie Newbigin, *Foolishness to the Greeks* (Grand Rapids: Eerdmans, 1986), p. 147.

rable. Pneumatology creates the space for mission. Reading the Gospels and Acts with one eye on the Holy Spirit and the other eye on mission, it certainly appears that David Bosch is right when he suggests that mission is a direct consequence of the outpouring of the Spirit, even though he dedicates only a few pages of his *Transforming Mission* to discuss pneumatology explicitly.

The Spirit is about movement. The Spirit is explicitly given for the mission of the church. Look, for instance, in the Gospels and the book of Acts: the renditions of the Great Commission in Matthew and Mark; the stories of the sending of the twelve and the seventy disciples; the last admonition of Jesus for the disciples to wait in Jerusalem until they receive the power of the Holy Spirit; Philip's evangelism in Samaria and his conversion of the Ethiopian eunuch; Saul's conversion and baptism; and Peter's work at the house of Cornelius. These instances, among many others, point to the fact that mission apart from the Spirit is mission impossible. Indeed, for Bosch, Luke's pneumatology in the Gospel and the book of Acts excludes the possibility of a missionary command because the promise of the Spirit implies that the disciples will, without a doubt, get involved in mission.[13] Arguably, John V. Taylor was correct to note in his book *The Go-Between God,* that "the Holy Spirit is the *chief actor* in mission," adding that "[the Spirit is] the director of the whole [missionary] enterprise."[14]

The story of the development of twentieth-century Christianity and mission was shaped largely by such factors as the worldwide rise of Pentecostalism and the southward shifting of Christianity's center of gravity. This opens up new ways to talk about the involvement of the Spirit in mission, especially when one bears in mind that most cultures that are coming into contact with Christianity in the global South still have a cosmology that allows for spirits and the spiritual world. The success story of the wild growth of Christianity on the African continent in the twentieth century underscores this point. Beginning that century with only nine million Christians, with the help of sweeping Pentecostalism and the spirit-type African independent churches, there were almost 400 million Christians in Africa by the year 2000.[15] In addition, the fast-rising numbers of Pentecos-

13. David Jacobus Bosch, *Transforming Mission: Paradigm Shifts in Theology of Mission,* American Society of Missiology series (Maryknoll, NY: Orbis, 1991), p. 114.

14. John Vernon Taylor, *The Go-Between God: The Holy Spirit and the Christian Mission* (London: SCM Press, 1972), p. 3 (italics added).

15. Lamin Sanneh, *Disciples of All Nations: Pillars of World Christianity,* Oxford Studies in World Christianity (New York: Oxford University Press, 2008), p. xx.

tals and charismatic Christians on the global scale went from zero to over 600 million in a space of a hundred years; today Pentecostals represent over 25 percent of all global Christians. These factors lead theologian-scholars to raise questions concerning how mission and pneumatology inform one another.[16]

Part of the complexity that both mission and Christianity as a whole have to face is that, in this globalized world, there will be cross-cultural encounters of theologies from different parts of the world, as Christians migrate from one place to another. On the one hand, the theological landscape has to be leveled. There is no theology superior to others. Ideally, all theologies will have to respectfully listen to *and learn from* one another. On the other hand, the average missionary ceases to be a white, middle-class, college-educated (if not seminary-educated) man serving in the jungles of Africa. The current average missionary might be a young Korean woman offering dance-worship lessons to teenagers while leading a Bible study group at her church and attending college in London, or perhaps a Nigerian pastor running a Nigerian Pentecostal church in Texas. And so, along with African migration to the West, the cosmological worldviews and their resulting theologies have come into the Western cities that were once the heartlands of U.S. Christianity. As this happens — at an accelerating pace as we go further into the twenty-first century — Western theology will have to pay more particular attention to the matters dear to African theology, such as those regarding the Spirit. For instance, the Swahili and Oromo ELCA congregations in the St. Paul area are steadily becoming voices worth heeding.

The reclaiming of Trinitarian theology as the foundational theology for mission and the understanding of mission as *missio Dei* have further enforced the theological underpinnings of the pneumatological background for missiology.[17] Decades of dialogue between missiology and pneuma-

16. In particular, the two resources from Michael Welker, *God the Spirit* and *The Work of the Spirit* reflect two positions on the issue of Pentecostals and their understanding of the Spirit and mission. In the former, Welker has some problems with the Pentecostal/charismatic emphasis on the spectacular, complicated by their inability to articulate the mysterious nature of the spectacular works of the Spirit. He suggests that there is just as much work of the Spirit in the ordinary day-to-day lives of the world. In the latter, Welker carefully engages Pentecostals in a mutually critical effort to understand the work of the Spirit. See Michael Welker, *God the Spirit* (Minneapolis: Fortress, 1994) and Michael Welker, ed., *The Work of the Spirit: Pneumatology and Pentecostalism* (Grand Rapids: Eerdmans, 2006).

17. International Missionary Council and Norman Goodall, *Missions Under the Cross:*

tology in the works of such thinkers as Karl Barth, Karl Rahner, Lesslie Newbigin, and the theologians of the Gospel and Our Culture Network have added weight to the understanding of the role of the Spirit in mission.

Missional faithfulness is not achievable without paying attention to the guidance, empowerment, and even the workings of the Spirit. Mission itself is founded on the work of the Spirit in the world, in which the followers of Christ have been invited to be participants. The Spirit is sent from the Father and the Son to heal, restore, and sustain the Father's creation and to establish the kingdom of God while bringing glory to the Son. While doing that, the Spirit calls and gathers together the church — the sweet fellowship of the Spirit — and invites it to partake in mission. This "sentness" of the Spirit implies a movement *away from* the sender, seeking to reveal Christ and the Father in those crevices of creation and society where the kingdom is not yet established. It is into this outward movement of God — *missio Dei* — that the church has been drawn. This outward motion of God to the world has implications for both our theology and our ecclesiology. At the very least, it implies that for all Christians there should be some form of intentional and continuous discernment to stay in tune with what God is doing through the Spirit, and where God is going in their community.

Western society, in its modern mindset, finds it hard to conceive of the spiritual world.[18] The Holy Spirit suffers the same treatment as anything else that cannot be explained scientifically, using reason. Because of this, Michael Welker says that "the secular common sense of the West has great difficulty in gaining even a distant perception of anything approaching God's Spirit . . . [and that] this [Western] understanding presumably only 'sees ghosts' in the doctrine of the Holy Spirit."[19] However, we have the privilege today of following Jesus in a world that, contrary to a few generations before, is beginning to believe in spirits and the spirit world once again. There has been a paradigm shift that has resulted in increased interest in spirituality, even though many still would not want to be identified as religious. In his *Planting New Churches in a Postmodern Age*, Ed

---

Addresses Delivered at the Enlarged Meeting of the Committee of the International Missionary Council at Willingen, in Germany, 1952 (London: Edinburgh House Press, 1953).

18. Other worldviews have little problems with this. From a very young age in Malawi, I remember hearing that the spiritual world is more real than the physical world. As a result, I have never questioned the effects of the spiritual world on the physical, like when an evil spirit causes sickness, or when the Spirit of God heals it.

19. Welker, *God the Spirit*, p. 1.

Stetzer notes that people are now open to "something mystical and spiritual."[20] Craig Van Gelder agrees with this, suggesting that the West now lives once again within a worldview that includes appreciation for spirituality within a dynamic and open universe.[21]

In their book *God is Back*, John Micklethwait and Adrian Wooldridge have brought to our attention from a secular perspective the fact that issues of the spirits and spirituality, even the belief in God's existence and God's active involvement in the world, have become acceptable in the world in this generation.[22] Just as Stanley Grenz once argued that postmoderns are spiritual people, this postmodern world in which we find ourselves is slowly opening up the public sphere for spirit talk.[23] For this reason, if the missional church is to "act its age" today, as Dabney proposes, it needs to reconsider its understanding of the work of the Spirit. It needs to open up more about the Spirit and the Spirit's key relationship to mission. Again, Van Gelder says that "it is crucial to understand the ministry of the Spirit if we are to comprehend that the ministry of the church is to participate in God's mission in the world."[24] In a perhaps overcited statement, John V. Taylor suggests that "our theology would improve if we thought more of the church being given to the Spirit than of the Spirit being given to the church."[25] Yes, a theology of mission that starts with the third article of the Apostles' Creed would be more relevant to our context.

It is not to be questioned that the excessive tendencies among some of the "people of the Spirit" in the past century have, in the long run, repelled some people who would otherwise have paid attention to the workings of the Spirit in the world. It certainly appears that some Pentecostals have scared people away from the Spirit of Pentecost itself. Welker politely says that "they scare common sense away."[26] Strange phenomena, like the classical Pentecostal insistence on speaking in tongues and the Toronto Re-

20. Ed Stetzer, *Planting New Churches in a Postmodern Age* (Nashville: Broadman and Holman, 2003), p. 137.

21. Craig Van Gelder, *The Ministry of the Missional Church: A Community Led by the Spirit* (Grand Rapids: Baker, 2007), p. 24.

22. John Micklethwait and Adrian Wooldridge, *God Is Back: How the Global Revival of Faith Is Changing the World* (New York: Penguin Press, 2009), p. 12.

23. Stanley J. Grenz, *A Primer on Postmodernism* (Grand Rapids: Eerdmans, 1996), p. 14.

24. Van Gelder, *The Ministry of the Missional Church*, p. 24.

25. Taylor, *The Go-Between God*, p. 133.

26. Welker, *God the Spirit*, p. 11.

vival, have understandably created an uncomfortable image of the Spirit.[27] Recently we have watched in awe, if not embarrassment, as news about exorcisms in immigrant Pentecostal churches that actually border on the abuse of children's rights have been made known to the public.[28] In spite of these excesses, Michael Welker declares that people have "without question" had experiences of God's Spirit — unless some 300 million Pentecostals worldwide are in error.[29]

However, a mission theology of the Spirit should be grounded in the conviction that the Holy Spirit is a missionary Spirit.[30] The Spirit not only *sends* the church as missionaries into the world, nor does it only *lead* in mission. The Spirit *does* mission. The Spirit itself is sent and it does mission — sometimes with little help from the church, and at other times in spite of both the church and the missionary. Stephen Bevans suggests that mission proceeds "not through 'strategies,' nor by alliances with 'worldly powers.' Its procedure is that of the persuading, cajoling presence of the Spirit." He adds that "the church is not so much 'sent' as much as it has become part of God's embrace of the world, an embrace made flesh in Jesus, but accomplished in the continuing presence of the Spirit."[31] Pneumatologically conceived, mission opens up a world of possibilities where the Spirit of God can surprise both the church and the missionary in many unexpected ways. Where the Spirit goes, there must the church follow. What the Spirit does, that the church must do also. This is mission. It cannot be otherwise.

Missional theology should, then, be comfortable with making the Spirit the subject of whatever missional life is happening in the community. The Spirit draws people to Christ. The Spirit equips believers for mission and ministry. The Spirit convicts. The Spirit speaks. One can confidently add that the Spirit heals and performs miracles, too. Yes, the Spirit

---

27. See M. M. Poloma, "Toronto Blessing," in *The New International Dictionary of Pentecostal and Charismatic Movements,* ed. Stanley M. Burgess (Grand Rapids: Zondervan, 2002), pp. 1149-52.

28. For an article discussing one such case that happened in London in 2005, see B. A. Robinson, "Demonic Possession, Oppression and Exorcism: A West African / Fundamentalist Christian Syncretistic Religion in the UK": http://www.religioustolerance.org/chr_exor5 .html (accessed October 10, 2009).

29. Welker, *God the Spirit,* p. 1.

30. See Roland Allen, *The Ministry of the Spirit: Selected Writings* (Grand Rapids, MI: Eerdmans, 1960).

31. Steven Bevans, "God Inside Out: Notes Toward a Missionary Theology of the Holy Spirit": http://sedosmission.org/old/eng/Bevans.html (accessed October 10, 2009).

saturates with *mission* everything that comes under its influence. Indeed, the same Spirit that incubated the precreation universe is the one that was upon Christ, leading him to preach the good news to the poor and proclaim release to the captives. It is the same Spirit that was sent by Christ and was poured out to empower the one hundred twenty believers in the upper room for mission. It is the same Spirit that is active as mission takes shape in the book of Acts and in the early church.

This same Spirit guided mission down the centuries as the church spread to Asia, Africa, and Europe. It guided mission when mission meant Anglo-Saxon missionaries from Europe and their American descendants left the West to go and convert the "heathens" elsewhere. However, it is also the same Spirit that guides mission today, when the mission field is now also in North America and Europe, and when local and foreign missionaries work together to embody God's kingdom in the West. Newbigin was right to say that the church's role is that of an attentive servant seeking the leading and empowerment of the Holy Spirit in whose mission the church participates.[32]

There will be a great deal to learn as Western theology comes into contact with non-Western theologies, especially those that are more deliberate on the issues of the Spirit because they were shaped in pneumato-centric cultures like those of Africa. The rise of the Pentecostal movement around the world brings into question most of the cessationist theologies that the Western missionaries brought along with them. In the African context, an unforeseen outcome of the pneumatological gap in the missionaries' theologies lives in the African independent churches. In Africa certainly — as well as South America and Asia — supernatural activities like miracles and wonders enhance mission again, just as they did for the early church in the book of Acts. It may be possible that some Western theological landmarks need shifting, and missional theology could be the perfect place for such a shift to start.

In addition, Western Christians can contribute to the conversation. For instance, the neo-Pentecostals and the Third Wave movement, which include church groups such as the Vineyard, are trying hard to find a balance between their evangelical theological convictions and the experiences of the Spirit that are identified with the Pentecostal movement.[33] John

32. Lesslie Newbigin, *The Open Secret: An Introduction to the Theology of Mission* (Grand Rapids: Eerdmans, 1995), p. 61.

33. See Bill Jackson, *The Quest for the Radical Middle: A History of the Vineyard* (Cape

Wimber's concept of "power evangelism" stands as an example here.[34] Power evangelism suggests the relevance here in the West of the experiential ministry of the Spirit, especially in mission and evangelism. A self-proclaimed fourth-generation pagan, Wimber himself stumbled on the power of the Spirit in evangelism and started a conversation that has resulted in two thousand Vineyard congregations worldwide in under twenty-five years.[35] Such an understanding of the work of the Spirit in evangelism and mission may be helpful for the missional church. Indeed, it may be that, in postmodernity, God beckons the church to redeem, refine, and put to use what was crudely developed in the Pentecostal and charismatic movements of the twentieth century.

The Spirit in the Missional Church Conversation

Looking back at the developments in global mission and missiology over the past century, it appears to me that the reclaiming of Trinitarian theology as the foundational grounds for mission greatly transformed the landscapes of mission theology. It has taken a huge paradigm shift to move from John Mott's *The Evangelization of the World in this Generation,* coming out of the 1910 Edinburgh World Mission Conference,[36] to *Missio Dei* at the 1952 Willingen Conference, to the publication of the *Missional Church* in 1998.[37] To finally understand the fact that mission belongs to God the Father, Son, and Holy Spirit — that it is indeed *missio Dei* and does not belong to the church — has been one of the greatest landmarks in Christian theology in the twentieth century. Twentieth-century world history could actually suggest that such a paradigm shift was necessary. When we factor in colonization, the World Wars, decolonization, Western secu-

---

Town: Vineyard International Publishing, 1999). See also Rich Nathan and Ken Wilson, *Empowered Evangelicals: Bringing Together the Best of the Evangelical and Charismatic Worlds* (Ann Arbor: Vine Books, 1995).

34. "Power evangelism" was built around the belief that the Spirit would perform miracles like healings and words of knowledge for the purpose of evangelism. John Wimber is the founder of the Vineyard Movement and author of several books on the topic, such as *Power Evangelism, Power Healing,* and *Kingdom Evangelism.*

35. Jackson, *Quest for the Radical Middle,* p. 44.

36. See John R. Mott, *The Evangelization of the World in this Generation* (New York: Student Volunteer Movement for Foreign Missions, 1900).

37. See Darrell L. Guder, ed., *Missional Church: A Vision for the Sending of the Church in North America,* The Gospel and Our Culture series (Grand Rapids: Eerdmans, 1998).

larization, globalization, and contemporary migration patterns, the paradigm shift in missions begins to make sense.

With the help of the Willingen Conference, mission scholars and theologians began to articulate the implications of *missio Dei,* especially for those engaged on the mission field. Mission theology had to be Trinitarian, with a strong emphasis on the involvement of God the Father, the Son, and the Holy Spirit. From the Western theologians' perspective, *missio Dei* has mainly had to do with the act of sending: the Father sending the Son, and then the Father and Son sending the Spirit, culminating with the Son and the Spirit sending the church. Consequently, from that perspective, the church is understood to be a community called, equipped, and sent to participate in God's mission in the world. On the other hand, theological scholars from the Eastern tradition have enriched the conversation through their notions of community and relationality in their Trinitarian theology. For them, the Godhead is relational community, and thus the church invites the world into this perichoretic communal relationship with both God and itself.[38]

This unleashing of Trinitarian theology has been very helpful to theology as a whole — and to mission in particular. The missional church conversation on both sides of the Atlantic Ocean works out a missional theology that has its foundations in a Trinitarian understanding of God. Even though the conversation was originally focused on the Western mission field, the scope of the theology articulated in *Missional Church* and the other works of the Gospel and Our Culture Network goes beyond the Western context. Indeed, if the church is missionary by its very nature, then it must be missional wherever it is, be it in New York or in Windhoek.

The missional church conversation, strongly influenced by Lesslie Newbigin's books, began to articulate what it means for the Western church to be missionaries to the West in a post-Christendom age.[39] However, there is still great room for dialogue, especially with other pneumatologies. Van Gelder, in agreement, suggests that "there is a need to develop a more focused understanding of what Spirit-led ministry looks

38. However, even with this relational theology and a mystical emphasis on the Spirit, the Eastern tradition has not been especially known for its mission endeavors. I wonder how the missional church conversation might be appropriated in Eastern theology.

39. The conversation has shown the effective role of the Spirit in missional theology in such works as *Missional Church, The Ministry of the Missional Church,* and Lois Barrett, *Treasure in Clay Jars: Patterns in Missional Faithfulness,* The Gospel and Our Culture series (Grand Rapids: Eerdmans, 2004).

like in a missional church."[40] For instance, Inagrace Dietterich's chapter in *Missional Church,* entitled "Cultivating Communities of the Holy Spirit," is a very hopeful chapter.[41] However, a larger portion is devoted to community itself, placing great emphasis on the distinctiveness of the missional church's communal life as a witness, and only a few paragraphs discuss the Holy Spirit's involvement in the process of mission. The chapter makes some critical points on the place of the Spirit in the missional community, making a bold suggestion that "the church owes its origin, its destiny, its ongoing life, its ministry — in short, its mission — to the divine Spirit of life, truth and holiness."[42] Nevertheless, it shies away from engaging the role of the communal gifts of the Spirit in a missional community for evangelism in the host society.

Lois Barrett's *Treasure in Clay Jars* has a chapter that suggests that one of the eight distinctive patterns of missional congregations is dependence on the Holy Spirit.[43] However, it is really a chapter on the importance of prayer in the life of a missional church. While it is understandable that prayer may imply dependence on the Holy Spirit, it is certainly not the only aspect of the work of the Spirit in mission or in the missional church.

The same thing could be said about Craig Van Gelder's *The Ministry of the Missional Church.* While it is a very engaging book, it leaves one wondering what could be said of the experiential dimension of the activity of the Spirit in a missional church. He does not engage any of the prevalent pneumatologies of the charismatic and Pentecostal movements, how they have shaped mission in the majority world, and how they can help the missional church conversation here in the West. As such, the very kingdom theology that shapes Van Gelder's argument does not get to be fully appropriated in the book. The eschatological kingdom of God, which is "already" but "not yet" fully here, cannot be articulated without accounting for the miraculous and the mysterious. Jesus frames this up when he says, "If I drive out demons by the Spirit of God, then the kingdom of God has come upon you" (Matt. 12:28; Luke 11:20 [NIV]).

In addition, though Alan Hirsch's contribution to missional theology is becoming increasingly influential in North America, *The Forgotten Ways,* one of his major works, only offers an implied pneumatology. The Holy

---

40. Van Gelder, *The Ministry of the Missional Church,* p. 17.
41. Guder, *Missional Church,* pp. 142-82.
42. Guder, *Missional Church,* p. 145.
43. Barrett, *Treasure in Clay Jars,* pp. 117-25.

Spirit is there, but seems hidden. Instead, his missiology is built strongly on Christology. Hirsch suggests that our Christology shapes our missiology, which in turn shapes our ecclesiology.[44] I wonder where pneumatology would fit into this formula. With the conviction that the Spirit reveals Christ, what if we started with pneumatology shaping our Christology — or even our theology — in a way that shapes our ecclesiology?

Given these observations on the place of the Spirit in the missional church conversation, one wonders whether our Trinitarian theology is any better now than it had been before. Are we Trinitarian in name only? Veli-Matti Kärkkäinen suggests, rightly in my opinion, that even though the church and theology have not lost sight of the Spirit, there is [still] a secondary, if not subordinate role, assigned to the Holy Spirit. Indeed, one wonders if the Spirit is still *theos agraptos* — the God about whom nothing is written.[45] Is the Spirit still the Cinderella of the Trinity, who was left home while the other two sisters went out to the party? Is it still the forgotten God? Is the doctrine of the Holy Spirit still the "orphan doctrine of Christian theology," as suggested by Adolf von Harnack?[46] While part of the problem has been addressed, with the many resources written now on the Holy Spirit from different perspectives, I agree fully with Jürgen Moltmann that a new paradigm in pneumatology has not yet emerged.[47]

With all this in mind, we now turn to the story of a church plant in St. Paul, Minnesota. The narrative of this process of discernment for the church plant seeks to embody the kind of mission theology that begins with the third article, to try out a missional theology for the development of a church that does as Dabney suggests and "acts its age."

St. Paul: A Case Study

We began the process of discernment for a church plant in St. Paul when several leaders in our network of friends felt an unexpected conviction that God was leading us to plant a Vineyard church in the city. Citywide

44. Michael Frost and Alan Hirsch, *The Shaping of Things to Come: Innovation and Mission for the 21st-Century Church* (Peabody, MA: Hendrickson, 2003), p. 209.

45. Veli-Matti Kärkkäinen, *Pneumatology: The Holy Spirit in Ecumenical, International, and Contextual Perspective* (Grand Rapids: Baker, 2002), p. 17.

46. John Bainbridge Webster, *The Cambridge Companion to Karl Barth*, Cambridge Companions to Religion (Cambridge, UK: Cambridge University Press, 2000), p. 177.

47. Moltmann, *The Spirit of Life*, p. 1.

conversations started, and several other friends confirmed that they also thought it was a good idea. Once we had established that, indeed, many people felt the Spirit was leading us to plant a church, the more contextual questions began. What is God up to in St. Paul? Where can we see the hand of God in the city's history? How did the city become what it is today? What are the historical landmarks in the city's narrative so far? What can we learn from them? Are there any discernible patterns of events that would point us to God's discernible fingerprints in the city?

While this chapter does not intend to provide a detailed history of the development of the city, it attempts to outline a broad sketch of the framework of events and people that informed our quest for a pneumatologically shaped contextual missiology for the city. First, I will provide a brief look at the history of the city, paying particular attention to ways in which religion played a role in shaping the city's life. I will then suggest three contextual warrants for a pneumatological missiology for St. Paul.

Brief History

In her extensive work on the history of the city, *St. Paul: The First 150 Years*, Virginia Kunz writes that the city was incorporated as a trading and transportation center in 1849, with only 910 people, under the name "The Town of Saint Paul."[48] It rose to prominence when it was named the capital of the Minnesota Territory by an act of the legislative assembly of the Territory of Minnesota in November 1849. St. Paul remained a town until March 1854, when it became the "City of Saint Paul, Minnesota Territory." In May 1858, when Minnesota was elevated to statehood, St. Paul became "The City of Saint Paul, State of Minnesota" (Kunz, p. 27).

It had started out in the late 1830s as one shanty that Pierre "Pig's Eye" Parrant, a French-Canadian whiskey-dealer, had erected for his business. Actually, St. Paul was first known as Pig's Eye because Parrant, who is credited with being its first resident, is said to have had only one eye.[49] In

48. This is significant growth from thirty families in 1845. See Virginia B. Kunz, *Saint Paul: The First 150 Years* (St. Paul: The St. Paul Foundation, 1991), pp. 21, 27. Hereafter, page references to this work appear in parentheses in the text.

49. Kunz says that, as early as 1839, one Edmund Brissette wrote a letter in his tavern in which, for want of a more euphonious name, he designated the place "Pig's Eye" in reference to the peculiar appearance of the whiskey-seller. The reply to the letter was directed in

1837, about two hundred Dakota Indians joined Parrant's cave shanty when they moved eastward from the Fort Snelling area (Kunz, pp. 1-5). Father Lucien Galtier built a log-cabin church, which he dedicated to the apostle St. Paul in 1841. In 1850, at his New Year's address, Galtier asked the town leaders that their community be officially renamed. With the approval of the people, he declared: "Pig's Eye, converted thou shalt be, like Saul; Arise, and be, henceforth, Saint Paul!" (Kunz, pp. 9-10).

The story of the early days of St. Paul is deeply shaped by the connection between John Ireland, James Hill, and Mary Mehegan (Hill's wife and Ireland's childhood playmate).[50] James Hill, nicknamed the "empire builder," came to St. Paul as a young man from near Toronto in 1856 to work as a clerk. Eight years later, Hill partnered with Norman Kittson to establish the Red River Transportation Company, whose main business was to operate steamboats on the Red River (Kunz, p. 23). Eventually, the two men acquired the St. Paul and Pacific Railroad and built it into the Great Northern Rail (Kunz, p. 24). Later, the Great Northern Rail expanded to include the Northern Pacific Railway, and together they were headquartered in St. Paul.[51]

John Ireland was born in Ireland in 1838. His family migrated to America when he was ten, and they moved to St. Paul in 1852. Ireland was sent to the preparatory seminary of Meximieux in France in 1853. He was ordained in 1861 in St. Paul and was appointed pastor at St. Paul's cathedral in 1867, a position he held until 1875, when he was named coadjutor bishop of St. Paul. He was promoted to bishop in 1884, and became archbishop in 1888, when his diocese was elevated and an ecclesiastical province of St. Paul was erected. John Ireland was thus the third bishop and first archbishop of St. Paul, a title he retained for twenty years, until his death in 1918.

Between the two of them, Hill and Ireland represented the culture that developed in St. Paul: a devoted Catholic working-class majority. They both had a passion for building and expansion, with Hill building his busi-

---

good faith to "Pig's Eye," and it was received in due time. See *St. Paul: Saga of an American City* (Woodland Hills, CA: Windsor Publications, 1980), p. 8.

50. Mary Lethert Wingerd, *Claiming the City: Politics, Faith, and the Power of Place in St. Paul,* Cushwa Center Studies of Catholicism in Twentieth-Century America (Ithaca, NY: Cornell University Press, 2001), p. 42.

51. The company is now called the Burlington Northern Santa Fe Railway. For a detailed history of the development, see "Terrific! It's Northern Pacific!": http://pw2 .netcom.com/~whstlpnk/first.html (accessed October 20, 2008).

ness empire and Ireland his diocese. Ireland became both a religious and civic leader in St. Paul. He created or helped to create many religious and educational institutions in the growing city.[52] Hill made generous donations to many of Ireland's endeavors, including $500,000 for the development of St. Paul Seminary. Also, with the help of Hill, Ireland secured the land in 1904 for the building of the current Cathedral of St. Paul, located at the top of Summit Hill, the highest point in downtown St. Paul. The cathedral was dedicated in 1915.[53] At about the same time, Ireland also commissioned the construction of the nearly as large Church of Saint Mary for the local Immaculate Conception parish in Minneapolis.[54]

Religious Development

The Roman Catholic Church has been formally involved in St. Paul from the days of Father Galtier. However, as Wingerd suggests, "there were already *many* Irish Catholics when Galtier arrived in 1841, such that his arrival to guide the official establishment of the church was widely celebrated."[55] Wingerd suggests that Protestants joined in the development of St. Paul a few years later than did the Catholics. By the time the first Protestant church, a Methodist church, was erected in 1848, the Roman Catholic Church was an established community institution (Kunz, p. 21). The Baptists and Presbyterians arrived in 1849, and within a few months, the First Baptist Church of St. Paul and the First Presbyterian Church were established. The first Lutheran congregation in St. Paul was established in 1854.

The early establishment of a Catholic presence served an instrumental purpose that would grant the church and its clergy an enduring status in the city, a status that remains to this day, with 50 percent of current St.

52. See Marvin Richard O'Connell, *John Ireland and the American Catholic Church* (St. Paul: Minnesota Historical Society Press, 1988). The achievements of Ireland are numerous. He is reported to have been personal friends with both Presidents William McKinley and Theodore Roosevelt. He founded the University of St. Thomas, St. Thomas Academy, Saint Paul Seminary, and DeLaSalle High School. He also helped fund the expanding Christian Brothers' school. John Ireland Boulevard, a street named in his memory, runs from the Cathedral of St. Paul to the Minnesota State Capital.

53. Wingerd, *Claiming the City*, pp. 61, 70.

54. It became the Pro-Cathedral of Minneapolis and was later to become the first basilica in the United States in 1926. For more information on the Basilica of St. Mary, Minneapolis, see: http://www.mary.org.

55. Wingerd, *Claiming the City*, p. 25.

Paul residents identifying themselves as adherents of the Roman Catholic Church.

Demographic Development

According to the 1850 census, St. Paul was largely a French-speaking town of 257 families and 1,294 residents from various countries. Ninety residents listed Canada as their birthplace, more than sixty claimed Sweden as their homeland, while England and Germany were each declared as the birthplaces of about twenty residents (Kunz, pp. 20, 30). St. Paul's population grew steadily over the years, nearly doubling between 1900 and 1960, when it peaked at 313,411.[56] The population slowly declined between 1960 and 1990, when it started showing signs of increase again. Throughout the city's history, the great majority of its residents have been of European (largely German and Irish) ancestry. However, that proportion has been decreasing as the number of African Americans, Asians, and Hispanics has grown; those three population groups now make up about one-third of the population (according to 2005 data). St. Paul is home to about 280,000 inhabitants.[57]

Contextual Missiology for St. Paul

An effort to develop a relevant and contextual missiology of the city of St. Paul has been undergirded by the belief that God's Spirit is always at work in the world. Therefore, our church-planting team also believed that God, through the Spirit, is currently at work in St. Paul — and has been throughout its history. Accordingly, we began a discernment process by which we intently tried to sense what the Spirit is doing in the city. After six months of prayer, listening, and conversations, we perceived that three points stood out: we identified postmodern spirituality, diversity, and hospitality to the needy as our three contextual warrants for a pneumatological missiology.

56. See *Encyclopedia*, s.v. "Saint Paul, Minnesota": http://www.nationmaster.com/encyclopedia/Saint-Paul-(Minnesota) (accessed December 18, 2008).
57. "2005 University Avenue Business Survey," St. Paul, Minnesota: The Most Livable City in America: http://www.stpaul.gov/index.asp?NID=158 (accessed December 10, 2008).

Postmodern Spirituality

The majority of the people in St. Paul are between twenty-five and forty years of age.[58] This statistic is not unique to St. Paul, but that's what makes it worth mentioning. In the first place, people in this age bracket are the least evangelized in the nation; in addition, it is an age group that, shaped by postmodernity, is intrigued by spirituality and mysticism. As a result, people in this demographic are responsive to the mysticisms of the emerging churches and the spirituality of the Eastern religions. Yet most of the people in this generation believe that it is acceptable to be spiritual without being religious.[59] Unfortunately, many of these young people thus leave the church and seek spirituality that is relevant to them — because they do not find it in Christian churches.[60]

Nevertheless, not all those leaving church are losing their faith.[61] Some are leaving the church to *preserve* their faith from the spiritless religion they experience in churches.[62] In this regard, postmodernity offers both an opportunity and a challenge to the church: an opportunity for the church to engage spirituality as it should have always done, since that is part of the church's identity, and a challenge because spirituality is not what comes to many people's minds when they hear about the church. As the culture around us becomes more open to the possibility of the spirits, spiritual powers, and spirituality, the church should be there to explain and answer questions.

As a matter of fact, evangelism in a culture that is spiritually open may become experiential again. Indeed, it is not unusual to hear postmoderns speak of deciding to follow Christ after *experiencing* God. This experience of God may take a form different from the miracles, signs, and

58. For a detailed look at the population distribution in St. Paul, see "Saint Paul, Minnesota," City-Data: http://www.city-data.com/city/St.-Paul-Minnesota.html (accessed October 9, 2009).

59. See William P. Young, *The Shack: Where Tragedy Confronts Eternity* (Newbury Park, CA: Windblown Media, 2007); see also Dave Schmelzer, *Not The Religious Type: Confessions of a Turncoat Atheist* (Carol Stream, IL: SaltRiver, 2008).

60. For a discussion of this phenomenon, based on a 2007 study by the Anglican Church in Great Britain, see Sara Savage, *Making Sense of Generation Y: The World View of 15- to 25-year-olds* (London: Church House Publishing, 2006).

61. See Philip J. Richter and Leslie J. Francis, *Gone But Not Forgotten: Church Leaving and Returning* (London: Darton Longman & Todd, 1998).

62. See also Stuart Murray, *Church After Christendom* (Milton Keynes: Paternoster, 2005), chap. 1.

wonders that are identified with the ministry of the Spirit elsewhere. Instead, it may be a deep sense of peace and calm, sometimes accompanied by a smile or a tear. In addition, mission in a spiritually sensitive culture has an opportunity to reclaim the spiritual nature of mission — which is part of its identity — and embody the missionary nature of the Spirit.

All the gifts of the Spirit have a missionary and evangelistic component to them. The power was given so that the disciples could be witnesses. It is power for mission. Prophecy, faith, words of wisdom, administrations, and so on — these are not just for the maintenance of the community. They are for mission as well. Add miraculous signs and wonders, plus Philip's experience of the Spirit nudging him to speak to an Ethiopian eunuch, and we can begin to understand why mission in the book of Acts looks so different from mission today. The varied experiences of God were given by the Spirit *for mission.*

Diversity

On the one hand, there is a great deal of cultural and ethnic diversity in St. Paul. The government statistics from 2005 suggest that almost 40 percent of the city is of non-Caucasian descent.[63] This category includes Africans, African Americans, Asians, and South Americans. As an example of this diversity, Caucasian students made up only 33 percent of the student body at St. Paul Central High School in the 2008-2009 academic year.[64]

Our church-planting team went to many cultural events in St. Paul, such as the Festival of the Nations, a multinational cultural festival where many nationalities living in St. Paul showcase their national cultural heritage; the Rondo Festival, which celebrates the history of the African-American Rondo community (going as far back as 1856); Hmong New Year celebrations; AfriFest; Winter Carnival; and St. Patrick's Day. Indeed, some of the most exciting seasons of the year in St. Paul are the times of the festivals. But in all these events it appeared that, while the various cultures were celebrated, they did not mix. Each lives within its own enclave, with apparently very little cultural mixing.

---

63. "St. Paul, Minnesota," City-Data: http://www.city-data.com/city/St.-Paul-Minnesota.html (accessed October 9, 2009).

64. "Central High School," St. Paul Public Schools: http://central.spps.org/profile.html (accessed October 8, 2009).

However, as our team looked further, we began to notice multicultural churches within the Minneapolis and St. Paul area. Such places as Church of All Nations and Sanctuary Covenant Church, both in Minneapolis, opened our eyes further to what was happening, on a small scale, in schools, business centers, and even in our own neighborhoods: people of different cultural heritages are intentionally coming together and living as a community.

We discovered several stories of the same things happening in congregations in St. Paul. In one story, the team learned of two monoracial congregations of different races that merged to form a multicultural one because they felt God leading them in that direction. In another story, a white congregation focused all its missional efforts on its immediate neighborhood, which was a minority community. Another white congregation, which wanted to live out its vision of leading in racial reconciliation in the city, lost its white pastor and chose to replace him with an African-American pastor. Many more stories like these came up during the time of our discernment, to the extent that the team agreed that the Spirit was drawing us in that direction.

While it is possible to interpret this diversity as the result of other factors, like the city's economic security and life opportunities, the discernment that the Spirit was at work in the city made it possible for the team to attribute both the cultural diversity and the move toward multiculturalism to the work of the same Spirit (see Jer. 29). For instance, when the historic injustices of the Rondo Conflict were discussed, and the tensions concerning the routing of the Central Corridor Rail in the Midway area of St. Paul (which potentially would not serve the neighborhood well) were brought to the table, we realized that this intentional attention to racial reconciliation through multicultural congregations in St. Paul could really be a work of the Spirit.[65]

It is characteristic of the Spirit to work out harmonious unity in diversity. Welker suggests that the unity of the Spirit does not only tolerate differences and differentiation, but it maintains and cultivates differences that do not contradict justice, mercy, and the knowledge of God. This unity becomes a reality when we cultivate creaturely differences and re-

---

65. The Rondo Conflict refers to the racial tensions that occurred in St. Paul when an African-American neighborhood was destroyed in order to construct the I-94 highway in the 1950s. See Evelyn Fairbanks, *The Days of Rondo* (St. Paul: Minnesota Historical Society Press, 1990).

move unrighteous differences. This is what our team saw in St. Paul. Welker continues to strongly suggest that the Spirit permanently fractures imperial monoculturalism, and moves us away from it. This one Spirit is poured out upon all flesh, irrespective of ethnicity. "When the Spirit of God is poured out, the different persons and groups of people will open God's presence with each other and for each other. With each other and for each other, they will make it possible to know the reality intended by God."[66] Jürgen Moltmann adds: "The acceptance of other people in their difference and their particularity is constitutive for the community of Christ. . . . It is only unity in diversity that makes the Christian community an 'inviting church' in this uniform community of ours."[67]

Further, when we talk about diversity, we come face to face with a cultural critique from both postmodernity and globalization. In a sense, postmodernity recognizes *difference* as something that could actually make the world a better place.[68] Difference does not have to be a threat. The postmodern notion of subjective truth builds on this recognition of difference. Indeed, within postmodernity, the truth is subjective to the individual: it totally depends on where that individual stands. Accordingly, many postmoderns believe that no one has the whole truth.

A culture that not only tolerates difference but also encourages it is on the rise. From the conversations that we had during the discerning process, we were told on numerous occasions that this multicultural generation feels that it is now desirable to have friends who do not look like you, to speak foreign languages, and to have foreign friends even when they speak your language with a foreign accent. In the process, we realized that it is culturally admirable to belong to a multicultural congregation.[69]

In addition, commercial globalization and ease of international travel, coupled with the refining of migration laws, have resulted in the arrival in the United States of many men and women of color from the majority world. As the global village continues to shrink, the West continues to become more and more variegated. Philip Jenkins observes that there will be no majority race in America in two generations.[70] While other in-

66. Welker, *God the Spirit*, pp. 22, 147, 151.

67. Moltmann, *The Spirit of Life*, p. 184.

68. For a helpful discussion of this, see Grenz, *A Primer on Postmodernism*.

69. Almost 100 percent of the people we talked to indicated that they *wish* congregations were more multiracial, but they do not know how to make that become a reality.

70. See Philip Jenkins, *The Next Christendom: The Coming of Global Christianity* (New York: Oxford University Press, 2002).

stitutions are desegregating, with diversified schools and workplaces, multicultural congregations will make more sense to the next generation than monocultural ones do.

The Spirit does not quash difference. Diversity becomes a way to a vibrant community. The pouring out of the Spirit creates a polyindividual testimony of Godself.[71] The polyindividual nature of the Christian community is called, in the language of Miroslav Volf, a *catholic personality*. It is "a personality enriched by otherness, a personality which is what it is only because multiple others have been reflected in it in a particular way." Volf then adds: "Each culture can retain its own cultural specificity. . . . Paul deprives each culture of ultimacy in order to give them all legitimacy in the wider family of cultures." He suggests that the church should have a catholic cultural identity. "Other cultures are not a threat to the pristine purity of our cultural identity, but a potential source of enrichment."[72] All this is possible through the work of the Spirit.

Hospitality to the Needy

Jürgen Moltmann argues that the Holy Spirit is our broad place in God, a place where "there is no cramping."[73] It is a place of freedom and growth, where God's love opens up the expanse so we can be free to live out our callings. It is God's hospitality to the world, for it is through our lives in the Spirit that we live, and move, and have our being in God. The Spirit is the comforter to those in distress, the liberator of the oppressed, God's life energy to the sick. It continuously extends Christ's invitation to the world, "All who are weary, come and have rest" (Matt. 11:28, paraphrased).

It was quite striking to our team, as we went through the story of St. Paul, that the city's narrative makes its sense of hospitality outstanding.[74] June Drenning Holmquist's historical work *They Chose Minnesota* is an account of an overarching story of ethnic groups accommodating one an-

71. Welker, *God the Spirit*, pp. 22-27.

72. Miroslav Volf, *Exclusion and Embrace: A Theological Exploration of Identity, Otherness, and Reconciliation* (Nashville: Abingdon, 1996), pp. 51, 49, 52. Christians can depart without leaving and thus maintain distance, but at the same time continue belonging.

73. Moltmann, *The Spirit of Life*, pp. 43, 178.

74. Hospitality to the stranger here does not suggest cultural mixing. It appears to me that strangers could share space and live in the city, but mainly within their own cultural communities.

other in spite of the conflicts among them.[75] Kunz adds that, by the 1857 census, St. Paul had 9,793 residents, of whom only 1,700 were natives of the United States; the remainder represented more than twenty countries (Kunz, p. 35). Our team realized that, even though the many cultures have not mixed well through the years, they have certainly made space for one another. For instance, Minnesota was generally a slave-free state, which made it attractive to African Americans, who poured in after the Civil War.[76] The landmark events of the *Dred Scott* case testify to this.[77] Over the years, African Americans became an important part of the ethnic mix in St. Paul, even though there was discrimination in many areas in terms of housing and other facilities. The Rondo Avenue district was a safe and hospitable place for the black community in St. Paul, where black churches, social-service agencies, and clubs flourished. Many citizens of the Rondo district were employed in the transportation business. Some owned businesses and lived well among themselves in the margins of the life of the city. In their own practices of hospitality, the Rondo district is said to have had extra rooms in homes that residents offered to visitors who came into town, since black people were not allowed in the hotels. The vibrancy of this community helps explain why the Rondo Conflict was such a passionate issue.

St. Paul is home to thousands of people who have sought asylum in the city due to wars, hunger, and other problems in their lands of origin. There is a Lao community, a Hmong community, as well as Liberians and Somalians, who have fled wars in Africa. When people in distress relocate, it is usually a difficult process. There is always great need for understanding and patience on the part of the host community. Many of the asylum seekers, from both Asia and Somalia, needed time to learn English and space for their worship services. Mosques and temples have been built in a city that would otherwise be without them.

Our team sensed the Spirit of God working in this area of hospitality.

75. See June Drenning Holmquist, *They Chose Minnesota: A Survey of the State's Ethnic Groups* (St. Paul: Minnesota Historical Society Press, 1981).

76. For an overview of black history in Minnesota, see also Earl Spangler, "The Negro in Minnesota," Manitoba Historical Society: http://www.mhs.mb.ca/docs/transactions/3/negroinminnesota.shtml (accessed December 18, 2008).

77. Scott is famous for suing for his freedom, though unsuccessfully, in the 1857 Supreme Court case of *Dred Scott v. Sandford*. See Walter Ehrlich, *They Have No Rights: Dred Scott's Struggle for Freedom*, Contributions in Legal Studies (Westport, CT: Greenwood Press, 1979).

The relational nature of Eastern Trinitarian theology implies a place for the "other," which leads to a conviction that, in this shrinking global village, there is a need for the Christian community to be intentional in being hospitable to the stranger and outcast. This is something that was close to the heart of God in the Old Testament (see Deut. 24:14-21). It is also emphasized in the New Testament: "Do not forget to entertain strangers, for by so doing some people have entertained angels without knowing it" (Heb. 13:2 [NIV]).

There are also encouraging stories of hospitality in the Christian churches in St. Paul. For example, the mission statement of Christ Lutheran Church says: "We are a diverse people, brought together by the grace of God to share with others what we ourselves have received." Their services use three languages: English, Khmer, and Eritrean. There are a few other congregations and ministries that are paying attention to ministering hospitality to strangers. For instance, there is a network of local Christians that invests a great deal of energy reaching out to Chinese students of the University of Minnesota. A great number of these Chinese students are actually based in St. Paul. The Minneapolis and St. Paul area synods of the ELCA have several recognized Oromo-speaking congregations in the Twin Cities, and have recently recognized a new Swahili-speaking congregation.

Conclusion

This reading of St. Paul made it possible for our team to imagine a contextual missiology that leans heavily on the work of the Spirit, through missionaries and in the context to be reached. The Spirit does more than call, equip, and send; the Spirit is actively involved in the *doing* of mission itself. This kind of missiology is inclusive and takes seriously the work of the Spirit in context. Such a missiology is deeply relevant to the developing postmodern culture. It opens up people to possibilities of surprises from God. God can show up in their neighborhood through people who neither look like them nor speak like them. It begins to locate answers for the question, "What is God up to in this community?"

In St. Paul, this contextual missiology opens up possibilities for understanding the ways God is working with and among the many nationalities that live there. It also opens up missionaries to God's surprising enabling of them to do God's work, and the gifts of the Holy Spirit become usable for mission. In the context of St. Paul we discerned the Spirit already working in three identifiable areas: postmodern spirituality, diversity, and hospitality to the needy. This feels like a *kairos* moment for the city. Such a pneumatological missiology has informed the church-planting efforts that have become the St. Paul Vineyard Church.

CHAPTER 8

Postbureaucratic Churches: Emerging Forms of Organization and Leadership

Todd Hobart

Introduction

What do theology and organizational theory have to do with each other? Perhaps more than one might think. In his book *Trinity and Society,* Leonardo Boff explains how sociopolitical theory and Trinitarian theology mutually informed one another in the early years of the Christian movement.[1] An a-Trinitarian, rigid monotheism went hand in hand with authoritarian and hierarchical models of social and political organization. This was also true of ecclesiastical organization, as that same type of monotheism led to a hierarchical form of church organization that disempowered the laity. Could this same connection between theology and organization be true today?

A shift is underway today in organizational theory away from emphasizing bureaucratic and hierarchical constructs toward focusing on networks, flattened leadership structures, and empowered employees. Some theorize that new knowledge- and information-related businesses are helping to spur these organizational changes, as well as the technological advances that speed communication and alter the ways humans communicate with each other.[2] Whatever the reasons, it is clear that the new

1. Leonardo Boff, *Trinity and Society,* trans. Paul Burns, Theology and Liberation series (Maryknoll, NY: Orbis, 1988), pp. 20-21.
2. Charles C. Heckscher and Lynda M. Applegate, "Introduction," in Charles C. Heckscher and Anne M. Donnellon, eds., *The Post-Bureaucratic Organization: New Perspectives on Organizational Change* (Thousand Oaks, CA: Sage Publications, 1994), pp. 6-7.

organizational forms that are finding their way into use in business today are also being used within churches. This is similar to what took place over the past century, as congregations and denominations adopted the organizational trends of their time.[3]

As organizational theory has been shifting in recent years, the doctrine of the Trinity has enjoyed some renewed interest from theologians. Jürgen Moltmann has played a key role in this process with his interest in the social doctrine of the Trinity. Moltmann's view of the Trinity places the cross of Christ at the heart of the Trinity and conceives of the crucifixion as a Trinitarian event between the Father and the Son that overcomes the dichotomy between immanent and economic Trinity.[4]

In *The Trinity and the Kingdom,* Moltmann challenges two historic ways of understanding God. One view places an undue emphasis on the single divine substance that unites the persons of the Trinity, which Moltmann labels "abstract monotheism."[5] Another view essentially reduces the Trinity to one divine subject in three modes of being (pp. 17-18). To supplant these views, Moltmann instead proposes a retrieval of the Eastern social doctrine of the Trinity, which he believes better represents a fully Trinitarian — and fully Christian — understanding of God.

This view understands that God's unity comes from the three divine persons in communion rather than from sharing a single essence or a single identification in the one divine subject (p. 157). Unity is instead based on the concept of *perichoresis,* which involves the mutual interrelatedness and circulation of the divine life between the three persons (pp. 174-76). In this view, being a person means "existing-in-relationship" (p. 172). Unity is thus seen through relationships instead of apart from them. This view of the Trinity corresponds to "a human fellowship of people without privileges and without subordinances" (p. 157). Following the work of Miroslav Volf,[6]

---

3. For a review of modern organizational ideas that have influenced congregations and denominations, and for examples in specific denominations, see Craig Van Gelder, ed., *Missional Church and Denominations: Helping Congregations Develop a Missional Identity* (Grand Rapids: Eerdmans, 2008); see also Van Gelder, *The Ministry of the Missional Church: A Community Led by the Spirit* (Grand Rapids: Baker, 2007), pp. 125-40.

4. Jürgen Moltmann, *The Crucified God: The Cross of Christ as the Foundation and Criticism of Christian Theology* (Minneapolis: Fortress, 1993), pp. 240-49.

5. Jürgen Moltmann, *The Trinity and the Kingdom: The Doctrine of God* (Minneapolis: Fortress, 1993), p. 17. Hereafter, page references to this work appear in parentheses in the text.

6. Miroslav Volf, *After Our Likeness: The Church as the Image of the Trinity,* Sacra Doctrina series (Grand Rapids: Eerdmans, 1998).

I utilize Moltmann's social doctrine of the Trinity in this essay as one of the key lenses through which to look at ecclesiastical structures and forms, which I will discuss in detail in the final section of this chapter.

If the doctrine of the Trinity and means of organization mutually informed one another in the early church, then it seems that that would be true today as well, and it would be beneficial to investigate congregations who are experimenting with new organizational forms. In this chapter I consider these questions via research I conducted in four different churches, which I chose based on their potential as congregations or groups who were embracing new organizational forms.[7]

One congregation, Christ is Lord Neighborhood Church (CIL), is a decade-old, multisite nondenominational church that has purposefully sought to subvert megachurch organizational forms and explore new ways of existing and working together as a very large congregation. Kingdom Community (KC) has similarly found a new way of organizing as a house church network that also challenges traditional ways of organizing. The Greater City Simple Church Cooperative (GCSCC) exists as a network of house churches and house-church networks that work together on a purely voluntary basis. However, this network has begun to explore a middle road of interdependence that subverts old understandings of disengaged denominational affiliation and do-it-yourself autonomy. Finally, Place of Grace (POG) is a congregation that has likewise challenged old methods of organizing through its insistence on a nonhierarchical team approach among the pastors and leadership of the church.[8]

Church	Key Emphasis
CIL	Large, multisite
KC	House church network
GCSCC	Meta-network
POG	Team-oriented

In this essay I will explore the modern organizational logic that guided congregations in the late twentieth century and the postmodern organizational forms that are emerging today. Then I will consider the re-

---

7. See Todd Hobart, "Organizational Postmodernity and Congregational Structures" (PhD diss., Luther Seminary, 2009).

8. The names of all churches and people in this narrative have been changed to ensure their anonymity.

sults of the research conducted in these four congregational groups. Finally, I will take a theological look at the observed organizational changes through the lenses of missional ecclesiology and the social doctrine of the Trinity.

Modern and Postmodern Organizational Perspectives

Stewart Clegg and William Wallace each take a common starting point to explain the difference between modernity and postmodernity in organizational theory.[9] They suggest Max Weber's theory of bureaucracy as the quintessentially modern organizational theory that best explained the functioning of corporations and large organizations for much of the twentieth century.[10] Weber's bureaucratic theory advanced concepts that supported a highly rationalized system of organization. These included five concepts that were later deemed more crucial than others and were quantified as variables in order to study the structure of organizations: specialization, formalization, standardization, centralization, and configuration.[11]

While there is some agreement on Weber's theory as the prototypical starting point for understanding the structuring of a modern organization, there is little agreement on how to understand postmodernity and organizations. Stewart Clegg, William Wallace, and William Bergquist have sought to discern postmodern organizational forms by using the conventional tools of organizational analysis.[12] In this chaper I will follow the work of scholars, such as the aforementioned, who have used conventional tools of organizational analysis to understand organizational postmodernity.

9. See Stewart Clegg, *Modern Organizations: Organization Studies in the Postmodern World* (Newbury Park, CA: Sage Publications, 1990). (Hereafter, page references to this work appear in parentheses in the text.) See also William McDonald Wallace, *Postmodern Management: The Emerging Partnership between Employees and Stockholders* (Westport, CT: Quorum Books, 1998).

10. For details on how Weber conceived of bureaucracy, see Max Weber, Hans Heinrich Gerth, and C. Wright Mills, *From Max Weber: Essays in Sociology* (New York: Oxford University Press, 1946); see also Max Weber, A. M. Henderson, and Talcott Parsons, *The Theory of Social and Economic Organization*, 1st American ed. (New York: Oxford University Press, 1947).

11. D. S. Pugh et al., "Dimensions of Organization Structure," *Administrative Science Quarterly* 13, no. 1 (1968).

12. See William H. Bergquist, *The Postmodern Organization: Mastering the Art of Irreversible Change*, The Jossey-Bass Management series (San Francisco: Jossey-Bass, 1993).

Two Additional Theoretical Perspectives

Modern and postmodern organizational disciplinary perspectives yield two sensitizing concepts that provide a focused framework for the research described in this chapter: *dedifferentiation* and *radical decentralization*. These ideas were not meant to form a rigid structure that influenced research findings, but they aided in the selection of congregations and in the initial analysis of the data. They emerged from the literature as broad concepts that potentially serve as important indicators of organizational postmodernity within congregations.

Dedifferentiation

Clegg's use of the idea of dedifferentiation forms the basis of this term as a sensitizing concept. He believes that actual postmodern forms of organization may be emerging around the world, and he takes the concept of dedifferentiation as a crucial one in his attempt to locate these postmodern forms of organization (Clegg, pp. 1-24). The initial impetus for Clegg's use of this term came from Scott Lash, who conceived of postmodernity as countering the tendencies in modernity toward increasing differentiation (Clegg, p. 11). Differentiation has taken place in modern organizations through an increasing division of labor (Clegg, p. 2). Thus, in postmodern organizations, this would be countered through processes of dedifferentiation, which would bring together disparate parts that had been previously divided.

Precisely how this could take place — or what it could potentially look like — is never completely specified in the literature. However, several authors give suggestions that are beneficial. Michael Hammer and James Champy suggest (among other ideas) that successful organizations should reengineer themselves to bring processes divided among many specialists under one generalist, who could then be empowered to make many complex decisions.[13]

David Nadler, Michael Tushman, and Mark Nadler describe High Performance Work Systems (HPWS), which are designed to maximize employee input and customer satisfaction through cooperative teamwork and constant monitoring for quality.[14] Additionally, William Wallace recom-

13. Michael Hammer and James Champy, *Reengineering the Corporation: A Manifesto for Business Revolution* (New York: HarperBusiness Essentials, 2003), pp. 53-68.
14. David Nadler, Michael Tushman, and Mark B. Nadler, *Competing by Design: The Power of Organizational Architecture* (New York: Oxford University Press, 1997), pp. 140-53.

mends systematic job rotation and cross-training in his proposal to remake modern organizations along the lines of employee-owner partnership.[15] The work of these authors provides potential indications of what processes of dedifferentiation might look like in churches. I have thus used the concept of dedifferentiation to help guide the selection of congregations and as an aid in data analysis.

Radical Decentralization

Relatively decentralized organizational structures have traditionally existed within many different of organizations; this is not in itself a novel development within postmodernity. However, while decentralization has been present in various ways in modern organizational forms, it appears to be of a much lesser level than the radical decentralization that is potentially emerging among postmodern organizational forms. One example of this kind of decentralization can be found in Clegg's description of the Benetton Group, which thrived for a time as a network type of organization. He points out here that the network nature of Benetton makes it difficult to determine where the organization begins and ends, and he questions whether it can be studied as a singular, complex organization due to its radically decentralized network structure (Clegg, pp. 120-21).

Many more examples of this radical decentralization can be found in *The Starfish and the Spider,* a book that describes two kinds of organizations at opposite ends of the spectrum of centralized power and control. On one hand, spider organizations lodge power, control, and information basically in one place in the organization — at the top.[16] On the other hand, starfish organizations have a structure that allows the entire organization to continue to exist and thrive even if one of its parts is cut off or dies. Thus power and information can be found throughout the organization, and control is maintained through peer accountability and shared norms instead of mandated rules.[17]

Radical decentralization is also meant to encompass the diminishing emphasis on formal hierarchy that seems to be part of the overall discussion of contemporary organizations, as well as the idea of permeable

15. Wallace, *Postmodern Management,* p. 148.

16. Ori Brafman and Rod A. Beckstrom, *The Starfish and the Spider: The Unstoppable Power of Leaderless Organizations* (New York: Portfolio, 2006), pp. 46-53.

17. Brafman and Beckstrom, *The Starfish and the Spider,* pp. 46-53.

boundaries both within the organization and with its environment. Organizational processes that use permeable boundaries, alternatives to hierarchy, and radical decentralization are still in their infancy. The authors discussed in this section provide limited glimpses of what these might look like today in churches. I used these concepts, along with dedifferentiation, to help guide the selection of congregations and as an aid in data analysis. In addition to their use in selecting congregations, I built on these terms in the research to explore new dimensions of organizational postmodernity that may not be as well represented in previous research and literature. I will discuss these new categories in the following section.

Congregational Research

Two important categories emerged from the data that could serve as the basis for a fully formed, grounded theory of postbureaucratic organization: the researched congregations were *interdependent* and *open* organizations. These two categories subsume a number of other important factors that I will discuss in each of the following sections.[18]

Interdependent Organization

The interdependent organization category subsumes two important lesser categories: seeking connection as a network and relational leadership. I will discuss the researched congregations in relationship to these lesser categories to provide a two-dimensional understanding of the nature of interdependent organizations. In the first category, seeking connection as a network, I will not consider POG because it is a congregation and not a network; the category is therefore not applicable to it. The second category, relational leadership, was similarly not applicable to one of the churches, CIL (so I will not discuss it in that section).

---

18. The following section describes much about the qualitative results. To understand how the survey and quantitative results influenced these findings, as well as finding a fuller description of the qualitative results, see my PhD dissertation, "Organizational Postmodernity and Congregational Structures."

Seeking Connection as a Network

Christ Is Lord Neighborhood Church   One of the unique and remarkable characteristics of CIL as an organization is its openness to change. This can be seen as it continues to adapt to its increasing size by changing the way it construes itself as a network. Lead Pastor Jimmy James likens the way CIL had been functioning while the research was being conducted and prior to that time as a server style of network.[19] That is, CIL had a Central Services department that supplied resources such as weekly worship bulletins and coffee materials to the worship centers as well as collecting money from them. Ten percent of a participating worship center's income would go to help fund CIL Central Services. The analogy that was in use was that of a computer server that was connected to other computers and that provided them with resources from a central location.

While the research was being conducted, CIL decided to embark on a plan to decentralize its network structure and instead rely on multiple hubs to serve the network rather than a Central Services department. While some financial and Internet resources would still be given from a central location, most of the other resourcing was instead encouraged to take place through the various worship centers themselves. This was in part inspired by the starfish metaphor from the aforementioned book. However, the idea of a CIL decentralized network is not just about sharing resources. It also involves sharing responsibilities among the various worship centers as well as involving everyday people in the CIL story in ministry to the network as a whole. All of this is to be facilitated by a more robust website infrastructure that could be leveraged to aid these kinds of interactions.

Kingdom Community   The KC network is more difficult to understand as a network in and of itself than either CIL or GCSCC. This is true for three reasons: (1) it began as one church and slowly evolved over time to become a network of home churches; (2) it is concentrated in a much smaller area; and (3) the house churches are much more relationally connected. Though the house churches of KC are functionally autonomous, it is difficult to imagine one of them ever deciding not to participate in KC. The relational bonds connecting the leaders of the home churches and many of the members are so strong that it is easier to imagine KC as one

19. Jimmy James, interview by author, May 15, 2008.

single church that is composed of smaller groups than it is to imagine it as several smaller groups that are bound together as one church.

Part of the strength of KC's unity likely emerges from its common mission. KC's core values and missional focus on its neighborhood so permeate the culture and thoughts of the people of KC that it serves as a strong unifying force. While espousing autonomy technically for the house churches, this was clearly the most tightly bound through relational connections of the three networks studied.

Greater City Simple Church Cooperative   The GCSCC network is much less formal than CIL and KC in that it contains no documents, has no paid or unpaid staff, and has no statements of common values or mission. It simply has a website of sorts and relational connections between its leaders. It is clearly the least tightly bound network of the three I studied; yet it has equally strong connections, only in different ways. The GCSCC is a network of smaller networks of home fellowships and individual house churches. None of these smaller networks or home churches has any formal or legal connection to one another, yet each is connected through relational bonds of friendship that have a unique strength that could potentially surpass the connections of formal bonds.

I should also mention that CIL and KC certainly also have strong informal bonds between their various house churches, worship centers, and leaders that complement the formal bonds of being explicitly together as one church. However, for the GCSCC network, the informal relational bonds are the only kind that unite the various house churches and smaller networks.

Network Comparisons   The three networks I studied — CIL, KC, and GCSCC — all have some striking differences in their scope and function. The CIL network has grown through adding leaders in additional locations and now considers itself to be one church meeting in many locations around the globe. It is a much larger network than the other two. KC began with a traditional kind of church structure and slowly evolved over time into the network of house churches that it is today. It focuses on roughly a six-block neighborhood instead of an entire city or the globe. The GCSCC is a purely informal network; in fact, it doesn't even really have a name. Most people who participate in it would not call it the Greater City Simple Church Cooperative, if they even had a name for it at all. Yet, despite its informal nature, there are many important activities and connections taking place because of it. The focus of the GCSCC is not on a small neighborhood, or around the world, but rather is on a greater metropolitan area.

While CIL is undergoing a process of decentralizing its network, KC and the Mountain Communities — a large house church network within the GCSCC — operate in more of a server style. This could be due in part to their relatively smaller size compared to the increasingly large CIL network. Both KC and Mountain Communities look to a central place to provide connection and resources for the rest of the network. The GCSCC does not really fit either type of network. It is more a relational pooling of resources and opportunities to connect than a server style that operates out of a central location or a decentralized network that uses multiple hubs to provide resources and share responsibilities.

Church	Key Emphasis	Network
CIL	Large, multisite	Worldwide, decentralizing
KC	House church network	six-block, tight
GCSCC	Meta-network	Citywide, informal
POG	Team-oriented	N/A

Relational Leadership

This category was difficult to name because all leadership is inherently relational. However, I chose the term "relational leadership" for this category because genuine, deep, and lasting friendships played a crucial role in the practice of leadership for POG, KC, and GCSCC. Therefore, *relational* is meant to signify that the deepest of friendships are a core part of this style of leadership. In many cases in businesses, churches, schools, and other organizations, leaders may consider one another to be good friends. But in these three groups in particular, the relationship between the leaders goes beyond simple friendship to instead form a crucial part of how leadership actually occurs. Suffice it to say that these groups would not exist in their current forms without those deep and lasting friendships as the catalyst for leadership occurring in the organization.

Relational leadership includes five interrelated factors: (1) a collaborative leadership culture, (2) nonhierarchical relationships, (3) consensus-oriented leadership, (4) egalitarian leadership culture, and (5) dedifferentiated job roles. Because of their close connections, I will discuss them by church instead of individually. These factors are not all relevant to each organization, but I will discuss them when they pertain to the individual groups.

Place of Grace   POG exhibits all five of the related factors. This begins at POG with an egalitarian leadership culture and nonhierarchical relationships. Though Jacquizz Robinson and DeAnn Brown have special roles as pastors that differentiate them from the rest of the staff and board, every measure is taken to ensure that the other leaders have equal say in the direction and functioning of the church. Furthermore, the board consists mostly of women and is representative of several different distinguishable affinity groups that regularly attend the church. The composition of the board also reflects several different age levels within the church. Though the board has a chairperson — and Robinson's and Brown's status as pastors distinguish them — there is no sense of hierarchy at POG. The very nature of the community as free-thinking and subversive precludes any emphasis on hierarchical relationships.

This egalitarian value is closely related to the collaborative, consensus-oriented leadership culture that is promoted at POG. Though Robinson and Brown are the paid pastors at the church, there was a clear sense at the board meeting (which I observed as a part of my research) that everyone was welcome to contribute. Indeed, without everyone's contributions, the functioning of POG's board as it is currently envisioned would not be possible.

At the staff level, the contributions of Donnell Roberts (music minister) and Shantay Bullock (children's director) were sought after and valued by both Robinson and Brown. Open sharing until a decision was mutually agreed on by the group seemed to be the rule at both the board and staff levels, and there was no attempt to impose a solution outside of consensus from the group.

One of the more noteworthy elements of leadership at POG is the emphasis on dedifferentiated job roles among the pastors. This feature is unique to POG among all the groups that were studied. It was mutually agreed on by the three founding pastors from the beginning of POG that both the joys and difficulties in pastoral work would be shared among the three of them. This originally meant that all three would share in the work of preaching, conducting Bible studies, working with the children and youth, and the many other tasks of pastoring a church. This evolved over time to where one of the pastors would take more responsibility over a certain area, such as working with the children or paying the bills, yet the idea of all sharing in the work together remained. No attempt has been made to give special or specific job titles or formally assign one area of ministry to a certain pastor. Currently, the work of preaching is split between Robinson and Brown based on Robinson's full-time and Brown's part-time status at the church.

Kingdom Community   KC is the most intense example of this relational style of leadership among the three churches. The current lead pastor, Keith Rhodes, the former lead pastor, Don Carter, and both their spouses have all taken vows of stability. They have essentially covenanted to remain together in the same area for the rest of their lives, unless God clearly calls them away with the blessing and acknowledgment of the KC community. Seven years after founding KC, Don Carter passed on the lead pastor role to Keith Rhodes. But Carter remains intimately involved in the life of the community. This requires immense trust in the relationship. Keith Rhodes described it as having "a lifelong commitment to one another."[20]

The emphasis on depth and quality of relationship in KC extends beyond Carter and Rhodes to include the way leadership happens on the pastoral council. The pastoral council at KC is made up of some leaders of the various house churches, as well as others who have established longevity, trust, and leadership potential within the community. It meets once per month for leaders to share their concerns about the condition of the house churches as well as discussing vision and practical issues related to the community as a whole. Rhodes envisions the monthly pastoral council meeting as a house church meeting time, which begins with a meal and emphasizes close, even intimate, relationships among its members.

Keith Rhodes does carry the title of lead pastor, which clearly distinguishes him from others at KC. This title, along with his charismatic personality, theological acumen, and leadership skills, would give every reason for him to emerge as the clear figure for everyone to defer to in leadership gatherings. However, during the pastoral council meeting that I observed, this was clearly not the case. His role seemed to be the person who helped to facilitate the emerging consensus of the group concerning the issue being discussed rather than the expert or person in power to go to in order to settle a dispute. The group would discuss an issue for a few minutes, with several options being offered from among its members. Eventually, a solution would emerge from the discussion with the tacit agreement of all. No attempt was made at any time to impose a solution on the group by Rhodes or one of its other members.

While Rhodes's title could lend itself to hierarchical conceptions, this

20. Keith Rhodes, interview by author, April 22, 2008.

never appeared to be the case at KC. This community, as well as POG, is full of artists and others who are gifted, independent-minded individuals who do not gravitate toward hierarchical constructs. Instead, Rhodes, Carter, Jordan Gallego (part-time paid administrator), the pastoral council, and the other leaders at KC all relate to each other as much as possible as equals.

Greater City Simple Church Cooperative   The GCSCC simply would not exist without the relationships between the various leaders of the house churches and networks. Not all of the relationships between the leaders would rise to the level of this relational type of leadership, but many do. In addition, there seems to be a striving for that kind of depth among those who participate. For example, Hei Jin Huang (Mountain Communities leader) and Dat Lam (Matthew 16 house church leader) enjoy a close relationship that is key to the functioning of the GCSCC. Dat Lam additionally meets regularly with Zhi Qiao (Kingdom of God Scriptural Community), and they enjoy a close relationship as well.

Like KC, the GCSCC did not evidence an egalitarian leadership culture and dedifferentiated job roles as much as a collaborative and consensus-oriented leadership culture and an emphasis on nonhierarchical relationships. Because of its informal nature, there is less power to be had in the GCSCC than in the other groups in the study. There are no formal or paid leaders of the group, and there is no money that is collected on its behalf. The completely voluntary nature of the group lends itself especially well to collaborative, consensus-oriented, and nonhierarchical conceptions, though counterexamples could likely be found of groups that are similarly voluntary but practice leadership completely differently.

Because the GCSCC is a cooperative effort between leaders of independent groups, consensus must be the order of the day. Otherwise, groups and leaders who did not agree would simply leave the cooperative. The term "cooperative" also shows the necessity of consensus. The idea behind the cooperative is to pool the efforts and resources of independent groups in order to achieve something greater than themselves while also effecting connections between these groups. This necessitates a dedication to ideals such as nonhierarchical relationships and consensus. Each group that is a part of the GCSCC also brings some of its unique resources to benefit the wider group, as I noted above. Without this emphasis on collaboration, the network would not be able to function, since it has no resources outside what is provided by its constituent groups.

Church	Key Emphasis	Network	Relational Leadership
CIL	Large, multisite	Worldwide, decentralizing	N/A
KC	House church network	Six-block, tight	Nonhierarchical, consensus, collaborative
GCSCC	Meta-network	Citywide, informal	Nonhierarchical, consensus, collaborative
POG	Team-oriented	N/A	Egalitarian, nonhierarchical, consensus, collaborative, dedifferentiated

Open Organization

Describing an organization as "open" is a bit ambiguous. What I mean here is that three of the four groups that were studied shared some or all of these characteristics: (1) they had significant leadership from men and women who are not ordained and who would not be typically thought of as leaders; (2) they welcomed organizational change; (3) they had little desire for bureaucratic structures; (4) they practiced a lack of central control; and (5) they empowered their lay leaders. Together, these characteristics suggest a general sense of openness to nontraditional leadership, change, influence from those within the organization — and the risk that all of this entails. CIL overwhelmingly provided the most data for this category, with KC and the GCSCC also making smaller contributions. POG was not represented in this category, though its organizational structure and leadership style would not necessarily conflict with these ideas. I will discuss the five concepts from this category as they relate to each group that I studied.

Christ Is Lord Neighborhood Church   CIL explicitly names empowerment as a value of the organization, and this is evident in the way this group encourages lay leadership in its various worship centers and small groups. One of the truly remarkable things about CIL is how they are now planning to extend that same value of emphasizing lay leadership to the network level. This aspect of CIL is yet to be seen, but it would be an extraordinary achievement if it could be accomplished because of the immense spread of the network across cultures and around the world.

One of the places where CIL has been most successful with its empowerment value is with its pastors of the worship centers and small groups. One of the strengths of CIL that distinguishes it from many other multisite churches is the freedom given to its individual worship centers and the pastors of those worship centers. CIL empowers those pastors to pursue their own vision for their worship center and allows each worship center to take on its own unique characteristics according to the passion of its leader — provided, of course, that it is in accordance with the overall mission, vision, and values of CIL. Thus, CIL Toledo has a strong focus on the teaching and preaching abilities of its pastor, William McNeal; CIL Light focuses on the importance of home-group gatherings and living missionally in neighborhoods, according to the passion of its pastor, Joseph Garrelli. Both locations fit well in the CIL story overall, but each has its own unique worship style, and those styles go beyond simple variations.

CIL has also not pursued methods used by other multisite churches to standardize church life at its various locations. Pastors are free to preach their own sermons at their individual locations; nor is one pastor's sermon broadcast to the entire network. Though CIL gives advice related to the preferred length of the worship service and ways to encourage worship through singing, it does not try to encourage a certain level of quality or professionalism to standardize the experience at each location. In this sense, CIL is open to the contributions of those who attend as well as those of the pastor(s) at each location, and it does not attempt to control the experience at each worship center.

A sense of openness in CIL also exists concerning the kind of leader who is drawn to serve in the network. These leaders have often experienced brokenness and pain in previous church leadership experiences, and they are not necessarily the typical kinds of people who would be sought for church leadership. Yet these leaders are often welcomed into the CIL story and have made significant leadership contributions in the various worship centers.

Kingdom Community   One aspect of KC that its members value is its openness to those members new to the community who are serving in significant roles in it. Although some aspects of KC are reserved for those who have established trust through their longevity in the community, there are still many ways that those who are new to the community can serve and are welcomed in doing so.[21] Like CIL, KC also attracts leaders from other churches who have experienced pain in ministry. Those leaders

21. For example, people who serve on the board of trustees and the pastoral council have gained that kind of credibility.

are welcomed into KC and encouraged to use their gifts when they are ready.

Lisa Miller is an example of someone who likely would not be thought of as a potential leader by many churches. As a single mother who had struggled financially, Lisa felt that many churches she attended prior to KC viewed her more as someone deserving of charity than as a gifted individual with the great potential. After coming to KC, Lisa felt immediately welcomed and was invited to serve — without any limitations placed on her by others as to what she could or could not contribute to the church.

The greatest strength of KC in this category has been how it has empowered ordinary members of the KC community to participate in ministry. This is likely true for at least two reasons: a lack of paid full-time leadership and the idea that the house churches form the foundation of the community. Without full-time paid professionals to lean on, this has meant that many in the community have needed to take on significant ministry roles. And the participatory nature of the house churches likely has also contributed to empowering members of the community to serve in exceptional ways.

Greater City Simple Church Cooperative Bureaucratic practices are even more absent from the GCSCC than they are from KC. This is because this network is based entirely on informal, relational bonds. Without these bonds, nothing would be accomplished within the network. There is likewise a lack of central control within the GCSCC network. Very little, if anything, exists in GCSCC that can be controlled. The network exists because of purely voluntary cooperation between the groups and close relational bonds. These ideas resist bureaucratic structure and central control.

Because of the informal, relational nature of this network, it must utilize empowered leaders from among its constituent groups; there is simply no other way to accomplish anything within the network. One of the strengths of the network is that it is open to participation from anyone who is willing and gifted (provided they have a connection with another trusted leader in the network). The network makes good use of the gifts of multiple groups within its ranks and does not seem to discriminate with respect to who participates. This was certainly true in the celebration gathering and the Matthew 16 house-church meeting that we observed. They were both open, participatory gatherings that welcomed the contributions of all who were present.

Church	Key Emphasis	Network	Relational Leadership	Openness
CIL	Large, multisite	Worldwide, decentralizing	N/A	Empowering, not controlling, nontraditional leaders
KC	House church network	Six-block, tight	Nonhierarchical, consensus, collaborative	Empowering, nontraditional leaders
GCSCC	Meta-network	Citywide, informal	Nonhierarchical, consensus, collaborative	Nonbureaucratic, empowering, not controlling
POG	Team-oriented	N/A	Egalitarian, nonhierarchical, consensus, collaborative, dedifferentiated	N/A

In the following section, I will provide a brief introduction to a missional ecclesiology. In the final section I will use a missional ecclesiology, along with the social doctrine of the Trinity, as key theological lenses through which to view the results from this study.

Missional Ecclesiology

Michael Goheen locates the International Missionary Council (IMC) at Tambaram in 1938 as the place where a truly missionary ecclesiology began to take shape. This occurred in part through Hendrik Kraemer's challenging question posed to the conference regarding the nature of the church and its obligation to the world. This, however, was still an ecclesiology that focused on mission as an activity of the church instead of proceeding from the life of the triune God. Later, following the 1952 IMC at Willingen, Germany, the *missio Dei* concept would be adopted as a way to encapsulate a focus on God as the author and initiator of mission. Lesslie Newbigin was significantly influenced by these advances in mission theology from the IMC and incorporated them into his own later thinking regarding a missionary ecclesiology.[22] Newbigin recognized the need for a missiology for Western culture when he returned to England after serving as a missionary in India.

The research I conducted follows the conversations about missional ecclesiology initiated by the Gospel and Our Culture Network and the seminal *Missional Church* in recognizing that missiology and ecclesiology cannot be separated because they are "interrelated and complementary."[23] This is because mission is not merely an aspect of the church's existence but belongs to the very essence of what it means to be the church.[24] Since mission is to be understood first as God's activity, and secondarily as the church participating in that activity, a missional ecclesiology holds that the doctrine of the Trinity is foundational for understanding mission. In the final section of this essay, I will frame an analysis of my research in light of the interrelated complementarity of missiology and ecclesiology as important theological lenses.

Theoretical and Theological Implications

In this section I will consider the theoretical and theological implications of the above research results according to the categories previously addressed: modern and postmodern organizational theory, the social doctrine of the Trinity, and a missional ecclesiology. First, I will discuss the associational bonds between churches and groups in this study in light of a missional ecclesiology; then I will discuss the implications for leadership and organization in light of the social doctrine of the Trinity, a missional ecclesiology, and theories of modern and postmodern organization.

New Congregations within Associations and Denominations

How do congregations cooperate with one another? What kinds of structures connect them and facilitate cooperative ministry? What is the pur-

22. Michael W. Goheen, "'As the Father Has Sent Me, I Am Sending You': J. E. Lesslie Newbigin's Missionary Ecclesiology" (PhD diss., University of Utrecht, 2000), pp. 22-24.

23. Darrell L. Guder, ed., *Missional Church: A Vision for the Sending of the Church in North America,* The Gospel and Our Culture series (Grand Rapids: Eerdmans, 1998); see also Craig Van Gelder, *The Essence of the Church: A Community Created by the Spirit* (Grand Rapids: Baker, 2000), p. 31.

24. J. Andrew Kirk, *What Is Mission? Theological Explorations* (Minneapolis: Fortress, 2000), p. 30.

pose of these structures? In the contemporary U.S. context, these questions naturally lead to considering the role and purpose of denominations. Yet denominations are not just structures that facilitate participation and ministry by constituent congregations; they also embody faith traditions that have deep historical roots. Denominations can be considered from many standpoints — historically, theologically, sociologically, and pragmatically. In addition, much has been written about the classification, purpose, and future of denominations.

However, when we consider structures that facilitate cooperation between congregations, denominations are just one of the subjects to be explored. Parachurch organizations; local, regional, or national networks; city- or county-wide ministerial associations; and ecumenical groups — all are ways of facilitating connection and cooperation between congregations. So how do denominations differ from those other groups? Where does a group like CIL or the GCSCC fit into those classifications? Or are new classifications necessary to understand those groups? These are questions without easy answers since denominations, parachurch groups, and various networks are ill-defined, not easy to categorize, and arise first from practice and only later receive theological reflection.

Craig Van Gelder has recently taken on the challenge of wading through the many-faceted perspectives on denominations and denominationalism. He follows historian Sidney Mead in showing that a denominational understanding of the church means understanding it as "an organization with a purposive intent to accomplish something on behalf of God in the world, with this role being legitimated on a voluntary basis." This follows, in part, from denominations emerging first in the United States, where ultimately no single Christian faith tradition was given a privileged place over the others. This allowed denominational ideas to develop out of the self-understanding of the European established churches, which existed "as the primary location of God's presence on earth through which the world can encounter God, with this authority being legitimated by the civil government."[25]

A denominational understanding organically developed without the constraint of the established churches of Europe to hold it back in the new

---

25. For a helpful review of the literature, see Craig Van Gelder, "An Ecclesiastical Geno-Project: Unpacking the DNA of Denominations and Denominationalism," in Van Gelder, ed., *The Missional Church and Denominations: Helping Congregations Develop a Missional Identity* (Grand Rapids: Eerdmans, 2008), pp. 12-41, esp. p. 18.

religious marketplace of the United States. This naturally leads to the question of whether there exists any other way for churches or interecclesial groups to understand their structures that facilitate collaboration and connection. Van Gelder ultimately commends a missional understanding of the church, which moves beyond the pure functionalism of denominations without moving back into an established church paradigm. A missional church exists "as a community created by the Spirit that is missionary by nature in being called and sent to participate in God's mission in the world."[26] Though a missional church is still called to *do* something, it both acts and organizes itself out of first understanding and living into its missional identity.[27]

The established-denominational-missional typology is helpful for understanding the churches in this study. Although they are both certainly on their way, it is clear that neither CIL nor the GCSCC has fully moved beyond functional understandings of themselves to embrace missional identities. Beyond saying that, it may also prove instructive to augment Van Gelder's typology with other ways of understanding denominations and networks in order to understand what is going on with CIL and GCSCC.

Van Gelder sees the newly emerging associational networks as possible further manifestations of a denominational understanding of the church; in the way that he has defined the denominational understanding, that is certainly true. Yet it is unlikely that a person would look at those networks and identify them as a denomination, even though they operate out of a functional understanding. There is something more cohesive and foundational related to the identity of the researched congregations that suggests that a denomination is necessarily different from an associational network.

In other words, though a church may participate in such organizations as the Willow Creek Association,[28] Purpose-Driven churches,[29] or an Emergent cohort,[30] it will likely first derive something foundational about

26. Van Gelder, "An Ecclesiastical Geno-Project," p. 43.

27. Van Gelder, *The Essence of the Church*, 37.

28. The Willow Creek Association claims to network more than 12,000 different congregations from ninety denominations in forty-five countries; see "About Us," Willow Creek Association: http://www.willowcreek.com/AboutUs (accessed February 2, 2009).

29. The claim is made that Purpose-Driven churches exist in more than 100 denominations and associations at "Who We Are," Purpose Driven Church: http://www.purpose drivenchurch.com/en-US/AboutUs/WhoWeAre/FAQ.html (accessed February 3, 2009).

30. Cohorts are local, incarnational groupings of individuals who wish to participate

its identity from its affiliation with a particular faith tradition (e.g., Methodist, Lutheran, Assemblies of God, and so forth). This would make the associational networks something distinct and secondary to a denomination, though they still would operate on functional, voluntary principles. For some congregations, however, their affiliations with those networks may provide more practical value to them than their particular denominational affiliation (provided they have one). Based on the idea of primary identification, some of these networks might eventually take on denominational characteristics.

From this analysis, the GCSCC would fit Van Gelder's denominational understanding of the church through its adherence to the voluntary associational principles and its understanding of itself as a cooperative that facilitates functional activities such as education, shared worship, prayer, and connection. Yet it would not be considered a denomination as such because all the constituent house churches and networks would primarily find their identities in themselves instead of the network.

There is a sense that someone would know denominationalism if he or she saw it. Perhaps it involves adhering to the theological distinctives of the particular faith tradition or incorporating that faith tradition in the name of the congregation. Whatever it is, however, it is impossible to look at a group of close-knit congregations that bear the same name and come from the same faith tradition — whether spread out over a single country or most of the world — and not think of that group in denominational terms.

So, is CIL a newly formed denomination or protodenomination? According to Van Gelder's typology, it would fit into the denominational classification primarily due to its functional self-understanding regarding evangelism and church planting, along with its adherence to principles of voluntary association. All of the constituent churches around the world have incorporated the CIL name, so it is also clear in some sense that there is a strongly shared, common identity between them. Yet, perhaps because of the time in history in which it has matured, it may represent a significant shift in denominational structure and organization, so much so that it stretches the boundaries of how traditional denominations have operated (as discussed in the previous section).

---

in the emerging church discussions. See http://www.emergentvillage.com/cohorts (accessed February 2, 2009).

Leadership, Organization, and the Triune God

A missional ecclesiology asserts that the church's mission is contingent on and finds its being only through the mission of the triune God. The church has the privilege of playing a part in God's redemptive purposes in the world. A missional ecclesiology further recognizes that the church exists as a creation of the Spirit, representing the present and future redemptive reign of God and living under the cross of Christ. As such, the church is intimately related to the Trinitarian life of God, and it has the privilege of representing that life through its leadership and organization. I will now reflect on the importance of interdependence and openness, the two main ideas emerging from this research, when it comes to the task and privilege of representing the life of the triune God through the leadership and organization of the church.

First, interdependence is an important component of congregations that function with shared responsibility and mutual accountability. Miroslav Volf points out how the doctrine of the Trinity addresses the tension between the one and the many that has classically arisen in philosophy.[31] Dual tendencies arise to either subsume the one in the many or the many in the one, with either tendency leading to distortions of the doctrine of the Trinity. These same issues exist in contemporary organizations that exist as single entities that are often composed of multiple parts in complicated ways. These parts could be the many skilled employees of the company, its vendors and contractors, or divisions and groups. The same tensions between the one and the many arise in congregations, with their many members and attenders, staff members, and various ministries. This is likewise true for larger groupings of churches through networks, cooperative groups, and denominations.

Modern organizations have sought different ways to alleviate the tension between the one and the many. Beginning with Adam Smith's *The Wealth of Nations,* modern organizational tendencies have emphasized the *many* through processes of differentiation and breaking down the one whole into its constituent parts.[32] However, an emphasis on the *one* could be seen as leading to massive conglomerate corporations that are composed of vastly different smaller parts. In churches, these same struggles could be seen as leading to immense megachurches that are composed of

---

31. Volf, *After Our Likeness,* pp. 192-93.
32. Hammer and Champy, *Reengineering the Corporation,* pp. 13-15.

many different ministries, while also leading to breaking down ministry roles into ever smaller pieces and specializations. What does the doctrine of the Trinity mean for churches as organizations that struggle with these issues?

The Trinitarian idea of *perichoresis* yields important insights into the category of interdependence that emerged from this research. Volf points out that relationships between churches — as well as relations within churches — have the opportunity to correspond to the communion of the divine persons.[33] Similar to other organizations, congregations with multiple pastors or staff members often find rising tensions about how to ensure that the various church tasks are adequately completed. This can be accomplished through assigning specific job descriptions and job titles, which can lead to ministry silos in which staff members fail to work as a team while they pursue their own narrow ministry goals. At the end of this scenario, the whole has lost out to the interest of the constituent parts.

In the perichoretic relationships between the persons of the Trinity, the tensions between what is *mine* and what is *not mine* melt away through the reciprocal interiority of the divine persons. Volf takes Jesus' statement in John 7:16 as an important verse to illustrate this concept: "My teaching is not mine but his who sent me." The teaching that belongs to the Father simultaneously belongs to the Son. This cannot be resolved by assigning it to one person or another; it properly belongs to both equally. In congregations with multiple staff members, one organizational consequence of this could be the idea that all ministry tasks related to the church as a whole properly belong to all staff members equally.[34] However, this idea would not mean that each staff member would share an equal role in completing each task. One staff member may take on the responsibility of completing a task, but ultimate accountability for that task, as well as for the good of the congregation, would lie with the group as a whole.

This team orientation helps to alleviate the organizational tension between the one and the many. It corresponds to the sharing between the Trinitarian persons while maintaining some differentiation between assigned tasks and titles. It also avoids an overemphasis on one staff member, such as the senior pastor, to the exclusion of the others. Place of Grace is a

33. Volf, *After Our Likeness*, p. 204.

34. For an explanation of this idea and some of its consequences, see Charles C. Heckscher, "Defining the Post-Bureaucratic Type," in *The Post-Bureaucratic Organization*, pp. 24-28.

good example of sharing and team-related ownership of pastoral responsibilities. Just as interdependence was valued between persons, so also did it arise as a category between congregations. These relationships also have the potential to correspond to Trinitarian relationships. If one conceives of church in a manner consistent with a multisite ecclesiology, then it is easy to see the potential for some of these same ideas of shared responsibility and group accountability to obtain between networks of groups or churches.

Openness was the second category that arose from this research. I mentioned that the churches in this study practiced openness to nontraditional leaders, change, influence from those within the organization, and the risk that is inherent in that openness. As interdependence, this openness is also analogous to the openness of the triune God. Jürgen Moltmann holds that "the relationality among the three Trinitarian persons seeks the inclusion of creation." Thus, God's openness and relationality "invites creaturely participation."[35] Regarding the cross as an inner-Trinitarian event, Moltmann explains that "God's being and God's life is open to true man."[36]

Openness here means risk and vulnerability from those who are other and different. It has the potential for new relationships and intimacy as well as for betrayal, disappointment, and pain. Just as the triune God is relationally open to creation, so also are churches open to other people and their surrounding communities; this openness carries the potential for both blessings and pain. Several authors likewise envision the mission of the church as being characterized by "openness to God and openness to the world."[37] They see mission as characterized by participation, which includes the idea of openness, an openness that leads the missional church outside itself and into territory that is foreign to it, where it engages in mutual hospitality. Here the missional church is a guest of the world and receives God's hospitality through the overtures of the world.[38]

35. Stanley J. Grenz, *Rediscovering the Triune God: The Trinity in Contemporary Theology* (Minneapolis: Fortress, 2004), p. 82.

36. Moltmann, *The Crucified God*, p. 249.

37. Jannie Swart et al., "Toward a Missional Theology of Participation: Ecumenical Reflections on Contributions to Trinity, Mission, and Church," *Missiology: An International Review* 37, no. 1 (2009): 85.

38. Swart, "Toward a Missional Theology of Participation," p. 85.

Conclusion

What is the future, then, of the new forms of organization discussed in this chapter? Some have wondered if perhaps these congregations will assume more traditional forms as they age or grow further. CIL is already quite large, and the Mountain Communities are nearing the end of their twentieth year of existence, so it seems plausible that these new forms are here to stay.[39] These organizational innovations have also weathered the test of time through many of the difficulties that are common to congregations, such as transitions in pastoral and staff leadership and the pain of broken relationships.

It is clear, however, that the adoption of these organizational forms and others like them is still in its infancy. There remains much more to be learned and discovered about the cultural and theological factors that are behind these changes. There will no doubt be further changes to come. I have explored in this chapter several important aspects of new ways that congregations can organize themselves and affiliate together, but I have only scratched the surface of the changes that are occurring. I hope that I have shown how these congregations practice a great sense of openness and seek interdependence and accountability over autonomy.

Just as new organizational practices were adopted in churches and denominations according to bureaucratic theory a century ago, it is also true today that new organizational forms are taking their place alongside the old. Undoubtedly, new research will continue to explore these facets of organization as congregations continue to seek to participate in God's mission in the world.

39. As of December 2008, CIL had about 17,500 attendees in twenty-six different countries. It had 1,200 small groups and 185 pastors; the vast majority of those pastors outside the United States were unpaid. Central Services director Dave Nelson noted that 5,000 of those counted were affiliated with the church and its other church plants that originally helped launch CIL. Those churches were still in the process of determining the nature of their formal relationship with the CIL network, according to Nelson (email message to the author, December 11, 2008).

A SERMON

As the Holy Spirit stirs our imaginations for planting missional congregations, we encounter a richly diverse world. How might we plant Christian churches in the soil of cultural and religious pluralism? Rooted in love, the gospel of Jesus Christ is born into the world through the intimacy, solidarity, and embrace that characterize God's faithful love throughout creation, as it takes shape in the lives of congregations. When we plant churches, we participate in God's love for the whole world. The church is planted in the gospel for all.

This collection of chapter studies concludes with a sermon delivered by Paul Chung during worship at the 2009 Missional Church consultation. As a mission and world Christianity scholar, Chung brings Scripture and theological scholarship together as he reflects on his own congregational experience as the planter of a multicultural congregation in California. Our thanks to him for weaving these rich perspectives together to proclaim the gospel to us in this sermon. Those who lead church-planting efforts are, first and foremost, hearers and followers of the Word. Poised to begin or continue church planting, we conclude this book with the proclaimed Word as the *final* word. We are rooted in the gospel of Jesus Christ crucified and risen for us — and for all.

Missional Church: Planted in the Gospel for All

MARK 8:29-30
ACTS 17:24-28

Paul Chung

May our Lord Jesus Christ be with you all in grace, peace, and reconciliation. Let me begin my sermon with an Asian story about a man and a horse in the Zen Buddhist community. The horse was galloping so fast that the rider on the horse appeared to be going somewhere important. Another man, standing alongside the road, shouted, "Where are you going?" The rider replied, "I don't know! Ask the horse!" This is also our story. We are riding a horse — we don't know where we are going — and we can't stop. The horse represents our habitual energy pulling us along, and we have become powerless. It has become our habit to always be on the run. We struggle all the time, even when we sleep. We are at war within ourselves, and we can quickly start a war with others.

We have to learn the art of stopping. To do this, we must read and listen with open minds and open hearts. Only then will the rain of the Holy Spirit penetrate the soil of our hearts. We live in a competitive world in which we are very used to thinking in terms of more speed and more progress. Somehow we feel as though our election demands another's rejection, that our uniqueness demands another's commonness. Considering the competitive nature of our world, the process of globalization today has become emotionally charged in public discourse. For some, it implies the promise of an international civil society, conducive to a new era of peace and democracy; for others, it implies the threat of American economic and political hegemony. This globalization process is reminiscent of the life of Willy Loman, Arthur Miller's famous salesman in *Death of a Salesman*, who rides on a smile and a shoeshine. Again, we have become the rider on the horse, not knowing where we are going.

Everything we read in the papers, hear on the radio, and see on television about the condition of the world seems to confirm the saying *homo homini lupus* ("human beings are wolves to each other"). And as our human intelligence invents ever more ingenious instruments of destruction, humanity comes closer every day to its own annihilation. However, the gospel breaks through these distinctions made in the context of rivalry and competition, which are also grounded in the privatization of faith.

When we enter into the household of God, we come to realize that God's house has no dividing walls or closed doors. "I am the door," Jesus says. "Anyone who enters through me will be safe" (John 10:9). East Asian people understand Jesus' saying as the Tao that embraces everybody without discrimination. Through Jesus-Tao we meet God in heaven. This was the mission principle practiced by Matteo Ricci in China during the sixteenth century. In the house of God we are consecrated to the truth, that is, we are part of God's betrothal with God's people. We truthfully belong together in God. This is the spiritual basis of our missional church in terms of embrace, companionship, and solidarity.

Publicly Jesus calls himself into question among his disciples. "But you, who do you say that I am?" (Mark 8:29). Reading from the Bible in the synagogue of Capernaum, Jesus proclaimed his mission: "The Spirit of the Lord is upon me, because he has anointed me to bring good news to the poor. He has sent me to proclaim release to the captives and recovery of sight to the blind, to let the oppressed go free, to proclaim the year of the Lord's favor" (Luke 4:18-19). Jesus' mission has social dimensions with the *ochlos* (Greek for "the people"), or *minjung* in Korean.

The exclusive claim of the gospel for the crucified God was foolishness to the Greeks, and it remained a stumbling block to many contemporaneous Hellenized Christians who felt ashamed of the cross. However, to the Athenians in front of the Areopagus, Saint Paul bore witness to *solus Christus* ("Christ alone"), in the conviction that everyone lives, moves, and has his or her being in the universal reign of God (Acts 17:22-28). Saint Paul recognized that Athenians were very religious. Instead of being iconoclastic toward the idol worship in Athens, Paul introduced God in Jesus Christ by utilizing the Athenians' devotion to an unknown God. God in Jesus Christ gives life and breath and everything else to everyone. Paul even cited some of the Athenian poets by saying, "In God we live and move and exist." From Paul's conviction we learn that God is missional and diaconal

— and working ahead of us. God maintains and prepares people outside the churchly sphere for the grace of Jesus Christ because they are also the children of God the creator.

For example, the first Christian missionaries to China in 635 CE recognized that Chinese people are God's children. When Matteo Ricci arrived in China in the late sixteenth century, he believed that dialogue and inculturation were the best ways by which to achieve his mission. Following Paul's conviction, these early missionaries attempted to listen carefully to how God was working in the life of Chinese culture.

In the earliest record of the life of the church in the Acts of the Apostles, we note that the fellowship of believers is established between Word and sacrament. Congregational fellowship always springs from the Word and finds its goal and completion in the Lord's Supper. The whole common life of congregational fellowship oscillates between Word and sacrament, and it begins and ends in worship. The daily growth of the church is a witness to the power of the Lord, who dwells in the visible church through Word, sacrament, and the people of God in the guidance of the Holy Spirit.

I planted this conviction about the power of the gospel in a multicultural congregation that I developed during my parish work in Berkeley, California. As a mission developer planting a multicultural congregation of the ELCA, I was always surprised and challenged, and I learned from people with non-Christian backgrounds who joined the congregation. I strongly sensed that God prepared them and invited them to a Korean Lutheran congregation. Learning about their differences and embracing their unique belief system nourished my previously abstract theological education, which derived from Europe, in a new and fresh way. My congregational work became a form of liberation.

Allow me to give an example of an experience in a public cemetery in Canada. A Caucasian family was visiting the grave of its departed loved one. They placed some flowers on the grave in memory of their beloved, and they bowed their heads in silence for a while. Some yards away, an Asian family prepared rice and food for the departed, knelt, and bowed in memory. Curiously enough, one of the Caucasians approached one of the Asians and asked whether the departed would return to eat the rice in front of the grave. The Asian person, a little surprised, responded to him by asking whether his departed would also return to sit and smell the flowers near the grave. To Asian people, a bowl of rice symbolizes a deep spiritual life in ongoing relationships with the ancestors in the same way as a bunch of flowers do for Caucasians. Rice and flowers are not the same, but they are two ways of expressing a memorial act on the part of the beloved with loving concern about eternal life.

Saint Paul declares in Colossians 1 that God created the whole universe *through* Christ and *for* him. Through Christ, God brought the whole universe back to Christ. God made peace through Christ's death, and he thus brought back Christ to all things, both on earth and in heaven. Therefore, our confession to the exclusivity of Jesus Christ cannot be fully understood apart from its dimension of the embrace of others. Reminded of Luther's saying, Bonhoeffer expressed his marvelous solidarity with others through these memorable words: "The curses of the godless sometimes sound better in God's ear than the hallelujahs of the pious."

God is also for people outside the walls of Christianity. God, who is reconciled to the world through Jesus Christ, will never give up on people no matter how indifferent, even hostile, they are toward God. This is the essence of God's *diakonia* of reconciliation in Jesus Christ for the world. We meet God's beautiful mind in his great compassion for the world by participating in his Son's life and death. This is the meaning of the gospel to which we are summoned to bear witness — with passion and gratitude to the promise of God through Word and sacrament.

In *A Beautiful Mind,* a Ron Howard film, I see a story of courage, passion, and triumph. John Nash, a brilliant mathematician, becomes entangled in a mysterious conspiracy on the brink of international acclaim. Overcoming his long psychotic trials with the great help and love of his wife, Nash was even competent enough to receive the Nobel Prize. On the occasion of the award, he made this moving and insightful statement: "I've always believed in the numbers in the equations and logic that led to reason. After a lifetime of such pursuits, I ask, What truly is logic? Who decides reason? My quest has taken me through the physical and the metaphysical and the delusional and back. I have made the most important discovery of my career, the most important discovery of my life. It is only in the mysterious equations of love that any logical reasons can be found."

"A Beautiful Mind" is rooted in love. Love is sometimes mysterious. As humans, we meet the mysterious beautiful mind of God in the life, death, and resurrection of Jesus Christ. Saint John expresses it in the following way: "The Word was made flesh and pitched his tent among us" (John 1:14). These words express the mystery that God, in whom all was created, has become part of that same creation. God, who was rejected by our sins, became sin for us in order to offer us a share in the divine life. The life, death, and resurrection of Jesus manifest to us the full intimacy of the divine embrace. He lived our lives, died our deaths, and lifted all of us up into his glory. The mystery of the incarnation reveals to us the spiritual dimension of human solidarity. We who belong to Christ belong to all of humanity. That is why Jesus prayed for his disciples with these words: "Father, consecrate them in the truth; your word is truth. As you sent me into the world, I have sent them into the world, and for their sake I consecrate myself so that they too may be consecrated in truth" (John 17:17-19).

We cannot live in intimate communion with Jesus without being sent to our brothers and sisters in the world. They belong to that same humanity that Jesus accepted as his own. Thus intimacy manifests itself as solidarity — and solidarity as intimacy. In the presence of love, intimacy occurs; in the presence of intimacy, embracing of others occurs; in the presence of embrace, solidarity begins. Christians are called to bear witness to the truth of gospel in which we meet Jesus' intimacy, embrace, and solidarity. May the Holy Spirit guide our missional church, which is rooted in the gospel of Jesus Christ through that intimacy, embrace, and solidarity — for the sake of the world.